Contents

Preface to the Third Edition

Since time does not stand still, I found myself joining the ranks of the privileged pensioners some years after writing the first edition of *Dinghy Cruising*. Joyfully, after a life of limited leisure, I now had time to fully indulge my hobbies. Quality time was a dream that at last became a reality.

In 1999, crewing my husband in our Wayfarer in Canada, sailing a Wanderer dinghy in Holland, and singlehanding my Gull Spirit in East Anglia almost every other week of the year, produced quality time afloat. Mobility of sailing area is the great advantage of the dinghy cruiser.

As time had gone by, I had found that pulling Wayfarers and Wanderers loaded with cruising gear up steep slipways and along soft sandy beaches had become problematic; however, taking on crew would have limited my freedom to sail where I wanted and when I wanted. As I watched my friends divert from dinghies – buying yachts, and then sailing less and less as they waited for willing crew and free moorings – I realised that this was not an option for me. Instead, I experimented with various types of sailing dinghies until eventually I fell in love with the 3.3 metre (11 foot) Gull Spirit. Once more, I was able to delight in the total freedom to sail where and when I liked.

While researching gear better adapted to my miniature cruiser, I discovered that modern technology had brought wonderful comforts, conveniences and safety afloat. In this new edition I have tried to share with you my fresh ideas.

MARGARET DYE

Dinghy

City Council

Newcastle Libraries and Information Service

☎ 0191 277 4100

Please return this item to any of Newcastle's Libraries by the last
date shown above. If not requested by another customer the loan
can be renewed, you can do this by phone, post or in person.
Charges may be made for late returns.

ADLARD COLES NAUTICAL
LONDON

DEDICATION
This book has been written with my admiration,
affection and thanks to *Wanderer* and *Wanderbug* and especially to
Frank who makes such things possible.

This third edition is dedicated to the memory of Ian Proctor who died
in 1992. I feel that he would understand why I now sail the Gull Spirit
and I am grateful to him for all the fun I am having with her.

Published 2006 by Adlard Coles Nautical
an imprint of A & C Black (Publishers) Ltd
38 Soho Square, London W1D 3HB
www.adlardcoles.com

Copyright © text Margaret Dye 1992, 2001, 2006
Copyright © illustrations Frank Dye 1992, 2001, 2006
First edition 1992
Second edition 2001
Third edition 2006

ISBN 0-7136-7934-4
ISBN 13: 978-0-7136-7934-2

A CIP catalogue record for this book is available from the British Library.

Note: While all reasonable care has been taken in the publication of
this book, the publisher takes no responsibility for the use of the
methods or products described in the book.

Typeset in Fournier.
Printed and bound in Great Britain by
Cromwell Press, Trowbridge, Wiltshire

Foreword

by Ian Proctor

Even before I begin to write this Foreword, I realise I will have to claim partial responsibility for many of the things Margaret Dye has written about in this book. However, it is an involvement that gives me great pleasure. The reason is simple. I was fortunate enough to be the designer of the sailing dinghies in which Margaret has done her cruising.

There is nothing unusual in that fact – and I am lucky to have designed over 100 sailing dinghies as well, of which 65,000 are presently sailing – but in truth, it can be said that no other dinghy sailors have had so much influence in the development of their boats, or commanded so much attention, in the best possible way, as Margaret and her husband Frank. They have a wealth of experience in dinghy cruising which I believe is unmatched. When they talk about it, you would be stupid not to listen very carefully.

To be honest, Margaret is not the easiest of clients. But undoubtedly she and Frank are the best. When she wanted a 4.2 metre (14 foot) dinghy, lighter than a 4.8 metre (16 foot) Wayfarer, and asked me to design it eleven years ago, I was given a free hand. The Wanderer class was the result, and as there are now over 1000 of them and Margaret still owns one, it can be termed a success. I can now sit back and relax, you might think.

Relax? What a delusion! Every year this determined small powerhouse has ambitious sailing plans and often, (or at least it seems pretty often!) she has new or different requirements for the boat. Frequently, these requirements seem conflicting. All Margaret knows is she wants them – she does not even pretend to know how to get them all into one little boat! That's *my* job, of course, but sometimes it is very tempting to dismiss her objectives as incompatible or just too difficult.

Are these objectives always sensible? Well, on occasions I may have been foolish enough to doubt it, but not any longer. Maybe her objectives cannot always be fully achieved, but one can always see good reason for each of them. It is a pleasure discussing them, thinking about them – and one always learns something.

The same applies to her sailing. In this book she shares with us some of her more treasured experiences in a dinghy cruising career especially rich in variety.

You will read of quiet places, where the only sounds are the sighing of the breeze in the reeds, the call of wading birds and the squelchy sucking noises of worms and little crabs busy in the shoreline mud.

In contrast to this there are moments of real danger, briefly described with stark matter of factness: 'Falling backwards out of the boat, unconscious with seasickness, my husband quickly taught me that determination and self reliance are vital factors in the enjoyment of dinghy cruising'! Just imagine that scene in a 4.8 metre open boat in the Minches, off Skye, in a gusty force 6 wind against tide, kicking up a big sea. I find that description awe-inspiring and very frightening, but Margaret dismisses it in a few words without the slightest attempt at embroidery.

It is indeed a privilege to be invited to share in the knowledge of these places. Some of them – such as the west coast of Scotland – may remain relatively safe from over-visitation (especially when people have read about Margeret's seasickness experience off Skye), but other haunts may suffer under pressure of popular public access. This is an an ever-increasing problem. But in any case, before such places lose the fascination of their peace and remoteness, Margaret has captured magic moments from them to put in this book.

In these days when maxi yachts are raced round the world at a cost of millions of pounds, financed by commercial sponsorship, aided by radio communication, satellite navigation, and all the complicated back-up of modern trans-ocean racing under the glare of international press publicity, it is perhaps reassuring to know that individuals, quietly and on their own account, can still find adventurous sailing and very special happiness afloat in suitable cruising dinghies at modest cost.

Thank you, Margaret, for helping to show us how.

Ian Proctor
Duncannon River Dart

Foreword

Even before I begin to write this Foreword, I realise I will have to claim partial responsibility for many of the things Margaret Dye has written about in this book. However, it is an involvement that gives me great pleasure. The reason is simple. I was fortunate enough to be the designer of the sailing dinghies in which Margaret has done her cruising.

There is nothing unusual in that fact – and I am lucky to have designed over 100 sailing dinghies as well, of which 65,000 are presently sailing – but in truth, it can be said that no other dinghy sailors have had so much influence in the development of their boats, or commanded so much attention, in the best possible way, as Margaret and her husband Frank. They have a wealth of experience in dinghy cruising which I believe is unmatched. When they talk about it, you would be stupid not to listen very carefully.

To be honest, Margaret is not the easiest of clients. But undoubtedly she and Frank are the best. When she wanted a 4.2 metre (14 foot) dinghy, lighter than a 4.8 metre (16 foot) Wayfarer, and asked me to design it eleven years ago, I was given a free hand. The Wanderer class was the result, and as there are now over 1000 of them and Margaret still owns one, it can be termed a success. I can now sit back and relax, you might think.

Relax? What a delusion! Every year this determined small powerhouse has ambitious sailing plans and often, (or at least it seems pretty often!) she has new or different requirements for the boat. Frequently, these requirements seem conflicting. All Margaret knows is she wants them – she does not even pretend to know how to get them all into one little boat! That's *my* job, of course, but sometimes it is very tempting to dismiss her objectives as incompatible or just too difficult.

Are these objectives always sensible? Well, on occasions I may have been foolish enough to doubt it, but not any longer. Maybe her objectives cannot always be fully achieved, but one can always see good reason for each of them. It is a pleasure discussing them, thinking about them – and one always learns something.

The same applies to her sailing. In this book she shares with us some of her more treasured experiences in a dinghy cruising career especially rich in variety.

You will read of quiet places, where the only sounds are the sighing of the breeze in the reeds, the call of wading birds and the squelchy sucking noises of worms and little crabs busy in the shoreline mud.

In contrast to this there are moments of real danger, briefly described with stark matter of factness: 'Falling backwards out of the boat, unconscious with seasickness, my husband quickly taught me that determination and self reliance are vital factors in the enjoyment of dinghy cruising'! Just imagine that scene in a 4.8 metre open boat in the Minches, off Skye, in a gusty force 6 wind against tide, kicking up a big sea. I find that description awe-inspiring and very frightening, but Margaret dismisses it in a few words without the slightest attempt at embroidery.

It is indeed a privilege to be invited to share in the knowledge of these places. Some of them – such as the west coast of Scotland – may remain relatively safe from over-visitation (especially when people have read about Margeret's seasickness experience off Skye), but other haunts may suffer under pressure of popular public access. This is an an ever-increasing problem. But in any case, before such places lose the fascination of their peace and remoteness, Margaret has captured magic moments from them to put in this book.

In these days when maxi yachts are raced round the world at a cost of millions of pounds, financed by commercial sponsorship, aided by radio communication, satellite navigation, and all the complicated back-up of modern trans-ocean racing under the glare of international press publicity, it is perhaps reassuring to know that individuals, quietly and on their own account, can still find adventurous sailing and very special happiness afloat in suitable cruising dinghies at modest cost.

Thank you, Margaret, for helping to show us how.

Ian Proctor
Duncannon River Dart

1

Dinghy decisions

Dinghy or yacht?

Most cruising is done in yachts, and people cruise the world using their cabin as their home. However, finding and keeping compatible crew, meeting ever-increasing marina costs, securing safe wet and dry berths, and craning in and out of the water, all add up to a considerable annual financial outlay. By contrast, a cruising dinghy and a reliable trailer greatly reduce these costs as well as bringing many other benefits.

Mobility

Cruising in a dinghy has many advantages over cruising in a yacht. The most obvious one is that a small, light, shallow-draft dinghy is much more mobile. You can explore a completely different sailing area every weekend. Sailing 16 kilometres in a dinghy can be as much of an adventure as covering 160 kilometres in a large yacht. In twenty-four hours it is possible to cover over 1600 kilometres (some 1000 miles) by trailer and have a totally different sailing area to explore, whereas a yacht may take several days to reach the same area and by then it may be time to start the return trip. Using a delivery crew is never quite so satisfying.

The range of cruising grounds are enormously opened up to a centreboard boat. Exploring to the head of a river, skirting the shallow sandbanks of an estuary, or creeping over a bar on the last of the flood tide into a safe harbour are delights well known to dinghy sailors, but not easily achieved in deep-keel yachts.

Navigation can be easier for dinghy sailors too, as they can sail into shallow water until they have to pull up the centreboard, then be away into deeper water, whereas larger boats may well be aground for the tide, or even longer! On a two-day cruise along the north Norfolk coast, work demanded that we returned home on the Sunday evening. Missing the ebb tide, we found a dry sandbank blocking our entrance to Wells-next-the-Sea harbour. Rolling the dinghy over the sandbank on our boat rollers was a laborious task, but it enabled us to get to the deep water channel and so reach the dinghy park by supper time.

We have shipped our dinghy to many foreign countries to sample a different kind of cruising: in Danish, Norwegian, Icelandic and American waters. People who charter share the same enjoyment in experiencing a wider variety of cruising grounds, but we have the added advantage of being able to live in our own boat using our own familiar equipment, as the following log of an American cruise shows.

CHRISTMAS IN THE MANGROVE SWAMPS

In November we built a cradle and lined it with carpet to provide Wanderer *with a fully fitted chine-to-chine carpeted boat cradle. With our wooden* Wayfarer *freshly varnished, we took her to Felixstowe and spent an exhausting day there packing all our gear – not forgetting an iced Christmas cake wedged between our oilskins and Christmas puddings tucked into the toes of wellington boots, which matured nicely as they travelled across the Atlantic!*

We planned to cruise the Intracoastal Waterway to St Lucie Inlet, then down the Gulf of Mexico, explore the Everglades, then the Florida Keys, and return to Fort Lauderdale where our cradle would be left.

Getting ourselves away from the UK was more difficult than organising Wanderer's *departure. The blizzards of December 1981 closed all runways at Heathrow for a whole day, and conditions were chaotic and overcrowded. When air traffic started again, we crushed and queued with a cosmopolitan company, but were pulled out of line before we reached the metal detector. Our luggage consisted of a bucket of hacksaws, files, nails, plywood patches, screwdrivers and normal dinghy repair kit tools. Officialdom took a dim view of our equipment, as there had been a hold-up attempt in mid-Atlantic only two days previously.*

Twelve hours later while UK boats were lashed and battered by storm force winds, snow and ice, we tipped *W48* into the *Intracoastal Waterway* and complained how hot *Florida* was!

Fortunately, a stern gale allowed us to plane up the *Intracoastal Waterway* effortlessly for two days and we made good time. Contrary to expectation, a week before Christmas, the waterway was uncrowded, the many bascule bridges presented us with no problems, the locks were easy to pass through, and the few boats that we passed were friendly and courteous. Everybody else's motor yacht seemed huge and people laughed to see that we carried no engine. They all motored up to each bridge, hooted and an obliging lock keeper stopped the road traffic to open the bridge for them. We astonished the lock keepers by sailing up to the bridges, dropping mast and sails all standing, and paddling our way through.

The first day we sailed past *Palm Beach*, where the twenty-storey hotels completely dwarfed the palm trees, and the high rise condominiums looked sparklingly white and brand new against a vivid blue cloudless sky. Millionaires' views gave way to fantastic private houses, all leading down to rolling lawns and sumptuously laid-out subtropical gardens, but there were hardly any people to be seen in the gardens or on the balconies; the landscape looked devoid of humanity. Larger than life plastic snowmen, lit-up reindeer-drawn sledges, Father Christmas profiles and artificial Christmas trees decorated the waterfront gardens. Sailing out from the populated area, we came to real wilderness in *Hobe Sound*, past St *Lucie's* inlet where a tumble of water meant that the tidal ocean was meeting the calmer water of the *Intracoastal Waterway*. Pelicans and heron fished, and the citrus groves and palm trees gave way to long majestic lines of *Australian* pines hung with swamp moss like long white beards.

It was dark by 1800 hrs each night, but the stars and full moon, and warmth of the subtropical evenings, made them magical times. There was no problem in camping; everywhere there were firm white shell beaches. Daily non-stop from dawn till dusk we sailed, the temperatures hovering around 24–27°C; the sun was bright, the sky blue and cloudless, and every sunset and moon-filled night sky was magical. After five days of travelling, our rucksack of tinned food was used up. However, our food supply was soon stocked up again; Sam, a lock keeper, invited us to walk around his garden as we waited for the lock gate to be opened. He gave us a big bag and

3

insisted that we picked fruit from his grapefruit, orange and lemon trees, while his wife insisted we take a pot of preserves back on our boat.

Thirteen bridges and three locks later, we emerged into Lake Okeechobee. There wasn't enough wind, and this large stretch of open water has a bad reputation for sudden storms. We sailed all that day, making no more than 10 kilometres (6 miles) and, like the previous two days, saw no other boat. Instead an alligator cruised close to us, and the pelicans seemed unconcerned at our presence. When we pulled back the tent after anchoring in a vast water lily bed in the lee of an island for the night, we were greeted by the sight of a family of otters playing close by and which stayed with us while we ate breakfast in the hot sunshine.

Turning eastwards we had our first glimpse of the Everglades, the region of 10,000 islands. Each mangrove clump looked exactly like the next and we began to take navigation seriously; it would have been easy to have got lost in the area. The sunset that evening was pink, calm and beautiful as the others had been, but we saw less of it than usual, as we rushed to put up the tents at dusk and light a mosquito coil. The mosquitoes were very active in the mangrove swamps.

The next night's anchorage was a disturbed one. We pulled into a little creek off the Gulf of Mexico at low water, with only a few inches of water beneath us, rowed into Clam Creek, and anchored in the middle of the deep-water channel. It was a dream anchorage. The high sandbank, separating us from the breaking surf on the seaward-looking beach, was like soft white sugar. The shells were beautiful and we collected some as the supper heated, identifying tulip shells, ceriths, conch and angel wing shells. In such places, dinghies score – because yachts cannot get near them. Pelicans flew homeward after the day's fishing; it was dark by 1800 hrs, and the sun was quickly replaced by a brilliant moon and a sparkly Venus.

Christmas Eve was quite the best we have known. We found an empty white beach in between the many mangrove swamps, and lit a camp fire. Supper was followed by a huge slice of mature Christmas cake dripping in walnuts, cherries and icing, then coffee, nuts and port. Looking out to sea, we saw miles of empty blue and turquoise water, the setting sun falling into it, and a blush of pink silence.

4

Once or twice bring harbour being by bad weather, we have shipped Wanderer on a local ferry as deck cargo or trailed her to another launch site and continued to cruise from a different harbour. If the unexpected threatens a well-prepared cruise, the adaptability of a smaller boat can often mean that a change of plan will still secure a sailing holiday. One year during a dock strike, Wanderer was locked in a London dock for the whole of July, so our plans to ship her to Bergen and sail on towards the North Cape had to be aborted. Later in the sailing season, though, when the strike ended, we drove Wanderer from London docks to the Newcastle ferry and shipped her instead to the Lofoten islands.

We spent the first day dozing and rowing and wondering about katabatic winds, whirlpools and fjords 5 kilometres (3 miles) deep and about 900 metres (3000 feet) high. The blue Arctic landscape was impressive and seemed to stretch into infinity, one mountain range rising into the next, with glaciers white tinged with turquoise falling off their peaks. The silence was frighteningly and wonderfully impressive. We both became ensnared by the magic of the Arctic; its isolation, vastness and silence needed to be experienced to be understood, but we would never have had the chance had we not been able to adapt our cruising plans.

Longer sailing season

If a boat is kept in a marina, the sailing season can be restricted because boats are put in and taken out of the water at the convenience of the boatyard or fitted into the marina schedule. By contrast, a dinghy kept on a trailer can often provide the unexpected day afloat, even in the depths of winter, as the following passage demonstrates.

BOXING DAY AFLOAT

We made a quick, unplanned getaway one Christmas. Bidding goodbye to our guests after a day's pleasant indulgences, we left behind our dirty linen, piles of presents, cards and excess food and escaped to Wanderer. Brancaster Staithe, north Norfolk, was peaceful and empty. Sailing out through the empty moorings, we gazed delightfully at the empty, flat salt marshes. All was quiet. The winds were SW force 3, and the offshore breeze was warm; our destination, Sunk Sand. Wanderer *lifted to the swell, and we slipped over the bar on the last of the ebb tide. As far as the eye could see there was nothing: seawards was a calm grey watery waste, the estuarine beaches behind glowed a wet gold as did the stubble fields beyond them.*

This place is like the very rim of the world; there is no emptier place to visit than the Wash in winter. Deep-draught boats shun these dangerous shallows, but centreboard dinghies can find great peace out here. Running about on the drying sandbanks to restore our circulation, we picnicked on the hard sand.

As the tide returned, we carried the last of the flood over a bubbling frothing bar, and the grey, calm afternoon lapsed into a black night. The gulls fell silent, and we later washed down the dinghy in a happy silence. It had been a good Boxing Day. Nothing special, just two Norfolk sailors sharing it alone in a Norfolk estuary.

Less work

Big boats require heavy anchors, large sails and heavy gear, all of which can deter the elderly, the less active or those of slight physique from handling them. By contrast, dinghies use light gear which requires much less physical effort to handle it.

Less expense

A dinghy involves lower intitial cost than a yacht and should depreciate less. Maintenance costs are even lower if the dinghy is kept at home and you are prepared to do your own varnishing, painting and repairing, whereas winter storage for a yacht and craning in and out of the water is a costly business at any boatyard.

Replacing or updating equipment on a dinghy will cost much less than for a yacht because items are smaller and cheaper, Crew costs on dinghies should also be lower since fewer people are required to sail them.

Bigger boats have to stay in deeper water, which can mean overnighting in anchorages that can be noisy, expensive, or crowded, but a dinghy can pull on to a quiet beach, giving the crew an opportunity to explore the locality as they take a rest away from the boat. Often, overnighting on beaches or riversides is free and usually more peaceful.

Freedom

Dinghies have an indefinable advantage over yachts in that a closeness to nature, and often an intimate contact with the elements, cannot be avoided. The ability to drop a mud weight or anchor on a windward bank or sunny reed bed and merge with the environment are things you rarely talk about but never forget. Last week, just after dawn on a misty May morning, I watched a kingfisher fishing off an overhanging alder branch. While rowing along river banks I have seen otters playing, heard cuckoos call, bitterns booming, seen cranes flying, and kestrels and marsh harriers performing aerial acrobatics above the reed beds of the Norfolk Broads. While sailing along the Gulf of Mexico in Florida we have watched mink and racoons gambolling with their young, and in Norway and Canada golden eagles have flown close to us. The ability to glide along silently using oar, paddle, praddle or sail enables the dinghy cruiser to be very intimate with nature. Bigger boats under power, even with quiet inboard engines, invade the environment far less gently and inconspicuously.

It is possible to extend the versatility of dinghy ownership by exchanging boats and homes with like-minded families in other continents. Such friendships can arise when families trail their boats abroad on their annual holiday. Quite by chance we were offered the loan of a Wayfarer in the Persian Gulf:

PERSIAN GULF CRUISE

We must have given many people cause to laugh as we left Heathrow Airport one January. Elatedly, my husband and I climbed aboard the plane and struggled out of wellington boots, life jackets and oilskins (easier to wear than pack!). Elegantly clad travellers nearby watched the disrobing with cool distaste.

Leaving a grey, foggy London to step out on sunny Sharjah airport was a climatic shock, but the cultural one was even more stunning. Gone were the winter-wrapped January sales crowds; here were olive-skinned men in white flowing robes moving with majestic elegance along sandy, sunny streets.

Our holiday plan was to identify and mend a neglected Wayfarer dinghy left on Dubai's offshore sailing club beach. It had been lent to us by a total stranger whom we happened to meet at a boat show.

7

The Dubai sailing club were friendly and helpful, and the much publicised war was never mentioned; the troubles between Iran and Iraq seemed worlds away. Within a few days, the 4.5 metre [15 foot] dinghy was stowed and ready for the month's holiday. Pushing out into the turquoise waters of the Persian Gulf, we laughed like children let out from school. Turning southwards from Dubai, we sailed on a broad reach, past a totally Eastern landscape of glittering gold and turquoise mosques and minarets. Sheikhs' summer palaces were built on the low sand dunes, and close by were white Arab houses clustered round cool courtyards. Laughing olive-skinned children, clucking chickens and chewing goats enjoyed the shade of palm trees. Itinerant workers' shacks, sheds, and garbage tips sprawled beyond the well-kept Arab villages. Contrasting oddly and towering above them, high-rise modern hotel blocks and conference halls linked two cultures 2000 years apart; we felt that we were in a time warp.

Sunset that first night as we camped at high water was a slow blood-red blush over the indigo calm Gulf. Almost immediately the sun sank and sparkling stars emerged in the velvet darkness. Close by, a sheikh's palace lit by a thousand lights looked like a fairy castle. Before we had completed supper, a jeep roared along the hard desert sand. Stopping beside our tented boat, three men in army uniforms jumped out, all carrying rifles. Holding tightly to one another we offered our passports, cups of tea and broad smiles. Later we learned that they were the sheikh's guards offering to take us to shelter in the police station for the night, assuming we had been shipwrecked on their beach!

Next day we continued southwards. A hot, humid calm hung over us. A new experience: a shamel was sweeping in. Onshore winds rose quickly to gale force, turning the whole coast into a lee shore. Well reefed, we sailed on. Finding a deep channel through the surf towards the desert, we turned into it. It was not marked on our charts, but shelter in such conditions should not be sailed past. We found that the channel was the beginnings of a new harbour. Round a sheltering corner was a huge crane. Eager hands took our lines and tied us to a barge. Several hours passed before the screaming hot winds died. While Frank drove off with the Korean labour force to telephone our friends, I sat happily in the dinghy, enjoying the enormous desert isolation. An hour after Frank had departed, a small dinghy driven by a spluttering outboard came straight towards me from the sea. *Fearful that a woman alone at night in the desert might not be safe, I looked straight at the man who climbed into the Wayfarer from his leaky tender. He merely held out a blanket and wrapped it round my shoulders. I offered some tea from our thermos flask and we sat in companionable silence watching a glowing sunset turn into a starry night.*

Farther south lay many miles of salt marsh and desert, but we were curious to explore new cultures and the Eastern lifestyle, and so we sailed back towards Dubai and onwards north towards Oman. The last camp of our month's holiday was the most spectacular. Rowing the last 12 kilometres [8 miles], as the wind dropped and the tide turned against us, was hot exhausting work, but it gave us time to absorb the magnificent scenery. Beyond the desert strip of land 300 metre [1000 foot] high mountains rose, bald and amethyst coloured, eroded by centuries of violent winds and scorching sun. They marked the Oman border. Without visas, we could not sail into the straits of Hormuz, so turning into the estuary at Ras Al Khaymah, we anchored the dinghy off the village of Al Ramms.

We were mesmerised by strange sights and sounds. Eagles soared high in the blue sky, resting in thermals above the purple mountain range. Blue and white herons fished in the shadows of a line of anchored dhows and a flock of flamingos waded along the turquoise creek. A large jade kingfisher used a wire woven fish trap as his fish-spotting territory. As a mullah called the faithful to prayer from a tall minaret in the middle of the village, a fisherman pulled his small row boat on to a nearby sandbank. He knelt on the damp desert dirt, turbaned head touching the ground, and his body bent low and long in silent prayer. Later that day, fishermen, splendidly regal in their customary garments of kaffiyeh and dishdashas (traditional white robes and head-shawls) – even while fishing – invited us aboard their dhow. Showing us how they used the adze to fashion their boats, they offered us thick bitter coffee. Later, we all sat round a communal supper dish of beans. Before the sudden subtropical dark descended, they took us ashore, walked us through a deserted village at the foot of the mountains, and proudly showed us their falcons.

Back in England I read the Bible with a new interest. We felt we had dinghy-cruised back into the Old Testament. This trip had not only tested our bodies and our minds – it had touched our spirits.

At present, *Wanderer V* sits in a friend's garden in the United States. Two years ago, Frank and I took early retirement. Shipping the boat to Miami in a container from Harwich, we later uncrated her in Port Everglades in Florida. Cruising the eastern seaboard of North America and sailing 1600 kilometres (1000 miles) each summer, Frank has reached Canada. He and *Wanderer* are still heading north. The variety of sailing adventures to be enjoyed and the marvellous range of a dinghy are endless. There is never time to get bored cruising a dinghy because there are such a variety of jobs to be completed, and with fewer people aboard there is more opportunity to take the initiative and make one's own decisions.

Choosing your boat

Every sailor has a dream boat in mind. I met *Wanderer* W48 quite by chance at a London boat show. It was love at first sight. Her simple lines were strong, and her battered gear spoke of high adventure. Thirty years on, the Wayfarer is still my ideal cruising home; however, I also enjoy singlehanding, and for me 4.2 metre (14 foot) is ideal for this.

It is pointless falling in love with an elegant or historic boat only to find her unable to cope with a stiff breeze or a foul tide, or to be unable to relax and sleep in her. If compromises have to be made in the choice of boat, the following basic characteristics should be born in mind:

1 Ideal length between 3 and 5.4 metres (10 and 18 feet); anything smaller could be unseaworthy and impossible to sleep in, and anything larger would be too difficult to get in and out of the water.
2 Good freeboard to keep the boat dry in a seaway.
3 Flat floorboards to sleep on and to enable the crew to sail with dry feet, above the bilge water, and to provide dry, flat places to stow gear.
4 Good sturdy and wide fore and side decks to work on.
5 Dry stowage lockers.
6 Good buoyancy.
7 Strong, sound construction.
8 Not too heavy.
9 Ample beam to afford relative stability.

As a generalisation, any dinghy can be cruised except the high-performance racing machines; these are usually too light, too wet and too tender, and often lack sufficient dry stowage spaces. Racing stresses a boat more than cruising, but the wear on a long cruise is greater, and so light racing fittings should be replaced by stronger ones. In particular, cruising boats need strong big cleats and fairleads. Frank suffered a dismasting 80 kilometres (50 miles) offshore in the North Sea as a result of a bent bottlescrew breaking. He now always replaces these with prestretched Terylene lanyards. Rudders and their fittings on cruising boats take real punishment in heavy weather, and the pintle and gudgeon fittings must be strong, and preferably through-bolted. The centreboard and its pivot bolt should be examined before every serious cruise, and shrouds, forestay and spreaders given similar checks. Our log when sailing to York from Norfolk recalls our near capsize as a result of inadequate and poorly placed jib sheet jam cleats.

YORK CRUISE

We were sailing our Wayfarer from Norfolk across the Wash, through the Humber, and up the Yorkshire Ouse to York. The wind was getting up and we should have reefed as we passed Goole Docks while still close hauled, but we didn't want to get caught by a ship coming out of the docks unexpectedly. The river turned up to windward in a short narrow channel, then bore away under the high level motorway bridge into a wide straight reach, ideal for taking in a leisurely reef, so we put it off. It was in the narrow windward channel that we got into trouble.

A sudden gust through a gap in the trees made Wanderer heel heavily; we luffed and let out the mainsheet. 'I can't release the genoa, the sheet has jammed,' I yelled, frantically trying to lift the rope out of the jam cleat. The next few seconds were spectacular, as we watched it all happen, almost in slow motion. The genoa blew the bows off the wind until the mainsail filled and Wanderer heeled until water poured over the lee sidedeck. 'We are over this time', I thought as we both scrambled to sit farther out, and prepared to swim.

We cursed racing fittings, which are so unsafe in a cruising dinghy. The trouble was that the jam cleats were fitted on blocks, so that a direct pull secured the sheet but an upward pull was needed to release it, which is impossible when sitting out. Only the Wayfarer's excellent stability kept us from capsizing.

Crewing for my husband in our 4.8 metre (16 foot) Wayfarer has been the most rewarding challenge I have yet met. However, I wanted to sail singlehanded in my own cruising dinghy as well. Over the years I contemplated a variety of small dinghies: the 3.3 metre (11 foot) Gull, the 3 metre (10 foot) Mirror, the 4.2 metre (14 foot) Leader, GP, Enterprise and Skipper, and several of the Drascombe range of boats. Toying with the pleasure of owning a wooden Tideway or a traditional Norfolk, I quickly realised I wanted to spend my available time sailing and exploring, not varnishing and caring for the dinghy.

While wooden boats have the advantage of lending themselves to simple modifications, those built in GRP generally need less maintenance and can stand more exposure to frost, sunlight and wet weather. Wooden dinghies need to be winter-stored in dry sheds, but GRP hulls are rot resistant, and if the gel coat is carefully preserved they can stand upturned outside during the winter. But remember that some of the best sailing can be during the peaceful winter season...

In searching for my ideal singlehanded dinghy, I had in mind a boat that would enable me to take a friend occasionally, but one that I could also handle on my own. Therefore, it could not be too tender because I enjoy spending many hours and days afloat, and I do not like to leap about trying to balance a lively boat in windy conditions – something that is very tiring. If the dinghy is too narrow, this also causes more acrobatics than required if the main object of cruising is to bird watch, explore and generally enjoy living aboard. If the dinghy is too heavy or too big, a small person (I weigh 44 kilograms [7 stone]) cannot be self-sufficient when launching and recovering the boat. Flat floorboards so that you can sail and sleep above the bilge water are something that I rate very highly for a cruising dinghy. Handymen may be able to make up their own floorboards, but I don't believe that amateurs can improve on the design of a professional draughtsman. Some boats are designed with a daggerboard so that a heavy centreboard casing is not needed. However, I prefer a dinghy with a centreboard because it lifts in shallow water, giving ample warning of running aground. A daggerboard hitting the shallows may jam and thus break more easily. A jammed daggerboard is also difficult to raise, and when it is in the 'up' position it reduces the space in the cockpit.

First-time buyers should look for a secondhand boat, or crew in as many different types of boat as possible, to discover the advantages and the disadvantages of each design. Heavy boats are more tolerant of mistakes than light ones; high-performance dinghies are a joy to control if the skipper has the experience necessary; small dinghies cannot be efficient load carriers; and old boats may be wonderful to own but tiring to push against a foul tide or headwind. My husband bought his first boat because he employed the engineer's maxim that 'If it looks right, it *is* right.' It would be difficult to love an ugly, unresponsive dinghy.

The choice of a dinghy depends on a number of factors:

- the area in which the boat is to be sailed. (Daggerboards are a problem when sailing in shoal water or over sandbanks or mudflats, as are fixed rudder blades, whereas centreboards and lifting rudders warn you of imminent grounding. High wooded valleys need tall masts, whereas in fjords katabatic winds could cause a violent roll unless the weight of the rig were low.)
- whether or not the dinghy is to be trailed often
- whether you plan to keep it afloat or launch it every trip
- whether help is at hand to recover when a new venue is used
- whether a car park is close to the launch site for loading and unloading gear
- access to a safe spot to leave trolley/trailer

My own choice is *Wanderbug*, a Wanderer class 4.2 metre (14 foot) dinghy; the MD version suits me perfectly. Being 4.2 metres in length means I can carry a crew or sail singlehanded as I choose. She is versatile for inland, sea or esturine sailing. Being 1.78 metres (5 feet 10 inches) in beam she is stable at anchor, so I can live and sleep aboard in comfort, as well as reef her afloat. She has a centreboard drawing 76 centimetres

(2 feet 6 inches) when it is down and 10 centimetres (4 inches) when up, so I can skirt shallows and sail along shelving river banks without fear of getting 'neaped'. There is ample buoyancy and dry stowage for my tent, sleeping gear and spare clothing. Her stability and strong foredeck and sidedecks allow me to work around the boat without fear of rolling her over. *Wanderbug*'s total weight is about 136 kilograms (300 pounds), so I can launch and recover her from most sites on my own. I can even move her on rollers if the slope is gentle. *Wanderbug*'s forestay is wire, spliced to a long rope tail which enables me to shoot bridges or overhead wires, and raise and lower the mast in its tabernacle while afloat. A large strong cleat, situated just behind the bow washboards, allows me to fasten or unfasten this rope while standing by the mast in the most stable part of the dinghy.

Dinghies that need to have the mast lifted bodily into position before the shrouds can be secured are not for me because the operation is so unwieldy. Neither are ones with a fixed gooseneck; I need a sliding gooseneck to reef more easily, and to tension the tent, and to give as high a ridge as is practical when I am living inside my tented home.

Wanderbug is constructed in GRP. Apart from fairly regular surface cleaning with a gel-coat cleaner, maintenance of her strong moulded hull is minimal. The hull is double chine, which is more stable in gusty weather than single chine boats, and I find her predictable and satisfying to sail when beating, reaching or running, either reefed or carrying full sail. She will heave-to, row, lie quietly at anchor, and dry out on a hard bottom quite happily, and she appears well built and strong. I have suffered no damage from floating debris or from glancing blows when sailing past submerged stakes or passing a river bank too closely. The clever shaping of the bow into an ample beam ensures a dry, stable, predictable, sea-kindly dinghy. My search for a suitable cruising boat is over!

After the hull shape and general construction have been considered, the rig and rigging is an important concern.

Standing and running rigging

Secondhand elderly dinghies may still have galvanised wire rigging, but stainless-steel standing rigging for shrouds and forestay is found on all modern dinghies because it is stronger and non-corrosive. Racing dinghies often use a tensioning lever to tension a wire halyard for the foresail because it enables the luff to be tightened better; but, generally speaking, cruising dinghies are looking for safety in preference to high performance, and rope halyards are preferable. They are nicer to handle than wire and they do not jam in the mast sheave or wear it as wire does.

Spars

Short spars that can be stowed inside the boat are convenient when towing or stowing. When a dinghy has two masts (for example, some of the Drascombe range) the sails are smaller and more easily handled, but the advantages can be at the expense of performance. However with the sail area shared between two masts an instant reduction in sail is achieved by dowsing the mizzen sail. I have also seen a simple reefing system being effected by dropping the mainsail and sailing the boat under foresail and mizzen only. The mizzen is a handy sail which will keep the boat moving along, or allow it to lie quietly head to wind while the mainsail is reefed. If there is no boom, another spar has to be carried to make a firm ridge pole between the masts over which to erect the tent. In my experience, having a rope stretched between both masts, or using the oars, is not as effective as using the boom for a tent ridge pole.

Short spars reduce windage and enable the boat to be rowed more easily; it will also lie more quietly at anchor. Such boats have a lower centre of gravity, so increasing their stability.

When a lugsail or a gaff rig is reefed, the heavy yards are dropped to the depth of reef required, thus increasing the stability of the boat. If high performance to windward is not a priority then the balanced lug, the gunter, the gaff and the una rig are all efficient, particularly off the wind. Their shorter spars can be easier to repair, are less likely to cause capsizes, and may be cheaper. Some boats have a boomless mainsail (convenient in an unintentional gybe) and need no kicking strap. Windward performance of these sails is less efficient, however, than the bermudian.

15

A bermudian rig is the most efficient when sailing to windward. The taller mast needs more care, of course, when rowing under bridges or when being towed, but reefing (either jiffy, slab or roller) is very easy on this type of rig, requiring mimimum effort. In strong winds the taller mast may make rowing, anchoring and righting after a capsize a little more of a problem, but in general this rig is highly efficient and popular. All things considered, it is good windward performance that enables the cruising boat to beat a foul tide and reach shelter before a storm breaks.

If wooden spars are your preference, you will find that they can be more easily repaired and adapted than alloy ones. Frank, sailing his Wayfarer from Scotland to Norway, met a force 9, capsized three times, and the mast lashed down in the crutch was shattered. At sea he and his crew were able to cut out the damaged wood, effect a jury rig with temporary lashings, and continue their passage to Norway some 320 kilometres (200 miles) away. Repairing an alloy mast would have been much more difficult. Wooden masts are more expensive and heavier than alloy ones and they need varnishing and storing carefully away from frosty and wet conditions. Also, they are buoyant. Aluminium alloy masts and booms need much less maintenance, but in the event of a capsize their lack of buoyancy may allow the dinghy to invert. Some dinghy classes use sealed booms, but the

Fig 1 Types of rig (opposite)
There is no perfect rig; every type is a compromise.
a Balanced lugsail A short mast, easy to rig. Weight of spars is low. A large sail area off the wind, and popular among workboats. Does not point well to windward.
b Standing or 'dipping' lug A more efficient sail than the balanced lug.
c Gaff rig A powerful driving sail off the wind, but the gaff sags off to leeward on the wind. There is a heavy gaff aloft and more complicated rigging.
d Gunter rig Requires short spars which will stow inside the boat. The size of reef that can be taken in is restricted to the length of the throat of the sail.
e Cat boat or 'una' rig An easily managed rig especially when singlehanded, and a large uncluttered deck area. Always combined with great beam. A very popular rig in the United States; developed from the oyster workboats of the eastern seaboard.
f Bermudian rig A very efficient sail to windward. It lacks drive when running, so the leech is cut full and fitted with battens to increase sail area. There is no limit to the depth of reef that can be taken in. A tall mast; the boom can be used as a tent support.

inbuilt buoyancy is not sufficient to prevent inversion without the additional use of sailhead buoyancy (see Fig 2).

Sails

Some people believe that heavier sails are needed for cruising than for racing. The standard sails are perfectly adequate, but it may well pay to reinforce the stitching where they rub. Reefing and stowing sails over a long cruise can cause chafe, and protecting them in sail bags is advisable when the sailing is over.

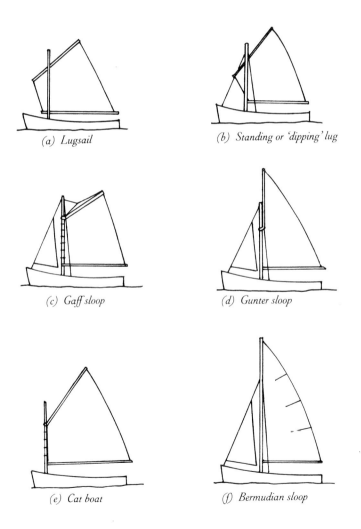

(a) Lugsail

(b) Standing or 'dipping' lug

(c) Gaff sloop

(d) Gunter sloop

(e) Cat boat

(f) Bermudian sloop

The ability to reef is important for the cruising dinghy. Often this can be done on land before setting sail, but reefing afloat needs to be practised too. Roller reefing means rolling the mainsail around the boom to reduce the sail area. A quicker method is 'slab' or 'jiffy' reefing. Without having to remove the boom from the gooseneck, the sail area is reduced by pulling down two lines attached through cringles in the luff and leech of the mainsail. These are cleated, and the ties across the sail are used merely to tidy the loose sail and prevent it blowing in the wind. The foresail, whether it be a jib or a genoa, can be quickly dowsed with a downhaul line or rolled up by a drum-type furling gear. Children like to help sail a boat, and two sails provide more training and give them a job to do.

Coloured sails are conspicuous and attractive and show stains and dirt less readily, but white ones are more generally used. Colour-coded bags that readily identify each separate sail provide a convenient method of stowage. If children or poor swimmers are on board, masthead buoyancy is a sensible precaution. This comprises a pad made of closed foam which is

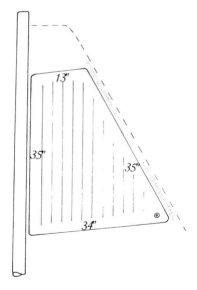

Fig 2 Masthead buoyancy
The inflatable pad inserted into a pocket at the head of the mainsail. It prevents the mast from sinking and aids capsize recovery.

slipped into a pocket sewn into the head of the mainsail; this prevents the boat inverting in the event of a capsize. Some people prefer to buy old racing sails and cut them down into smaller cruising and heavy weather sails, but I prefer to use full-sized ones and rely on the reefing system to shorten sail when conditions deteriorate. Carrying a small sail repair kit consisting of sail needles, Terylene thread, sail cloth patches and waterproof glue will enable you to attend to a simple tear, torn sail batten pocket, chafed corner, or unstitched seam before the damage worsens.

Ideally, a dinghy should be largely controlled by her sails, with the rudder used to make final adjustments.

Overall the disadvantages of dinghies over yachts for cruising seem small in comparision to the advantages. Dinghies offer less protection from the weather than cabin yachts, there is less stowage space, and the accommodation is smaller. The penalties for bad preparation, poor judgement and inferior sailing and seamanship skills are high in a dinghy, but this applies equally to both yachting skipper and dinghy helmsman.

2
Stowage in a dinghy

Whether a dinghy is used to cruise for a few hours, a weekend or a month, the basic principles of stowage are similar: keep it simple; make it safe.

It is important that the cockpit where the crew live and work is as uncluttered as is practical, nor must the sailing performance of the dinghy be affected unreasonably.

Our Wayfarer was once exhibited at the Earls Court Boat Show. Ian Proctor, her designer, came to visit. His eyes panned over *Wanderer*, recently returned from her cruise to Norway – two big anchors and a length of chain weighing 9 kilograms (20 pounds), masses of warps, tools, food, clothes, charts, and buckets were displayed in the dinghy cockpit. His face was a study in controlled surprise. 'When I designed the Wayfarer, I never visualised her carrying such loads,' he remarked.

The basic principles of storage should be:

1 Things needed once a day or less (bedding, tent, spares, charts not in use), to be stowed in less accessible parts of the boat.

2 Items likely to be required in a hurry or needed frequently (paddle, lifejackets, chart in use that day, 'nibbles' and drink, torch, white flares, pump, oilskins, camera and binoculars) to be stowed where they can be reached easily.

3 All loose items to be secured to the dinghy by shockcord or lanyard if bad weather is expected.

4 Heavy gear to be stowed as low as possible and as central in the boat as is practical.

5 Metal tins, tools, engine and bosun's stores to be stored as far away from the compass as possible (iron is the worst metal for causing compass deviation).

6 Anchors should be padded or laid in chocks and shockcorded to floorboards so that they cannot move in rough seas and thus damage the hull. Anchors need to be made ready quickly in case of an emergency, and must be stowed so that they can be released easily.

Fig 3 Stowage in Wanderbug

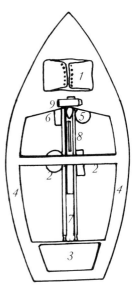

1 Tent rolled as it will be unrolled over the boom; stowed on under-deck shelf.
2 Heavy items shockcorded beneath the thwarts: cooker and crocks bucket, and water jar.
3 Spare clothing in waterproof bags, chart, torch, deflatable boat rollers, sleeping bag, air mattress.
4 Clipped beneath side seats: pump, tupperware box of 'nibbles', sunglasses, gloves, sailing hat, binoculars.
5 Anchor, chain and warp in bucket.
6 Spare water bottle.
7 Long oars, one either side of centreboard case, shockcorded together to prevent them moving over the floorboards.
8 Paddle tucked inside oars.
9 Thermos, behind the mast.

NB Everybody has an individual plan for stowing gear. I like to keep everything always in the same place, with heavy items in the centre of the dinghy and lightest gear in the stern.

7 All heavy gear should be secured well away from either end of the dinghy.

8 Work out the most satisfactory place for each item, and keep to this stowage plan so that you know instantly where to find each object.

9 Store dehydrated food in watertight containers clearly labelled or colour coded. Wrap clothing in watertight plastic bags.

There is satisfaction to be had in scouring the hardware shops for exactly the right shaped containers for your boat's individual dimensions. Square and rectangular plastic containers take up less space than round ones, and watertight buckets with lids and handles act as double-purpose shopping containers and for stowage of easily damaged objects like a primus stove or pieces of fresh fruit.

Some dinghies have sufficient space to stow some tinned foods beneath the floorboards. (They should have their labels removed and be marked with waterproof pen for identification.) There is nothing more refreshing than to reach beneath the floorboards and pass round cool tins of beer, orange juice or bottled water. Fresh milk keeps well, too, beneath the boards, cooled by the water against the hull. However, everything bought in glass bottles or jars should be transferred to plastic containers; broken glass in a dinghy is lethal.

Most dinghies have at least one watertight locker. The stern buoyancy compartment of a Wayfarer, for example, can be used to stow light kit like clothes and sleeping gear without prejudicing its main function, which is to provide buoyancy. Some dinghies have a shelf beneath the bows which is reasonably protected from spray and rain; watertight bags can protect light items stowed here. Other dinghies have sidedecks or side benches beneath which gear can be secured.

The construction of some dinghies is not easily adapted for gear stowage; in these cases, nylon netting or a plastic bag that does not shrink or rot can be strung beneath foredecks or side benches in a hammock-like shape, to hold light items like sunglasses, gloves, sun cream, binoculars or a camera, which can be reached easily when needed.

At a winter weekend at the National Sailing Centre in Cowes when I was Cruising Secretary for the Wayfarer Association, I asked people to demonstrate a stowage plan in an empty dinghy. It soon became obvious that there were as many different ways of stowing gear on a dinghy as there were skippers.

Inexperienced cruisers always take far too much equipment when they first start to cruise. It takes experience to know what to leave behind. A shallow saucepan, for example, can eliminate the need for a frying pan. A jibstick or batten can be used to hook gear out of an awkward corner of a long compartment, or an asbestos fire blanket carried to douse a fire can be used to wrap around containers of hot food to help them to retain their heat. If objects have two uses, stowage becomes simpler.

It is fun to hunt for exactly the right tool. In Sweden one year we discovered a tiny beautifully made stainless steel tin opener

A view of *Wanderbug*'s cockpit, ready washed down and prepared for an evening meal, showing storage arrangements:
(a) Note flat floorboards, essential so that cruisers may work and sleep dry above the bilge water.
(b) Oars shock corded in the centre of the floor ready for immediate use and where they are not in the way during sailing or sleeping.
(c) Pump and bailer ready for instant use – beneath side bench.
(d) Mast in a tabernacle – easy to raise and lower singlehanded.
(e) Everything heavy is shockcorded and stowed centrally so that the sailing performance of the dinghy is not impaired.
(f) Tupperware bucket with watertight lid acts as storage for kettle and billy can, as well as acting as a built-in windshield. Water bottles beside it.
(g) Open bucket stows anchor and warp. It can also be used as a bailer and loo bucket. Tupperware box contains 'nibbles' – nuts and dehydrated food for a quick snack whilst sailing.
(h) Plastic watertight tupperware boxes with colour coded lids contain crockery and other cruising gear. They are light and watertight, and when sailing they stack on shelves beneath the foredeck where only light gear is kept. *Photo: Len Tate*

with no projecting handle or moving part to jam, and I have a friend who day sails in a dinghy which carries a light folding bicycle that fits exactly in the stern locker.

Overloading a dinghy can be dangerous and, even after twenty years' experience, my husband and I were still guilty of this. After taking early retirement, we planned to cruise *Wanderer* for 'as long as it was fun'. Two weeks before her departure on a container ship, the lounge floor was covered in colour-coded sail bags and containers. A spare suit of sails, rudder, tiller, centreboard, cooker and shrouds were carried abroad in addition to our normal gear. A month later in Fort Lauderdale, Florida, we spent a whole day sorting and stowing all the gear. For several weeks we enjoyed good sailing and the cockpit was always clear of unwanted gear; we felt comfortable and well organised. Then one day, while running along Bogue Sound in North Carolina in a near gale, the seas began to break, and a long fetch and confused sea with wind against tide caused us to take in a second reef after reducing the foresail from genoa to working jib. Sitting well back on the stern of the dinghy, we were still planing fast. Large American motor cruisers came close to take a look, for a small dinghy travelling the Intracoastal Waterway is a rarity in America. The wake these cruisers threw up caused us further concern. The boat's bows were repeatedly imitating a submarine, and large breaking seas kept washing right through the cockpit; *Wanderer* refused to lift to them. Clearly, we were carrying too much gear too far forward in the dinghy. A day later, finding a friendly marina, we offloaded spare sails, oilskins, cooker and anchor. It is all too easy to overload a dinghy and spoil its sailing performance.

We had friends who planned their summer holiday cruise meticulously one year. Jumping out of the car some 160 kilometres later to rig their dinghy, they discovered that the sails had been left in the garage! A cruising checklist avoids such embarrassing mistakes. The following may provide a helpful basis.

Cruising Checklist

Address book and telephone numbers
Anchor, chain and warps
Bedding (sleeping bag and sleeping mats)
Binoculars (not more than seven times magnification)
Boom, boom crutch

Bosun's box (spare shackles, split pins, bolts, nuts, hand drill and bits, plastic insulation tape, whipping twine, screwdriver, small general-purpose saw, metal file, mole wrench, water pump, pliers, cutting pincers, marlin spike)

Buckets with watertight lids
Bungs
Camera and film
Centreboard bolt, nut and sealing washers, plus mast pivot pin
Charts, road maps, Ordnance Survey maps
Clothing
Compasses (hand bearing and steering)
Cooker and fuel
Cutlery sets
Engine and fuel, outboard bracket
Fenders
Fire-fighting equipment
First aid kit
Fishing tackle
Flares (white and red)
Fog horn
Food
Forestay
Gooseneck (spare)
Grease gun for trailer bearings
Hatch covers
Insurance papers (personal and boat)
Kettle (folding handle)
Kicking strap
Knives (shackle knife and floating knife – folding blades)
Licences – relevant to the waterways to be cruised
Lifejackets or buoyancy aids
Lights, torch, lantern and fuel
Log book and pencil/pen
Long warps
Mainsheet and blocks
Mast
Matches
Money
Nautical almanac
Oars
Oilskins

Paddle or praddle
Plastic plates, bowls and mugs
Pots and pans (a set of nesting billy cans saves space)
Pump and/or bucket – boat bailers
Radio receiver in waterproof box (cheap ones do not pick up Long Wave Radio 4 for the daily shipping forecasts)
Rowlocks
Rudder
Sail battens
Sails and sheets
Sponge and soap
Tent and tent supports
Tide tables
Tiller
Tin opener and bottle opener
Toilet bag and towels
Toilet paper
Torch
Water. Separate 4.5 litre (1 gallon) containers are easier to carry and fill than one big one
Wellington boots and spare walking shoes

For more extended cruising, a few extras may be necessary such as:
Bill of Sale (to identify ownership of the boat in the event of theft or accident)
Boat repair kit (small marine ply patches, mastic, GRP repair kit)
Boat rollers (canvas rollers are light to carry, easily inflatable by mouth, and easy to deflate and stow when not in use; large plastic ones are more robust and resistant to chafe, but,

since they are airline-inflated, they need to be carried inflated which adds to the boat's buoyancy. These pneumatic rollers make it possible to pull the dinghy up a beach when the trolley and trailer have been left at base. Rollers also make excellent fenders!

Courtesy flags, club burgee

Lifeline and harness

Lightning conductor (jump leads clipped to the shrouds are effective)

Medical insurance documents and any medication that you regularly take

Passports

Pilot books, tidal flow atlas, travel guides

Radio direction finder (RDF). This consists of a radio receiver with a hand-bearing compass designed to pick up the direction of coastal radio beacons and thus establish the boat's position in poor visibility

Second pump (diaphragm or semi-rotary pumps are more effective than the small piston designs)

Small Craft Registry documents

Visas

Rain has now started to fall and has stopped me writing this chapter in *Wanderbug*. It is time to put up the tent and prepare supper before the light goes. Since *Wanderbug* is my floating home, most things are stowed where they are to be used – as with most homes. First the tent goes over the boom, so it is stowed close to the mast on the shelf beneath the foredeck. This convenient shelf also stows my warps. The anchor sits in a bucket shockcorded beneath the port thwart, centrally in the dinghy where the heaviest weights need to be kept. The warp and chain are flaked down in the same bucket. The anchor can be carried forward or aft as required.

Once the tent is erected, I can sit on the centre thwart to prepare a meal. The gas cooker in a bucket with watertight lid, and a 4.5 litre (1 gallon) container of fresh water, are shock corded beneath the starboard side thwart. Kettle, cutlery and food are all within arm's length on a shelf beneath the bows on the starboard side. When I'm ready for bed, my sleeping bag and night clothes, stored in waterproof bags, are found in the buoyancy locker at the stern, which is where I need be to close the back tent flap. Radio, torch, thermos of tea and a book are placed beside my bed. No humping of heavy gear around the dinghy for me!

3

Clothing for cruising

A dinghy does not have the luxury of a cabin in which to shelter from the elements. The full glare of the sun, the biting cold of a northerly gale, chafe from badly fitting clothes, and regular dollops of spray or breaking waves which sweep the cockpit have to be planned for. Carefully chosen clothing enables skipper and crew to carry out tasks efficiently, and in comfort, and lets them enjoy their sailing without needing to return too often to the showers and shelter of the sailing club.

Protection from water

While wetsuits are excellent for racing and out-of-season day sailing, they cannot be considered practical for extended use. After a few hours these close-fitting neoprene suits – whatever style they are – become very uncomfortable because they prevent the skin from breathing normally. The skin starts to look white and dead, rather similar to the 'trench foot' experienced by soldiers during the First World War. Wetsuits work on the principle of holding a layer of water close to the skin; this is warmed by the heat of the body. Since water is a poor conductor of heat, the insulation that it provides prevents exposure.

A drysuit, by contrast can be worn over normal clothing which will absorb perspiration easily, like a thermal tracksuit. This drysuit is close fitting the wrists, ankles and neck. Air has to squeezed out before the hermetically sealed suit is zipped up, but even so there will be a residue of air trapped in the inner clothes; this tends to unbalance a capsized person as he tries to keep feet down and head uppermost in the water.

The most important outer garments for dinghy cruisers are the best-quality oilskins you can afford. Of all the foul-weather gear for the small-boat sailor, they are the most important, and care should be taken to avoid them getting torn. It is a matter of individual choice (and expense) whether you choose a one- or two-piece suit, chest-high trousers or waist-fitted ones, lightweight or heavy-duty material, a fitted hood or a separate sou'wester hat; whether you choose woven nylon, plastic impregnated nylon, Terylene or PVC material; and whether the seams are stitched, welded or taped. It is worth remembering that white oilskins reflect the sun's rays and thus keep you cooler when sailing in a hot climate.

We had two-piece, lined oilskins of nylon specially made for us. We chose stitching so that if the seams gave way we could repair them while afloat; welded or taped seams are more difficult to repair because the surfaces need to be cleaned and made salt-free before a good seal is effected. We chose large deep hoods into which we could retreat, shielding our glasses from the salty spray in bad weather. The trousers are high waisted with braces that cross over and don't keep slipping off the shoulders. The jackets have double-breasted openings with heavy-duty plastic zips overlaid by a wide strip and sealed with Velcro as a second line of defence. Stormcuffs at wrists and ankles bound by elastic keep the water from seeping up the arms and legs, and they seal in body warmth. If jackets are chosen instead of smocks you can loosen or unzip them should you get too hot. We chose waterproofs that were one size too large; they are more comfortable around the hips when sitting for many hours on the thwarts; they allow you to pile on more clothes in cold weather, and they allow more freedom of movement. For offshore sailing, one-piece suits are better for keeping the sea at bay, but two-piece suits allow better ventilation and are easier to struggle out of should you have the need to 'spend a penny' while sailing. Some oilskins at the top of the range incorporate built-in harnesses, but these are perhaps better suited to offshore yachts where bulk is not such a problem and the crew work outside the cockpit.

Hands can get cold, numb and very wet. Waterproof gloves – those with the fingers cut away so that knot manipulation and rope handling is easier or just ordinary domestic waterproof washing-up gloves can be used to protect your hands. Because we prefer to keep our feet dry and warm we wear wellington boots – two sizes too large so that they can be kicked off in the event of a capsize. Other people prefer soft shoes, wet socks, or even bare feet. Shoes or sailing boots with a good grip mean that moving about wet GRP surfaces is safer.

Protection from cold

When rigging and launching on a sheltered beach it is difficult to remember how cold it can be at sea. Any significant drop from the normal body temperature of 37°C causes lack of concentration and efficiency. Heat is lost fastest from the parts of the body where there is least fat to insulate it; thus the skull, backs of hands, knee caps, the shinbone area of the legs and the shoulder blades most need clothes that insulate and are poor conductors of heat so that they trap air in their fibres. Woven or woollen clothing is less efficient when wet and more comfortable when dry. Moisture builds up inside oilskins from excessive sweating and from condensation, so if several thinner layers of clothes are worn, the inner one absorbs the sweat and the outer one the condensation, they can be changed before the damp meets in the middle.

When I was planning my first offshore cruise, Frank gave me a bale of quilted material to make a two-piece suit for myself. Before we set sail one evening from a sandy beach on Skye bound for St Kilda, an offshore island some 50 kilometres (30 miles) west of the Outer Herbrides, I was literally pushed into seven layers of clothes. First I donned a long-sleeved woollen vest and 'long johns', winceyette pyjamas, string vest, three fine-wool jumpers, corduroy trousers and a canvas smock, then covered this outfit with a one-piece oilskin suit with inbuilt buoyancy. A neck towel, woollen balaclava helmet, three pairs of socks and heavy PVC waterproof gloves completed my wardrobe. Needless to say, 'spending a penny' was extremely difficult!

Modern outdoor equipment and clothing are extremely good for warm gear. Skiwear shops, Army & Navy stores and mountain and walking shops all stock what is needed, which is hard wearing, attractive-looking thermal tracksuits and light absorbent outdoor clothing, which is easy to launder and reasonably resistent to creasing, and which takes up little space.

For a three-week cruise I now pack two complete changes of clothes, consisting of thermal long-sleeved vest, tee shirts, wool and cotton shirts long enough not to ride up when tucked into trousers, cotton and corduroy trousers, long and short trousers, long and short wool socks, wool gloves, waterproof gloves, woolly hat and neck towel. Each garment is separately wrapped in a clear plastic bag, and a big clothes sack retains the entire wardrobe. Dark clothing shows up dirt less than light colours. Everything worn is of natural fibre (cotton, wool, canvas or silk) except the one dress I take. This is usually made of manmade crease-resistant material. If there is a concert, a church service or an invitation to someone's home, I like to wear something feminine and unobtrusive. 'Yachty' shore-going clothes have no place in the limited space of a dinghy.

Planning the essential clothing for cruising is all about anticipating the weather you are likely to encounter. Unpredictable weather should not catch you out with the wrong clothing, as happened to us on one occasion. We took our annual holiday in 1976 in Florida where the winter temperatures were expected to average 21°C; we packed for a warm-weather cruise. That season great damage was done to the citrus fruit harvest all over Florida as a result of a huge northerly depression sweeping down from Canada, bringing sub-zero temperatures. Beneath our canvas tent on the third night, anchored off West Palm Beach, we were too cold to sleep. That first week we had to wrap our heads, legs and shoulders in sail bags, towels and spare socks before generating enough warmth to sleep as ice formed nightly on the dinghy decks.

Protection from heat

I once sailed all day wearing only a swimsuit. The hot, breezy conditions were a delight after a sun-starved English summer, but by nightfall I was suffering from heat stroke. For several days, peeling burning skin and a blistered face and shoulders made the cruise difficult to enjoy. You only make that kind of mistake once.

For light-air sailing and when air temperatures are high and humidity is a problem, loose light pale-coloured garments help the body lose heat and stay comfortable. Synthetic fibres do not absorb body moisture and will not be comfortable. A wide-peaked cap will protect the eyes from glare and the head from intense heat. The lips, backs of the hands and tops of the feet need protection from exposure to excessive ultraviolet rays.

The most miserable conditions I have ever experienced in a dinghy were in Chesapeake Bay, in the United States, one July and August. America was in the grip of an unbearable heat wave. For six weeks the daily temperatures rose to 38°C, dropping at night only to 32°C. Our skin, tempers and energy levels suffered badly. In an open dinghy in calm conditions there is no protection from the sun's rays or the reflection of sunlight from the water. Draping wet towels over our heads we floated about wilting in the heat. In desperation we found a hardware shop and bought a large blue and white umbrella, and then took turns helming and relaxing beneath its shade. In such conditions large loose linen or cotton garments are the best. Sun block cream to protect against the sun, and lipsalve for lip protection should always be kept handy in the cockpit of the boat, and good sunglasses (on a lanyard to prevent them falling overboard) are very important.

Safety first clothes

Some people are scornful that I sail in large wellington boots. They are not elegant, they can be a little clumsy, but they do protect the legs and support the ankles and they are not dangerous if they are large enough to kick off easily in the event of a capsize. Stepping out of a dinghy into polluted water, or on to beaches that may hide broken glass, rusty wire, unexpected holes between rocks, or quicksands in local pockets may cause sprained ankles or cut feet. I was very glad to be wearing rubber boots in Lake Okeechobee in Florida. Standing on the bows, anchor in hand, ready to step ashore, I ignored Frank's request to 'Hurry up', feeling that danger was lurking somewhere. As I delayed my jump to the bank, a dark shadow passed from the shadows under the dinghy. It was an alligator that had submerged as we drifted in on the last of the evening breeze. I was relieved to be wearing boots even though the protection they offered in this case was illusory.

Harnesses should be worn whenever conditions are bad, when sailing at night, and by all small children on board.

Whether you choose to buy a webbing harness or make up a lifeline from prestretched rope, the principle is the same. They should be long enough to let the person who falls overboard be able to float or swim clear of the dinghy (about 5–6 metres (16–20 feet long); they should be designed to keep the person's head and shoulders above the water if towed for any distance; and they should be securely tied with a bowline to the strongest part of the dinghy – in our case, the thwart. A snap shackle or safety clip ensures a quick release. Never use an ordinary carbine clip as it can open unexpectedly if the rope lies across the gate.

That my life was probably saved by wearing a lifeline is illustrated by Frank's log entry; I was suffering from acute seasickness in the Minches at the time.

OVERBOARD IN THE MINCHES

I look behind me from my position on the thwarts where I was working on my navigation. Marg has gone overboard, backwards, unconscious, with her feet still jammed beneath toe straps. I grab her lifeline and try to lift her aboard. I shout to her, but no sign of life – eyes wide and staring – horrible. Wanderer gybes heavily, and I almost get her inert, heavy, water-logged body aboard, but the rush of water turns her body sideways putting even more strain on her back. Oh God! Head under water; I began to panic, then manage to get a grip on myself and start to think. I must remove her feet from the toe straps, tip her overboard, then recover her head-first. A brutal remedy, but the only possibility as she is unconscious and cannot help herself. Unfortunately, her built-in buoyancy in the collar of her lifejacket is not inflated, but at least she is clipped on to the boat.

There should be a buoyancy aid or a BS approved lifejacket aboard for every member of the crew. Needless to say, they should always be ready for instant use. For serious dinghy cruising, lifejackets are preferable to buoyancy aids. Lifejackets are bulky, consisting of a close-fitting jacket filled with closed cell foam, with additional inflatable airchambers in the collar, and they can be difficult to work in because of their bulk. These airchambers are blown up on entering the water – providing the person is conscious and able to fully inflate it himself, but even if unconscious the inherent buoyancy will prevent them from sinking. They are designed to turn a person on to their back, keeping their face above water even if they become unconscious.

Lifejackets fitted with a whistle and a battery light make it easier to locate a person in the water. A bobbing head is easily lost from view in the next wave trough. A buoyancy aid, which is like a sleeveless vest with foam-filled pockets, has the advantage of being less cumbersome in a dinghy, but it has less buoyancy and will only help a conscious person to stay afloat – they do not automatically turn the person in the water face uppermost.

Lifejackets, buoyancy aids and oilskins will last longer if rinsed in fresh water and stored dry.

Protection against chafe

Racing sailors usually return to a hospitable club at the end of the race. Cruising sailors, by contrast, tend to stay afloat for longer periods of time. Thus clothes should fit well, particularly at the neck, wrists and ankles; whereas a simple chafe to the skin is easily ignored on land, it can become most uncomfortable, after several days at sea. Broken skin or a cut is slow to heal if exposed to salt water, and it is difficult to keep the skin dry to heal.

Before going on a major cruise, I nightly apply methylated spirits to my hands, heels, and particularly my behind. This hardens the skin nicely. Before I started doing this, I suffered boils and skin irritation on my posterior as a result of the long hours sitting on a hard thwart.

Dress

It does the morale good to be able to live well in a sandy, salt-encrusted dinghy. Tonight, when I have finished writing this section, I shall dress for bed. The nights are still chilly. A warm pile tracksuit replaces corduroys. Nobody will see my hat and woolly socks, but I shall sleep all the better for being warm.

In my spare clothes sack is my concert-going dress, since I plan to sail in *Wanderbug* to visit the Aldeburgh Festival soon. There is nowhere that I have yet sailed to that creates such a sense of 'place' for me. Snape Maltings is Benjamin Britten's county and the Alde estuary is most evocative of his music. The low long skyline, its intimacy with the grey rumbling North Sea, and the call of cuckoo and curlew over the empty grey-gold reed beds are all part of his music. To visit a concert from a dinghy, elegantly dressed, is a great pleasure.

4

Trolleys and trailers

The mobility of a dinghy is one of its great advantages over the cruising yacht. With a reliable car, a good trolley and trailer, you can cruise any part of the world that can be driven to.

Trolleys

Always choose a trolley strong enough to support the boat and whose cradle shape will support the hull at the strongest points – which is the keel, not the hull itself. A jockey or nose wheel on the trolley or trailer enables the dinghy to be moved about more easily. The wheels of the trolley should be large and wide to ensure that it moves easily over soft ground and does not become bogged down. If the wheels are kept correctly inflated they will move the dinghy more efficiently, and note that plastic trolley wheels are more resistant to corrosion than galvanised steel models.

In fresh water, a painted finish is adequate protection against rust, but for sea use galvanising is necessary to keep salt water corrosion under control and is best for a low-maintenance, rust-free serviceable life. If, after launching, the trolley/trailer can be given a fresh water rinse before you begin your sea cruise, you will add considerably to its life span. In any case, the launching trolley should be removed from the slipway so that other people may launch easily.

Recovery of the dinghy usually takes place after a cruise when it is heavily laden with gear. Because it will be heavy you will want to adopt the easiest method of recovery and the one that requires the least effort. All heavy gear, like rudder and anchors, is best off loaded to avoid the trolley bending under the weight. A low-loading launching trolley that allows the dinghy to be floated off in only a few inches of water should be chosen.

There are various ways of supporting the dinghy on the trolley: an adjustable steel cradle padded with a PVC 'D' section fendering, or carpet; a centre block or roller under the hog or keel to take the weight and adjustable supports at the chine; a premoulded cradle of GRP; or a sling of thick wide webbing. Whatever the type, the dinghy must be positioned centrally and supported correctly with the weight on the keel before it is trailed home. The angle of the crossbar, rollers or cradle should be checked regularly to ensure the dinghy is not being nipped, particularly at the chines or bilge stringers or stiffening ribs along the hull.

Trailers

Look at other people moving their boats about, and watch how their trailers perform before choosing your own. A model with a mast support saves you having to pad and secure the mast of the boat on to the hull for transportation, and note that the rear hull support cradle needs to be as far aft as possible to ensure that the maximum length of hull is supported. The 'A' frame type of trailer allows greater strength and rigidity than the centre frame model.

Good suspension to protect the hull from vibration while travelling is important, as are correctly inflated tyres. (It's a mistake to fit heavy-duty 6 ply tyres because they are much harder and the vibration transmitted to the hull is noticeably more.) A frequent maintenance check and regular lubrication is needed on all rollers, wheel bearings and brakes, as well as regular hosing down with fresh water if launching into salt water. Never launch a boat off a road trailer immediately after a long journey when the bearings are hot, as water may be sucked into them.

It is possible to have docking arms fitted to enable the dinghy to be floated on to its trailer or trolley and positioned accurately before pulling out. If you plan to sail singlehanded, a winch on the trailer will enable you to recover the dinghy with minimum effort.

Frank's last present to me before he set out on a long singlehanded cruise from America to Canada was a trolley winch enabling me to recover *Wanderbug* alone. I rely on this a great deal.

A jockey wheel on the trailer makes a combination trolley/trailer and dinghy so much easier to move along a beach or any flat area. Note the long handle on the jockey wheel which avoids the need to bend low to drag the boat along. *Photo Anglo Marine Services Ltd*

Trolley/trailer

By far the best equipment is the combination trolley/trailer. This unit is driven to the water's edge, the trolley (and boat) is unloaded, the trolley is then pushed into the water, and the dinghy floats off. It is quick, easy and the expensive trailer never enters salt water. Combination trailer/trolley units are expensive, but well worth it if they protect the dinghy and the owner's back – from strain. The most popular makes are:

Bramber Combi 650/17
Moores Escort Easiload 16
Rapide Super C
Snipe L & L 15p
Sovereign 100T

On some models the jockey wheel is an optional extra.

Trailing

To safeguard against the possibility of the ball joint becoming detached while travelling, a safety chain is a sensible precaution. It is wise to check the trailer hitch after parking for any length of time – it is just possible that some youngster may have been playing with it to see how it works.

Regulations regarding trailing boats vary in different countries and it is the responsibility of the driver to comply with the rules. In the UK these are set out in Vehicle Construction and Use Regulations 1986 No 1078, and Vehicle Lighting Regulations 1984 No 812, available from HMSO.

Currently the permitted speed for towing a boat is 60 mph on motorways and dual carriageways, and 50 mph on other derestricted roads where a lower limit is not in force. A sticker or plate with '50' on it must be displayed on the trailer facing backwards. Alternatively, it can be attached to the lighting board.

A car may tow a gross load (trailer, boat, engine, and any other contents) up to 50 per cent of the kerb weight of the towing vehicle without needing overrun brakes, up to a maximum gross load of 750 kilograms (118 stone). If the towing vehicle is less than 2032 kilograms (2 tons), the maximum width is 2.3 metres (7 feet 6 inches) and the boat and trailer must not exceed 7 metres (23 feet). A trailer without brakes must not weigh more than 60 per cent of the kerbside weight of the car. This weight must be marked on the car and on the trailer.

The rear lights of the car (stop, indicator, tail and fog hazard light) must be repeated on the trailer lighting board, which must also have two red triangles facing to the rear. It is an offence to use a trailer where the tyres, lighting, coupling or mudguards are faulty. The police will prosecute the driver, not the owner, should the law be broken.

The possibility of continuous flexing stress to the mast and dinghy when trailing must be borne in mind, so both must be lashed securely to the trailer, and the webbing or synthetic rope lashings should be padded where they could cause chafe to the hull. The lashings holding the boat on the trailer should pass over the boat and down to the trailer on the other side – these straps merely hold the boat down; the design of the trailer should prevent it moving sideways. Straps across the foredeck of the boat ensure that the boat does not slip forward on the trailer. Many trailers are fitted with a padded 'V' on the mast support for the stem to fit into which is an excellent arrangement. The bows of the boat must be lashed securely to the front of the trailer frame, but not over-tensioned because this puts a heavy load on the hull as the trailer flexes at high speed and on bad road surfaces. Also make sure that the mast is tied down securely on to the mast supports at either end.

The weight of the boat should be supported by the trailer on the hog rather than on the chine or bilge stringers, preferably with the cross bearers or rollers beneath the forward bulkhead and the rear of the centreboard case, where the hull is strongest. The side supports should be adjusted to steady the boat rather than take any weight. Some trailers have three keel supports; these should be adjusted so that all are in contact and support an equal load.

The trailer should be loaded slightly nose-heavy to prevent 'snaking' at speed. All gear should be secured so that it cannot blow out of the boat during the journey, and so that nothing can move and cause chafe. The centreboard should be pinned or tied in the raised position to prevent it being damaged during the journey or when launching.

When you have travelled a few miles, stop in a layby to check that the lashings have not worked loose, that there is no chafe, and that the wheel bearings are not heating up. If the bearings are hot, there is little you can do other than wait for them to cool, all the while fretting that you will lose the tide. Generally it is better to grease the bearings thoroughly before setting out to ensure that they do not dry and then overheat.

Launching

All padding, ropes, webbing and ties used in securing the boat to the trailer should be put into a bag and left in the car with the lighting board. Road trailers with bearings still warm from the journey should not be run into the water unless the hubs are of the sealed type, and even then it pays to grease them first.

If the self bailers were opened to drain the rainwater out of the hull during the journey, they should be closed before launching.

Check that all bungs are in place in the hull and are secure and a good fit. Inspect the slipway before using it and, if launching off a beach, a good prod around will ensure that no partly submerged rocks, stakes or debris that could damage the dinghy are in your path.

I like to walk a prospective beach or untried launch site at low water (this makes an excellent excuse for winter forays to new places). At this state of the tide it is possible to discover the firmest ground, and whether there are underlying mud holes where the trolley may get bogged down, or submerged stakes, or outcrops of rocks.

I once drove from my husband's marina in Cheshire to East

Anglia and, desperate for a sail before the tide rushed away from a narrow gulley leading to the sea, tried to manhandle my boat afloat at high water without first walking over the area. We all of us – *Loon* (my Gull), my trailer, trolley and I – pancaked into a deep shelf of mud. It took me an hour to extract us all, and I didn't get a sail until the next tide!

Do not fall into the trap of wrapping the dinghy painter around your hand when launching. I once saw a singlehander trying to control the boat's launch and the trolley. As the boat picked up speed and hit the water too fast, the painter, which snarled in its coil, tightened around his hand; the poor chap was dragged into the water with the trolley on top of him.

I have no bung holes in my newest Wanderer, preferring to sponge out water or use a pump. This is because I once saw an

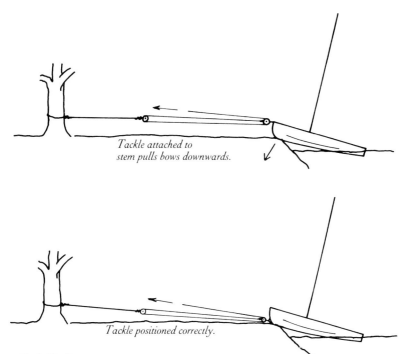

Tackle attached to stem pulls bows downwards.

Tackle positioned correctly.

Fig 4 Hauling out
A three or four part tackle (use the mainsheet if the blocks give sufficient power) can be used to pull the dinghy on to a bank. A hauling out eye fitted low down on the stem gives a better angle of pull; if it is too high, the bows will be pulled downwards, making the task very difficult.

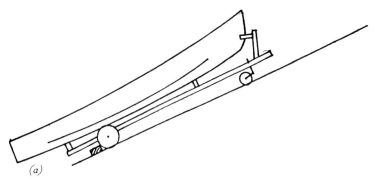

(a)

Fig 5 *Recovering boats on steep slipways – by hand*
a Too steep!
b A narrow slipway. Use bricks/timber as wheel chocks.
c A wide ramp. Zig-zag the boat and trolley up the ramp.

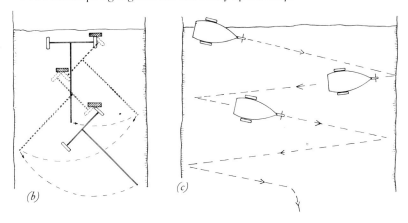

(b)

(c)

owner carefully checking his bungs at the transom before launching. By the time the man had returned from depositing his trolley back in its place some way off, the dinghy was filling with water. He discovered that the dinghy had hit a shelf on the edge of a decaying slip before floating off the trolley, and the bungs had been dislodged from their position in the transom edge.

Recovery

Recovering our dinghy one dark night from a slipway covered in deep mud and slime we threw a rope ashore and used the car to break the suction and pull her across the soft mud to the solid ground. It was many miles farther on that we discovered that we had holed *Wanderer* by sliding her over some sharp object buried beneath the mud!

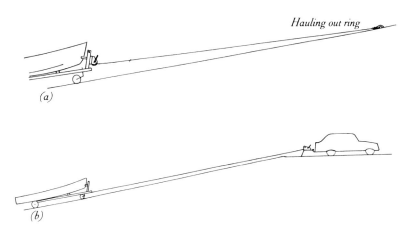

Hauling out ring

(a)

(b)

Fig 6 Recovering boats on steep slipways – by winch
a A winch can be fitted to the trolley to enable singlehanded recovery.
b A winch can be mounted on the car ball hitch to recover boat and trailer up a ramp which is too steep for the car to negotiate.
c The winch rope should be braided prestretched rope and should lead on to the lower part of the drum to reduce the leverage on the mounting post.
d If the winch post is likely to bend or break from a horizontal pull, lead the rope through a snatch block on the trailer tongue.

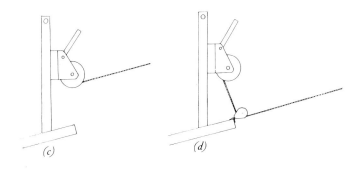

(c)   (d)

Recovery of a dinghy is usually more difficult than launching, and it is often done when one is most tired. We have an eyebolt, through bolted, *low down* on the stem to which we attach a three part block and the tackle to facilitate pulling her ashore up a steep or difficult slope. All heavy gear should be off loaded from the dinghy before she is brought out of the water.

Nobody should stand behind the dinghy when she is being recovered; if a heavy-laden dinghy slides back into the water, you could be run over by it.

Putting bricks behind the wheels and tacking or zig-zagging the trolley or trailer up a steep slope helps if nobody is around to help you recover your boat. Recovering a dinghy at high water also helps reduce the work load.

A boat that has been sailing should always be hosed down or washed in fresh water after its cruise.

5

Anchors and anchoring

Never economise on ground tackle; the safety of boat and crew may depend on it. No cruising boat should sail without an anchor, and sometimes two are necessary.

The holding power of any anchor is dependent on its design and weight. Because of the difficulty of stowage it is not easy to choose a conveniently shaped model of the right weight. The five most reliable types, shown in Fig 7, are as follows:

Fisherman   This has good holding power on a hard bottom and rock. it is easy to stow because it stows flat when the crosspiece is unpinned and folded along the stock. The disadvantage of the fisherman anchor is that is has to be assembled each time it is required, the stock being held in position with a pin or wedge. Also, it can foul its warp around the upper fluke when the tide turns and the boat and warp are pulled downstream.

Danforth   This is a good general-purpose anchor with good holding power in gravel and sand. It stows flat, which makes it easier to carry.

CQR or 'plough'   Designed by Sir Geoffrey Taylor who intended calling it the 'Secure' anchor (phonetically CQR), this is an excellent type of burying anchor with good holding power in most types of ground. However, its shape makes it difficult to stow in a dinghy.

Bruce   A one-piece shaped burying anchor. It is said to be a good general-purpose anchor, but various trials have suggested that one small enough for cruising dinghies is not particularly satisfactory.

43

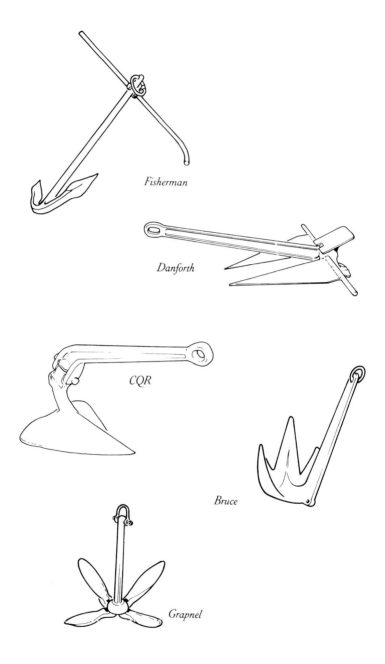

Fisherman

Danforth

CQR

Bruce

Grapnel

Fig 7 Anchor designs

Folding grapnel The four flukes of this type fold inwards and a sliding collar holds the points into the stock, making it a very convenient anchor to carry. However, it does not penetrate the bottom as well as the other types, and it drags easily through soft sand and mud. It is not to be recommended as the main or 'bower' anchor.

Dinghy anchor (non-folding grapnel type) This is a type that is rarely seen these days. In many ways it is similar to the fisherman anchor, but the crosspiece can be turned on the shank for easy stowing. Frank uses his with the crossbar slid up to the head – that is, as a proper rigid grapnel. It is an excellent anchor with good penetration and has never dragged yet.

Our original Wayfarer, now in the National Maritime Museum at Greenwich, has a 2.2 kilogram (5 pound) CQR 'bower' anchor and a 3.1 kilogram (7 pound) grapnel dinghy type for the secondary 'kedge' anchor. We now carry 45 metres (150 feet) of warp which rolls neatly on to a wood drum screwed to the side of the mast tabernacle. The anchor warp is 8mm braided prestretched Terylene with 2 metres (6 feet 6 inches) of 8mm galvanised chain shackled to the stock. The chain helps the anchor to bite, acts as a shock absorber, keeps the pull horizontal, and prevents chafe from rocks or shells. The bitter end of the warp is tied to the drum as it is only too easy to lose the whole lot overboard. Each anchor is shockcorded to the floorboards, one either side of the mast. This keeps the weight low and in the centre of the boat.

In *Wanderbug* I carry a 2.2 kilogram (5 pound) plough-type anchor shackled to 1 metre of 5mm galvanised chain, then 30 metres (100 feet) of plaited prestretched 6mm Terylene warp which is neatly coiled into a bucket with the anchor lying on top and shockcorded in position. The bucket sits beside the mast and the free end of the anchor warp is permanently cleated to the bow cleat which is the strongest part of the boat.

Nylon is the preferred rope for anchor warps. Its advantage is that it is light, strong, flexible, rot-proof, and has great elasticity which reduces snubbing – which might cause the anchor to drag and lift out. Too much stretch in a warp is not a good thing when it is used for some other purpose (such as pulling a boat up a bank or across a beach), so we tend to carry rope that can be used for all jobs – braided prestretched Terylene. Whatever type of warp is chosen, it should be inspected regularly for signs of chafe. A diameter of 8mm is satisfactory as it gives a margin for safety. One should carry enough anchor rope to allow you to anchor safely in the depth of water you expect. As a general rule, the ratio of anchor cable to water depth should be 4:1 in favourable conditions and 6:1 in unfavourable conditions – although for most short cruises in known sailing areas, four times the depth is acceptable. All these figures assume that an adequate length of chain is shackled between the warp and the anchor.

There are many stories of crews paying out an anchor warp and watching the unsecured end go overboard, but I once saw a crew throw out an anchor without checking that it was even tied to the warp! The bitter end of the anchor cable should be tied to the strongest part of the boat, usually a bow cleat or round the base of the mast, then out through the fairlead, and the other end tied to the anchor using either an anchor knot or fisherman's bend. The knot ends can be 'moused' or whipped for extra peace of mind. If a shackle is used, the pin should be wired or 'moused' to prevent it working loose.

How to anchor

It is not an uncommon sight to see a boat sailing fast into a harbour with the crew throwing a bundle of chain, warp and anchor overboard when yelled at to do so by the skipper. To lay out an anchor properly to prevent it fouling or dragging takes time and needs practice. Ideally, the dinghy should be sailed on a beam reach to the chosen area for anchoring, luffed to stop the boat, and at the moment when the dinghy starts to drift backwards the anchor should be dropped overboard. The warp should be handed out to prevent it snarling up as it snakes out through the bow fairlead. After giving the anchor time to dig in, a good tug on the warp will indicate whether or not it has a good hold. Taking a transit on two fixed objects ashore (possibly a tree and a house) should establish that the anchor is not dragging. Then the centreboard can be raised and the sails lowered. If there is any doubt about its security, the anchor should be hauled in and a second attempt made. Sometimes it is a good idea to row the dinghy backwards from the anchor to double check a

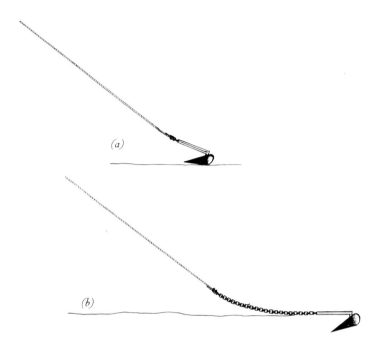

Fig 8 How to anchor
a Anchor drags owing to the upward pull of the warp.
b Anchor bites and holds better as the weight of the chain pulls down the stock
of the anchor.

doubtful hold. A snatch tug will tell the skipper whether all is
well, as the feel of an anchor dragging over the bottom is quickly
recognised.

If a second, or kedge, anchor is to be laid out, its purpose is
usually to prevent the dinghy sheering about or sailing round
her anchor, so that in restricted moorings you do not swing on to
another boat, or a sandbank, or across another boat's moorings.
The heaviest anchor should then be chosen to keep the boat head
to wind or tide (whichever is judged to be the stronger) and the
kedge will prevent her swinging.

Where there is little or no tide, one technique for landing is to
drop the main anchor as the boat glides into the beach with a
stern line taken ashore. By carefully planning where to drop the
anchor and by pulling the boat into the beach on the stern line
and letting the bows ride to the bower anchor, the crew can step
ashore with dry feet.

Another method of anchoring when the tidal waters (and on a flood tide) is to secure the boat on the main anchor, with a trip line attached to the crown of the anchor and taken ashore. When ready to sail again, the trip line can be tugged from the shore, the anchor broken out and pulled to the beach, and the boat recovered by its anchor warp.

In tidal water when the tide is ebbing, the better method is to sail on to the beach, lower sail, place the anchor on the bows of the boat, and flake its warp beside it. The trip line fastened to the anchor is held from the shore and the boat is pushed off the beach into deeper water where a jerk on the trip line should pull the anchor off the boat to anchor it. To retrieve the dinghy when the picnic is over or when the tide has fallen can be done by hauling in on the shore-secured trip line. Whenever the dinghy is left afloat with the crew and skipper ashore, a watch must be kept in case a passing speed boat sets up a big wash causing damage to the dinghy by pounding her into the bank or pilings. The main object is to keep the cruising dinghy just afloat, but accessible whenever it is required.

On our American cruise, we experienced several thunderstorms which, when combined with a northerly front, are particularly violent; the wind can jump from a light breeze to gale force with little warning. When such conditions were expected, Frank anchored with more than usual care, laying out two anchors from the bows towards the NW at roughly 70° to each other, and rowing in each anchor in turn. Anchored in Oxford harbour off Chesapeake Bay one July evening, the wind jumped from a light SW breeze to NW storm force within 20 seconds (it was recorded ashore at 65 knots) catching *Wanderer* beam-on with her tent up, and it blew for 15 minutes. Fortunately *Wanderer*'s anchors held (although our inflatable tender, tied to our stern, was torn away), but several large yachts anchored around us dragged badly.

Before committing the anchor, time should be taken to consider the state of the tide, currents, position of nearby boats, and how they are lying to their anchors. Some people lash the tiller in position but we remove both rudder and tiller and lay them on the stern locker, where they cannot be trodden on or damaged. Then rudder and tiller are usually tied to the dinghy horse so that they cannot go overboard.

The nature of the sea bottom can be read off the chart (eg sh= shingle, m= mud). The best types of ground to choose for a good hold are those firm enough to secure the anchor, but granular enough to let the flukes penetrate. Soft mud, loose sand or silt do not provide good holding, but firm sand, firm mud and soft clay are excellent. If you suspect your anchor may foul on rocks or underwater rubbish, a trip line secured to the crown of the anchor should disengage it without you having to swim down the warp to free it by hand!

On one cruise sailing a borrowed dinghy we anchored at

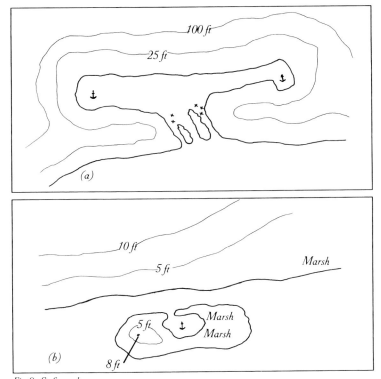

Fig 9 Safe anchorages

a A rocky cove sheltered from every direction The islets and rocks in the entrance break up any swell. Anchor anywhere here, but move to the head of the cover close under the land for a lee if a gale is expected.

b A sheltered lagoon in a marshy island Although there is little shelter from the wind as this is a low-lying area, and there are no trees or high land to deflect the wind, a comfortable night can be had as the seas cannot build up swell.

Umm Al Quiwain in the Persian Gulf among the local dhows, assuming that the local boats had anchored in the best place. Next day we prepared to sail on, but attempts to break out the anchor failed. Unwilling to swim in water reputed to have deadly sea-snakes in it, we spent a frustrating hour rowing the dinghy backwards and forwards on a shortened anchor warp, attempting to snatch the anchor free. The penalty for not fixing a trip line to the anchor crown was that we missed the tide and had a long fight to get out of the estuary against the incoming flood. We should have used a trip line too when anchored in a Norway harbour beyond the Arctic Circle. Rowing round Harstadt harbour for half an hour one cold sunless August evening, we chose our spot carefully and lowered the plough anchor in perfect textbook manner. Next morning I had great trouble lifting it. On the end of it was a large bag of dumped empty mussel shells.

Anchoring out of shipping lanes and in shallows where big boats cannot enter is the obvious choice for cruising dinghies. A riding light secured as high as possible in the rigging (see page 154), with a powerful torch and white flares handy, and tiller and rudder kept in position but lashed should the need arise for a quick move are also sensible precautions. Listening to the weather forecast before planning where to anchor may save you an uncomfortable night. If, for example, the forecast is for SW winds but you have an easterly breeze, you are probably experiencing a local sea breeze and may expect the predicted SW wind to establish itself by nightfall, when the sea breeze created by rising convection currents over warmed land will have died.

Fig 10 (opposite) *Where not to anchor*
a *Cliff cove* This is a spectacular anchorage and often recommended by the sailing guides for that reason. There is little else to recommend it. It is usually very deep under the cliff and the anchor will be unreliable, being almost 'up and down'. The cove will be uncomfortable in wind from any direction. Winds from the north and east send waves into the cove which are reflected back from the cliffs; a southeasterly wind causes a swell to run up the fjord and round the headland; winds from the south roar over the headland, funnelled into violent gusts through the col and then beat down on to the anchored boat; and southwesterly, west and northwesterly winds form vicious squalls which fall vertically from the high cliff tops with considerable risk of capsizing the boat.
b *A bay open to the prevailing wind* A swell will run into this cove for many hours after the wind has died down. Do not anchor here.

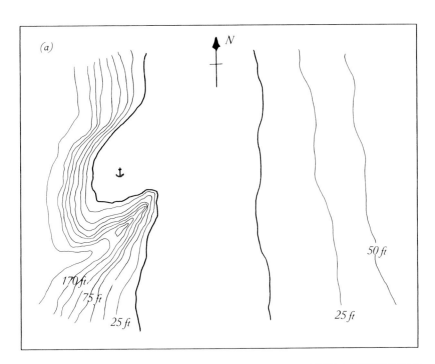

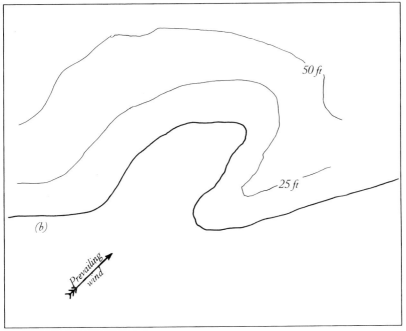

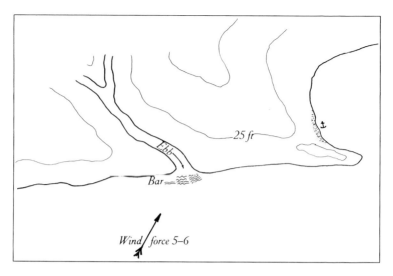

Fig 11 Finding an alternative anchorage
A dinghy should not attempt the estuary entrance because of the heavy breaking seas on the bar caused by the ebb tide running against the strong onshore wind. Anchor instead in the lee of the farther headland. A dinghy would be able to anchor close in or pull ashore on the beach, whereas a deep-draught yacht would anchor farther out, and might roll uncomfortably if a swell comes round the headland.

Also, choose a place where protection can be expected from most wind directions, and where there is not a long fetch for waves to build up. (A 'fetch' is an exposed open stretch of water.) Anchoring behind a sandbank, or downwind of a chain of islands, behind a reef, or even a reed bed, should provide shelter from swell, leaving a smooth area in the lee. For choice, never anchor near a lee shore (one on which the wind is blowing) nor in a small cove with steep cliffs all round, because if bad weather comes in and a swell sets into the cove it could be difficult to get clear of it in the event of a wind shift. Remember, too, that swells tend to run round behind an island. The waves are retarded in the shallows near the shore, swinging the waves round the island and causing an uncomfortable sea where the two systems 'mix'. The only possible anchorage in an emergency is *very* close under the land.

In mountainous areas, beware of katabatic winds and squalls funnelling down off steep cliffs.

Anchor dragging

If the anchor drags shortly after the boat has turned on the tide, it will have tripped out and you can expect it to dig in shortly as the pull on the warp causes it to bury again. If it continues to drag, it is probable that the warp has taken a turn around one of the anchor flukes, and you will have to pull it up and re-anchor. This is always annoying as it is usually dark, you are probably tired, and it may be raining as well!

If the anchor drags when the wind gets up or the tide rises, pay out more cable as this will improve the angle of the anchor – but you have probably underestimated the scope required in the first place. (A scope of 5:1 in depth of 6 metres (20 feet) amounts to 30 metres (100 feet) of warp, which seems a great length when you are paying it out.)

If the anchor drags and you suspect poor holding ground, you may improve the situation by increasing the length of cable, but you will be safer in the end to anchor elsewhere. If this is impractical, use two anchors in tandem. You can judge if you have stopped dragging by taking a transit on objects ashore, and by holding the anchor warp you will feel a dragging anchor.

Anchor snubbing

Nothing is more miserable than being unable to sleep because of a boat snubbing or jerking against her anchor. It happens rarely with a rope warp but is more common with chain. Try letting out more cable or hanging a heavy weight (such as a coil of rope) halfway down the cable to absorb the shocks.

Rolling at anchor

Rolling is very uncomfortable and is usually caused by the boat lying to the wind (or tide) but across the swell. The remedy is to swing the boat into the swell by some means. On one occasion, anchored in a tidal river, we were woken from a deep sleep by the boat rolling badly as the tide flooded upriver. Frank fixed a 'spring' from the boat's quarter on to the anchor warp, adjusting both ropes until the dinghy was lying across the wind but with her bows headed into the swell. We then went back to sleep. Sometimes it is necessary only to replace the tiller and rudder, and lash them to one side in order to swing the dinghy's head to the swell.

Retrieval of anchor

Hoist the mainsail, then pull the dinghy forward on the main anchor warp until it is 'up and down' from the bow. Break out the anchor (standing as close to the centre of the cockpit as possible to ensure you are in balance with the dinghy), backing the jib slightly to ensure her bows fall off in the correct direction, and lift the anchor over the windward side, taking care not to damage the hull. If singlehanded, dump the dirty anchor in a bucket and sail off. With a crew there is time to remove weed, clean mud off the anchor and warp, and stow it ready for use again by flaking the warp neatly in a box or plastic container and shockcording the anchor over it, or rolling the warp round a drum.

Each time I anchor *Wanderbug* I frap the halliards, clipping them away from the mast, so that they do not keep me awake by tapping against it all night long. There is nothing more frustrating than having to climb out of a warm sleeping bag to silence them in the middle of the night.

That an efficient anchor saved a nasty shipwreck of *Wanderer* is shown in Frank's log. We were returning from St Kilda, had recrossed the Minch, and were approaching the mainland of NW Scotland. It was dusk on a wild early August as we turned Cape Wrath.

ANCHORING

Intend to anchor in Kyle of Durness, but Loch Eribol would be better. As we round the large island at the loch entrance, it looks more like the entrance to Loch Eribol. The double light flashes from a lighthouse confirm this too, over on the opposite hill, but it does not happen again, so maybe low cloud now obscures the lights.

Tremendous gusts whistle off the cliffs, and we reduce sail yet again. It is now quite dark and we feel our way along under the cliffs to windward until we hear breakers ahead. We free off but find rocks awash to port. Am completely baffled – there should be a long loch ahead. Wind is gale force westerly, but we are sheltered by the lee of the cliffs. Margaret puts out the anchor, and we lay out about 30 metres [100 feet] of line. It is so dark. I can feel it, and I reflect on the stupidity of approaching an unlit coast in worsening weather, at night. We put up the tent and heat food as we badly need a hot meal. I check the position every four minutes. I can hear the roar of breakers on the sands to port and breakers on rocks ahead, and to starboard as well. *Unpleasant if she drags.*

At 0100 hrs the weather has worsened, wind veered into the north and blowing force 8 and gusting – it is driving straight into the fjord and putting up a big swell; the dinghy is sheering about wildly; 0130 hrs: still pitch black, wind increasing. Heavy seas coming into the loch from the sea. Anchor still holding. Glad of the springiness of nylon rope otherwise this snubbing must lift anchor from ground. Wished I had my CQR to lay out as well. I let go another 21 metres [70 feet] of rope to try to reduce snubbing on anchor. If we drag I intend to attempt to sail to the strip of sand on the other side of the loch, as across there is a lee under the land and I prefer to be blown ashore on to sand rather than on to rock if we drag. 0400 hrs: becoming lighter. Still in the same position. Anchor still holding, but only just, I think. 0430 hrs: daylight. Tremendous swell up the loch. Last night we were sheltered and safe, but this switch in the wind means that we are now dreadfully exposed. Situation very dangerous. Main concern is anchor dragging; we may drag ashore before we can get sail on her. 0650 hrs: boat almost rolled over. I scramble on to stern in a desperate bid to balance her. The swell running down on us: almost vertical 4 metre [12 foot] walls of water, breaking heavily. We almost capsize twice more, and have to sit out violently as breakers roar over us. There is a continuous line of surf just to leeward on to the beach. Nasty!

NB The correct timing of two flashes were not, as we thought, the expected lights on shore, but the headlights of two cars driving along the cliff. That we only saw them once – but suspected low cloud to be the reason – emphasises the common mistake; that one sees what one is looking for!

6

Dining in a dinghy

My first cruise was in a large yacht with the Island Cruising Club. Feeling cold and seasick for the most of the first day, I looked forward to an evening meal in a sheltered harbour. Basking in sunshine on deck, the galley crew passed up steaming plates of macaroni in a cheese sauce. The flat shallow plate did not keep the food warm, and it was difficult to chase macaroni lumps around in a runny sauce. Had I been alone I would have drunk it!

Those who cruise need to consider what to cook, how to cook it, and in what to cook, serve and store the food. When to eat, especially the main meal, is also worth planning.

What food to take

In a loaded cruising dinghy fresh fruit and vegetables are difficult to carry. The vegetables that store best are root ones: carrots, potatoes, turnips and onions all last well. Salads, however, are not worth carrying; within twenty-four hours tomatoes and lettuce are hardly worth the space they take up. Fruit such as apples and bananas bruise easily, but oranges and grapefruit last well and provide good vitamin value. Going ashore to buy fresh bread and vegetables makes an enjoyable break from the dinghy during coastal hops, and exploring local markets is always fun. On my first solo cruise, I was so worried about possible damage to the dinghy that instead of visiting shops I stayed aboard; my stores consisted of only eight tubes of dehydrated curry packs and oranges and Mars bars!

56

Dried food is lighter to carry than tinned, but considerably more fresh water has to be carried to reconstitute it. In an isolated fjord in Arctic Norway, Frank and I had run out of everything except for one dehydrated packet of shrimp risotto and less than a pint of water. Determined to find 'a vegetable' I dragged seaweed out of the water. Noticing that the water was less saline than normal, I thought cooking the risotto and seaweed in 50 per cent seawater would save enough fresh water for a cup of tea. Needless to say, supper was revolting – but just after we had stopped laughing about it two Lapps paddled by, offering us two skinned reindeer (we think!) almost as large as our dinghy!

Tinned food, although heavy, bulky (magnetic) and more expensive than fresh, can provide wonderful hot stews when you are tired and cold. Ready meals in self-heating cans are a real boon to the hopelessly undomesticated sailor, or when you are too exhausted to spend time preparing a meal. The 'Hotcan' provides a hot meal within minutes. This firm now provide five choices of 400 gram meals. A metal tool is provided to pierce the tin's outer rim, and the meal in the inner insulated tin heats as a result of chemical reactions in the outer rim. Dried food, and convenience dehydrated packs, are light, take little stowage space, and can be made quite tasty – but only if fresh water is easily available. But whether your preference is for tinned, fresh or dried foods, most meals taste good after an exhilarating sail and a successful landfall!

On my first offshore cruise with Frank to St Kilda, we had had a hard outward journey. On our return sail towards the Outer Hebrides at dawn, Frank invited me to stay in bed while he made breakfast.

I listened blissfully as he hove-to and cooked a meal on a calm dawn sea. I visualised at least a hot mug of tea and a bacon and egg sandwich. To my amazement I was handed a billy can of unidentifiable stew-like mixture. 'I've made green pea soup and scrambled egg in one dish,' explained a cheerful Frank 'Eat it quickly while its hot – the warmth will do you good.'

Fresh meat does not last long in an open boat, and cooking it takes time and a significant amount of fuel. A better protein substitute is fish, which you can catch yourself, or buy when you sail past a fishing boat. We were once thrown some delicious dabs by a local fishing boat while we were sailing in the Kattegat. Entering Brancaster harbour from a trip across the Wash we sailed towards a shrimper, boiling up his catch while waiting for the flood tide into the drying-out port. A bucket of steaming fresh shrimps made an excellent supper dish. Collecting mussels can be a delightful occupation while exploring on a pollution-free shore – quick to prepare, easy on fuel, and needing only blanching in boiling water, they are an economic and delicious, meal.

Fresh bread is the most difficult item to carry if cruising far away from shops. Sliced white bread appears to be the type to go mouldy the quickest. We always carry hard biscuits for when the bread runs out. Though rice and noodles can replace bread for some meals, some people prefer to bake their own bread over a camp fire on the beach. Some crews are not happy without a bacon and egg start to the day; however, this can only be provided on short cruises, as bacon, cheese and butter are best stored in an icebox. Fresh milk is a luxury; the powdered kind is easier to transport. Long-life milk is bulky to carry and difficult to stow without spilling. Fresh water can be stored in 5 litre (1 gallon) screw-top plastic jars; we carry at least two jars with a third one empty, always available to fill up.

Storing food

We carry two small canvas ex-army haversacks for stores; one carries only savory dishes, the other contains sweet foods. Each can be easily identified. If the foods are tinned, the labels are removed and a waterproof pen is used to identify them. Food that needs to be kept dry like bread, biscuits, bacon, nuts, teabags and coffee are stored in colour-coded square boxes (round ones take up too much space). For a short cruise, food can be frozen in a container, and even whole precooked meals can be frozen into these square containers and stacked in the rucksacks. They stay usable for several days. Tupperware containers seem to be the best on the market. The lids seal well and are watertight, and the plastic material is flexible and hard wearing. They carry a lifetime guarantee against chipping, breaking or peeling, and the different coloured lids are useful for colour coding the contents. Tupperware also sell waterproof labels to stick on to the containers to establish dates and contents.

Ways to cook

There is a wide choice of cookers available. Considerations to bear in mind before buying one should be compactness, efficiency, safety while in use, and availability of fuel.

In the early days of the Wayfarer Association, I invited members to bring their dinghy cookers to a winter weekend conference and to share their experiences. We timed each cooker boiling a pint of water to assess its efficiency. Each cooker was then used on a seesaw base to check out its stability, then placed in a wind machine and timed again when boiling a pint of water. Each cooker was measured and weighed. Availability, and where fuel could be bought ashore, was discussed. The conclusions were as follows:

1 A two-burner stove and grill is popular for sheltered cruising.

2 A one-burner stove is better for coastal cruises, because of its reduced weight and the reduced stowage space needed.

3 Solid fuel tablet stoves are only used as an emergency. They are useful for making a hot drink only.

4 If cooking is to be done while under way, a simple stove with windshield is advisable.

5 The Optimus petrol stove (using lead-free or two-star petrol) was shown to be highly efficient. It boiled water fastest, had a controllable flame, spilt fuel evaporated rapidly leaving no smell, it was·very stable – being low and square in design, it supported a kettle or billy can quite safely on a wide base, and it stowed in a tin box which also acted as a windshield. However, it is difficult to obtain petrol in small quantities, and the stove needs regular pricking and cleaning to prevent carbon build up and sooting. The Optimus stove that uses paraffin also performed well, and was stable and easy to stow. Paraffin is also a safer fuel than petrol, both to use and stow. The fuel is easily obtainable and burns with a hot flame.

6 A butane Camping Gaz stove with a wide-based large refillable cylinder was quick to light, fairly fast in bringing water to the boil, especially if used in conjunction with a windshield, and replacements are sold universally. Its one drawback is that, without weighing it, there is little indication of when the bottle is going to run out, and heat output is reduced as the fuel is used up. Smaller Camping Gaz disposable cartridges are more

expensive to use, take up more stowage space (spares have to be carried as the canisters are small), and are slow to boil unless a windshield is used. However, they are convenient, quick to light, and spares are readily obtained.

7 Kerosene or paraffin Primus stoves are wide based, easy to stow in a box or bucket, but they do need preheating with methylated spirits. So two fuels have to be carried, plus prickers to to clear a blocked jet. The Primus flame is fierce but controllable, and the stove is robust but not heavy.

8 The Coleman unleaded petrol stove is small, reliable and compact, giving faster burning as a result of its hotter flame. It is easier to light and less volatile than automotive petrol with its special additives to prevent clogging.

9 A pleasant alternative to cooking aboard is to find a likely looking driftwood-covered beach and cook by campfire. Insects keep away from wood smoke – another advantage. Soaping billy can and kettle bases protects them from sooty coatings and they are easily washed clean. Carrying soot-stained saucepans back on to a dinghy is not a good idea.

Fire is an obvious hazard if you cook afloat regularly. A small asbestos or wood mat on which to stand a hot pan, as well as a small fire blanket and a chemical or powder fire extinguisher, should always be carried.

A feast in Florida: *Wanderer V*, laid out with lunch ingredients including local pink grapefruit. We were using the reliable compact Colman stove on this cruise. *Photo: Author*

Cooking utensils

Some people enjoy cooking and eating afloat in true 'cordon bleu' style and take great trouble when producing meals. Personally, I find a collection of greasy pans and dishes a disgusting end to a meal, so I carry only one kettle and one pan and eat very simply. Some people cook in a pressure cooker, which is the most efficient use of fuel.

Lightness and compactness are the main criteria of cooking vessels. Nesting saucepans and coated non-stick ones are good types to choose. Pans with detachable handles or hand grips pack more easily than ones with fixed projecting handles. A kettle with a folding handle is also a better choice for dinghy use. A chopping board, stainless-steel kitchen knife, wooden spoon or spatula take up little space. Rolls of kitchen paper stored in plastic bags make hygienic throwaway dish cloths.

Serving dishes

Food should look attractive, be easily served, and easy to eat on a long cruise, especially if the crew are tired or feeling seasick. We simply carry coloured bowls and coloured insulated mugs for all our meals. They pack well, do not damage easily, and keep food both hot and cold. We have stopped carrying plates as food slides off them, cools down too quickly, and they are too big to hold, or to stow. Metal plates and mugs lose heat rapidly and, being good conductors of heat, can be painful to hold or drink from; their only advantage is that they are unbreakable. Plastic ones are light, non-corrosive and easy to keep clean. Nice as it is to enjoy a glass of sherry, wine, or liqueur, carrying glasses on a dinghy is asking for trouble. (I have never known anyone refuse a sherry or an after dinner whisky because it was in a plastic cup!)

Meals afloat

Everyone will have their own pattern of mealtime routines. Frank and I like a cold quick breakfast. A banana or a sardine sandwich, tea or coffee, and cereal if milk is readily available, starts our day. Other people prefer a more relaxed start to their sail. Bacon, egg and mushroom smells wafting along the waterfront on a misty morning are very appealing.

The significant energy used during open-boat cruising

requires a high calorific value of food intake. Cold meals are no less nutritious than hot ones however, though a hot drink is an instant morale booster with a quick release of energy. During the day I like to keep favourite 'nibbles' like peanuts, dried fruit, chocolate and sweet biscuits in plastic containers ready to hand while sailing. We tend to eat whenever we get hungry. Before setting sail, I fill two thermos flasks with boiling water, so that hot coffee, tea, soup or cocoa is simply a matter of choice while sailing and is quickly available. If a wide-necked flask is carried, boiling water poured over rice and carried all day in the sealed flask provides the basis for a hot meal as soon as the day's sail is over.

One of the pleasures of exploring a new place by boat is going ashore to shop for food or to eat in a local restaurant, pub, or with local people. Our main meal of the day is the evening one. It is relaxing to find a sheltered spot, snug down the boat, and enjoy a leisurely hot meal. We nearly always eat on the boat, usually a hot dish like fish, stew or a vegetable hash, followed by fresh fruit (if we are close to shops) and a hot drink. Water can be flavoured with fruit juice crystals, but carbonated sweet drinks and alcohol can have a dehydrating effect.

Do make sure that you drink plenty during hot weather. The penalty for becoming dehydrated was horribly brought home to us while cruising in America. The temperature had not dropped below 38°C for the three weeks we were there and we suffered greatly from the heat and humidity, as it is difficult to take shelter in any open boat. One evening in a marina in Washington, Frank doubled up with abdominal pain. A day later in hospital he passed a kidney stone, the consequence of severe dehydration. It is more important to drink than to eat if sailing in very hot weather.

Enjoying dinghy cruising is all about being flexible. Over the years we have been invited to eat fresh reindeer steaks with Lapps; enjoyed caviar and salmon steaks washed down with champagne overlooking Biscayne Bay entertained by American millionaires; shared barbecued fish on the beach with Arab fishermen while the mullah called the faithful to prayer at the nearby mosque; and been invited on to a dhow in the Persian Gulf to share the crews' supper – a communal dish of beans to be dipped into and eaten with the fingers. Eating with local people breaks down the barriers of nationalism and prejudice, and many warm friendships have begun over a steak barbecued on a campfire, or a shared sandwich.

As I finish writing now, aboard *Wanderbug*, I am reminded that dining in a dinghy can be elegant or casual, alone or with a crowd. Tonight others may stream into the city, queueing at fast food cafes, or eat elegantly at a beautiful restaurant. Out here, moored quietly in the reed beds, there is no traffic or commuter noise. The wind has dropped, and the evening sunshine is warm. The calls of birds bedding down their young is like a chorus from an opera. A full moon will rise over my tented dinghy, while in the morning I shall be woken by the dawn chorus. At this moment, my billy can is beginning to steam. Shrimps, vegetables, rice and hard boiled eggs make up a juicy risotto. Yesterday I made a summer pudding, collecting wild strawberries and other fruit from the country lanes close to the river. That will make a nice desert. A small brandy to follow will complete a lovely day with *Wanderbug*.

7

Alternative propulsion

In windless conditions a dinghy will need a paddle, oars, or an engine. A paddle is only efficient to move and steer a dinghy around a congested harbour. Strong long oars and well-positioned rowlocks raised, to prevent the oars chafing the sidedecks or coamings, provide a slow but steady means of propulsion, but the work can be tiring if the wind is strong or the tide is against the rower. A tow, though acceptable on occasions, only takes you to where the other boat is travelling.

Oars should be as long as possible given the dinghy's stowage area. Some people carry them shockcorded to the floorboards, one either side of the centreboard case. Others lay them either side of the boat, along the side seats. One dinghy cockpit construction did not lend itself to either position, so the owner lashed them on the outside of the dinghy hull, one either side. Another tied his to the boom, while another carried his along the mast.

Every item carried in a dinghy should have at least two uses. Oars justify their bulk, as their main function is propulsion, but they also make excellent depth sounders and bottom probers in a drying estuary. Some people use them as tent side supports. I have even seen one skipper transport a jar of marmalade across the water from his boat to his neighbour's by means of an oar!

Straight-bladed oars are stronger and more suitable for sea work than spoon-design blades, and spruce oars are lighter than ash and therefore less tiring to use. Oar tips can be damaged very easily; protecting the tips with glassfibre tape will prolong their

Rowing *Wanderbug* along a backwater on the Norfolk Broads. By removing rudder and tiller, and lifting the centreboard so that it is only about a quarter down, you can steer the dinghy by watching the bank. Note:
(a) The rowlocks are slightly raised in the dinghy to lift the oars and thus to avoid rubbing the decks or fendering.
(b) Claw-shaped rowlocks keep a good grip on the oars.
(c) The painter is tied to the bow ring and led back into the cockpit so that it is easy for the singlehander to locate it and step ashore. *Photo: Stan Telling*

life. As for rowlocks, the galvanised type will not bend as bronze or plastic ones will.

In a small cruising dinghy, an engine and its fuel present difficulties of stowage, but they do enable you to get home if the wind falls light, or you have to sail to a timetable. However, the size of engine suitable for dinghy use may not be powerful enough to drive you through really rough seas. Neither Frank nor I have ever owned an engine, believing that if conditions are too bad to sail in, we should not go out. However, in the crowded anchorages of many UK harbours, and to get in and out of marina berths, often the only safe way to proceed is to take down the sails and use the engine. Most dinghies can be driven easily by an outboard engine of 2.5–4hp with a standard length shaft, but a tiller extension makes for easier control.

In a wooden boat, transom pads can be fitted easily, but on a GRP transom care needs to be taken in fitting the screw fastenings. An outboard bracket is a better way of attaching an engine to the boat's hull. A strong cord or chain should be fitted for safety to ensure that the engine is always attached to the dinghy, since lifting a heavy engine over the stern of a boat into position demands good balance in choppy water, and a strong lift. Putting the centreboard of the dinghy down slightly may stabilise the boat somewhat during this operation, and when refuelling the engine also. (A metal can with flexible spout and hose should make refuelling easier when afloat.) When not in use, the engine can be carried on the transom (take care when gybing or going about that the mainsheet does not drop over the engine and jam) or in the stern locker, under a side deck, or shockcorded to the floorboards by the aft bulkhead.

The box of engine spares should include the engine handbook, a spare spark plug, a plug spanner, sheer pin, and a propeller pin. Newspaper or cotton rag to mop up spilt fuel is useful, as a tiny drop will spread all over the dinghy.

A magnetic compass will be badly affected by close proximity to metal objects. Should you carry an outboard motor, the compass reading could be inaccurate as a result of deviation caused by the different positions of the metal outboard and fuel tank close to it.

Whether an outboard or an inboard engine is chosen largely depends on the construction of the dinghy. In general, outboards use more fuel than inboards, they are noisier, but they are easier to trade in for newer or more powerful models. The propeller can be tipped up to clear off weed or underwater litter, like plastic bags and fishing lines, and they can be taken off the dinghy to protect them from the weather, thieves, and when pulling up on a beach. Inboard engines tend to give longer service, are more robust and reliable, and are easier to sound proof. However, they cannot be taken ashore for servicing.

Whether petrol or diesel is chosen is again a matter of personal choice. There is more risk of fire with petrol engines; they are somewhat less reliable than diesel engines; they may need more service checks; and they use more fuel. However diesel engines may be noisier, heavier, and more costly to buy than petrol ones.

Occasionally the engineless dinghy sailor will find the river is too narrow for efficient use of his oars, and the headwind too strong for the efficient use of the paddle. If there is firm ground or a towpath beside the waterway, towing your dinghy on foot may be the easiest way to travel. The towrope should be taken from its cleat in a turn round the mast so that the person on the bank can walk forwards without pulling the dinghy's bows into the bank. As he leans into the towrope, which is passed over his shoulder, the rope should be high enough not to foul the vegetation growing on the river bank. A long towrope improves the angle of pull for the person on the towpath. The helmsman in the dinghy needs to steer just off the bank, sitting well back in the boat; putting the centreboard down a few inches will enable him to steer more efficiently. If singlehanded, the tiller needs to be lashed to steer the boat off the bank. The sails should be loosely tied down to avoid them affecting the steering if a gust of wind catches them through a gap in the trees.

A socket at the transom for a sculling oar, mounted offcentre so that it can be used without removing the rudder, is another means of propulsion. A spare rowlock should be carried with a leather gaiter or plastic protector fitted over it so that the sculling oar is not damaged.

8

Weatherwatch

———

The most successful dinghy cruisers are those who have an instinctive feel for the weather trends. Weather forecasting can be an art as well as a science. However, this art form can only be acquired after years of experience in watching the weather. Fishermen generally have this ability; they are not often caught out. Many of the old countryman's sayings denote years of weather watching, for example:

Red sky at night, shepherd's delight.
Red sky at morning, shepherd's warning!

and

Long foretold, long passed.
Short notice soon past.

and finally

If the sun sets clear as a bell,
  Easterly winds you may foretell.
If the sun behind a bank does set,
  Westerly winds you're sure to get!
When the rain's before the wind
  Topsail halyards you must mind.
If the wind's before the rain
  Soon you'll make plain sail again
If the wind shifts against the sun
  Trust it not, for back 'twill run!

Other signs I have noticed during my most recent summer afloat in *Wanderbug* were nearly always an accurate indication of the weather ahead. For instance, a bright yellow sky in the evening indicated wind and rain, while a red morning sky told of unsettled weather to come. A soft blue sky was an indication of settled weather, while a hard, darker blue sky warned of a change in wind direction, with heavier wind on the way. If I saw a large halo around the moon because of water particles in the atmosphere, I would always fix my tent with especial care, expecting rain. High cirrus clouds, commonly known as 'mare's tails', indicate that a blow is on the way. A Norfolk fisherman told us to 'Take account of 'stays'ls from the setting sun and green light in the sky'. Nearly always these signs foretold bad weather on the way.

Watch for the break up of the long spell of settled weather when very high clouds begin to form. And when clouds of different levels move in different directions, usually the wind changes to the line of movement of the highest clouds that day.

Quite recently, I happened to be in the Alde estuary in Suffolk. *Wanderbug* was anchored just off Iken Cliffs at the end of a long day's sail. The weather had been warm, fine and settled for over a week. Supper was steaming, the tent half up, and I was looking forward to a good night's sleep. Suddenly a short sharp rain storm and wind blew through the boat. I hastened to complete the tent fastenings. The air temperature dropped, while the humidity increased very noticeably. The gulls began to get argumentative on the drying mud banks. Looking out of the tent, the sky had a bright coppery light to it. The weather had been so settled for days that I had not bothered with the shipping forecast, but a combination of all these signs made me turn on the radio. 'SW gales imminent' announced the forecaster. I took down at the tent and after supper, used the ebb tide to row back down the river to a sailing club slipway some 6 kilometres (4 miles) away. The SW winds blew force 6–7 for two days, so I was glad my weather watch had been put to good use.

Clouds

Sailors afloat have the time to study clouds, which form as a result of water vapour in the atmosphere. Some clouds form by convection, but most are the result of the dynamic effort of approaching fronts. Cloud formations at dawn and sunset invariably give an indication of weather trends. Soft clouds usually mean fine weather and light winds, while hard clouds indicate strong winds to come. Observation of clouds, coupled with wind changes and barometer readings, can tell the sailor a lot about the weather trends.

Clouds are classified by the heights at which they form and by their shape. Cloud is said to be 'high' above 25,000 feet and 'low' when it forms below 8000 feet. Stratus or layer cloud is usually formed in stable air. Cumulus clouds, usually found in unstable air, are puffy with a flat base. If their rounded tops push upwards, expect rain or wind.

The main cloud types give a reliable guide for the sailor, by illustrating weather trends:

- *Cirrus* clouds composed of ice crystals are in the vanguard of an approaching depression. Often these cirrus formations (or 'mare's tails'), which are feather-like high clouds, indicate bad weather approaching from the west, particularly if these clouds are moving from north to south.

- *Cirrostratus* over 20,000 feet looks like a thin white veil of continuous cloud. If this type of cloud collects after cirrus and the barometer falls, a deterioration in weather is highly likely.

- A 'watery sky', indicating that rain may be on the way, is indicated by the presence of *altostratus* above 19,000 feet, a thickish, grey, continuous sheet of middle cloud.

- *Stratus*, the lowest clouds of all, are associated with a warm moist airstream and can bring fog.

- *Nimbostratus* clouds look grey, dark, and they are low – about 3000 feet. Continuous rain or snow and poor visibility will accompany them.

- Fair weather *cumulus* clouds are a welcome sight for the dinghy cruiser. Fluffy, light and white, formed by thermal convection, they indicate pleasant dinghy sailing weather conditions.

Barometers

A few dinghies carry barometers. These instruments measure air pressure. When this is steady, stable weather can be anticipated. When the barometer rises slowly, good weather can be expected. When the barometer falls, however, a deterioration will probably follow, and if the fall is rapid then stormy weather can be anticipated. The barometer rises for northerly winds (between NW and E) giving less wind and drier weather, and it falls for southerly winds (between W and SE) with more wind and wet weather to come.

Average air pressure is normally 1013 millibars. A barometer measures this pressure accurately so that you can be forewarned of approaching fronts. On a weather map points of equal pressure are joined by lines known as isobars. The closer they are together, the stronger the wind will be.

Wind

Winds blowing from the SW tend to be warmer and wetter over the UK because they pass over the Atlantic Ocean. Often too they bring cloudier conditions. N and E winds generally bring dry, clear, colder weather. Wind strength is measured by an anemometer.

When the forecaster speaks of strong winds or gales he gives a time prediction. These are:

Imminent – within six hours
Soon   – between six and twelve hours
Later   – twelve hours after the broadcasted warning

When winds 'back' they go in an anticlockwise direction. If a wind is predicted to 'veer', its direction will be clockwise, and it will tend to drop in strength.

The following extract from Frank's log records the time we nearly lost our dinghy when the weather caught us out badly. We had sailed several hundred miles around Britain, starting from our home port in north Norfolk. After six weeks we had reached north Cornwall. 'That's an evil sky,' I said as we entered Portreath harbour. The early evening light was a dull oily bronze colour, and the air was humid and unusually hot.

PORTREATH HARBOUR

Portreath harbour has a long entrance, with vertical walls of sharp-edged slate rock. The inner basin dries out and there are strong smells of decaying seaweed. This is a private harbour and visiting yachts are not encouraged. We had little choice. This whole coastline is quite inhospitable – the beds of rocks have been distorted into tortuous whirls and inclines; faults, slips and anticlines have been hollowed out by weather and sea. We tied alongside the northern wall of Portreath inner harbour, carefully rigging boat rollers to protect Wanderer's hull from the sharp rocky edges. We also rigged long bow and stern lines to allow for the rise and fall of the tide. The 1755 hrs radio forecast told of storm force winds NW force 10 gusting 12 – straight into the harbour mouth. There was also a heavy ground sea from the gales out in the Atlantic.

I walked across the bed of the inner basin; it was sand and mud, good holding ground. I dug in our plough-type anchor as deep as possible, just as a precaution, and we rigged the tent. By 2000 hrs it was blowing a full gale, and the tide was flooding fast into the inner basin, and there was a ground swell. At 2100 hrs it was very dark and Wanderer was begining to rise and fall violently alongside the wall, with the rollers squealing on the sharp stones. Violent gusts tore through the harbour entrance and vicious wind eddies screamed down the cliffs. By 2130 hrs Margaret was very unhappy about the pounding the boat was taking, fearful that the rollers must puncture soon.

At 2140 hrs I decided to move Wanderer out to swing on her anchor. It was going to be tricky as a wind eddy could hold us and pound us into the wall. I climbed the harbour wall ladder and I found I could hardly stand up against the strength of the wind. The rain squalls were horizontal. I led the mooring line ends back to the boat so that we could cast off from inside the tent. Then I led the anchor warp outside the shrouds and tent, and through the fairlead with a check rope in case it jumped out. The wind was roaring, there were heavy swells, and it was pitch black at water level. I waited for a lull then Margaret let go the mooring line and pushed off violently from the wall, on top of a swell. Suddenly all hell was let loose. Wanderer got clear of the wall all right, but a vicious squall tore off the tent and it disappeared into the air above us. The dinghy did not round up to her anchor but tore it out of the ground, despite the fact that I had buried it very deeply, and took off downwind. She shot down the length of the basin under the force of the tent which had tangled itself halfway up the mast and was spread out by the battens, forming a square sail. Horrified, I realised that the boat would be shattered at the far end of the basin and we would be cut to pieces by the sharp slate in the heavy swell before we drowned. The walls were quite impossible to climb, and it was too dark to see when we were about to hit.

Suddenly the mast and tent engulfed us in the mass of splintered wood and canvas, and the dinghy slowed and then stopped. All went quiet except the roar of the storm 3 metres [10 feet] above us. We seemed to be in a tunnel. Margaret managed to find a torch and shone it around her, believing I had been flung out of the boat and crushed or drowned. Incredibly, Wanderer had sailed herself up the narrow slipway, and with the force of the wind she was almost clear of the water. The mast had hit the gangway across the slip, broken the stemhead block and had fallen down as we slid up the seaweedy slip, bringing the tent square 'sail' down with it. There was just 15 centimetres [6 inches] to spare either side of the boat. Incredible but true! We pulled Wanderer up the slip on rollers and stowed the gear by torchlight as well as we were able. It was just 2215 hrs but we had lived a lifetime in seconds.

Winds cause the earth's atmosphere to move, with the high pressure and low pressure areas reacting to cause pressure gradients. As the sailor understands how the weather is caused he can plan his cruises with some expectancy of what weather he will meet.

Depressions

Depressions are low pressure systems during the passage of which the sailor may expect bad weather. The winds in a depression blow in an anticlockwise, or cyclonic, direction. The pressure system will travel in a northeasterly direction and the barometer will drop. Cirrus clouds will have formed to cirrostratus, giving a 'halo' around the sun or moon. The stratus will deepen and drop in altitude as the winds freshen and back to the SE.

The next stage in the depression will be the appearance of low, grey, nimbostratus clouds. Rain may be expected as the winds move to the SW and freshen. Such a simplified picture of depressions enables the sailor to know how and when to avoid bad weather, and to plan a passage that takes into account the likely wind shifts that will be encountered during it.

A cold front may accompany the tail end of a depression. Winds can then increase violently and become gusty. If the area of depression is a large one, other low pressure systems may move in behind the first within a space of about twelve hours.

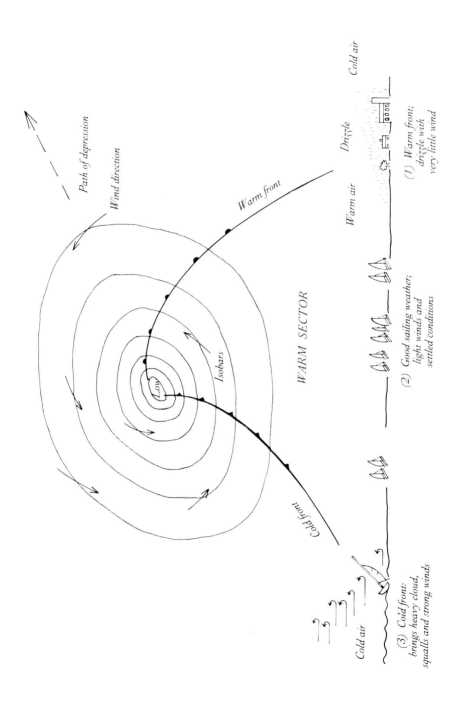

Path of depression

Wind direction

Warm front

Isobars

Low

WARM SECTOR

Cold front

Cold air

Warm air

Drizzle

Cold air

(1) Warm front;
drizzle with
very little wind

(2) Good sailing weather;
light winds and
settled conditions

(3) Cold front:
brings heavy cloud,
squalls and strong winds

Cold air

Fig 12 (opposite) *Low pressure system (depression)*
In the UK depressions pass to the north west of the observer. The observer will experience winds from the east, becoming southerly, then backing round to the west and north west as the depression passes. The warm front is formed by warm air sliding gently up over the denser cold air, producing drizzle, followed by a period of good sailing weather in the warm sector. Prepare for deteriorating conditions as the cold front, caused by colder denser air forcing its way beneath the lighter warm air, builds up. This will result in boisterous weather and strong winds.

Anticyclones or 'highs'

These give the sailor good settled weather for cruising. Pressure will be high. On a weather map the isobars will be well separated, indicating light winds with little cloud and good visibility. High pressure systems tend to drift about, and do not normally have a predictable path as depressions do. Around the UK, winds circulate within the anticyclone or high in a clockwise direction, with light winds near the centre of the pressure system. When two weather patterns merge there will be a period of unsettled weather, known as an *occlusion*.

Fog

Fog is the most frightening and dangerous of conditions for the sailor. During periods of anticyclonic pressure, the occasional absence of cloud may cause the Earth's land surface to radiate heat away. The air in contact with the land will therefore also cool, and water vapour collects. In summer, the mist thus formed will soon be dispersed by the heat of the sun, but, when the sun's heat is not sufficient to do this, radiation fog may persist. Sea fog is caused by warmed land air blowing over the cooler sea.

During periods of fog, dinghies can creep along the shallows where deep-draught boats cannot go, to avoid the danger of collision. It is even better to get ashore or anchor until visibility improves. On one fog-bound cruise we made around the Cornish coast, neither of these alternatives was practicable.

A FOG-BOUND CORNISH CRUISE

We had left Mousehole in Cornwall with a good forecast. The morning was sunny and the wind filling in as we left the charming little harbour on our route around Land's End to St Ives. A mile or two out of harbour, we heard the murmur of a fishing boat, but on

75

looking round could see nothing. Suddenly, out of the mist the boat bore down on us: only then did we realise how quickly the mist was closing in – a thick damp fog suddenly descended. The coastline was blotted out and the wind dropped to nothing. Frank had chosen the strongest tides of the year to sweep us round the coast, and even with sails hanging limply, the tide rushed us along. Visibility was possibly less than 90 metres [100 yards] approximately. 'The tide will keep us clear of the rocks,' said Frank cheerfully, as he prepared to row. Mile after mile I steered, peering into a white cotton wool world. Occasionally, I would yell out that we were approaching rocks. The water seemed to boil around them, and I shuddered to think what would happen should we be swept over one and holed. The coastline, which was invisible, was anyway quite unclimbable.

After six hours of favourable tide it suddenly changed, and we found ourselves being rapidly swept backwards. Frank thought we could land at Sennen Cove. As we approached where we thought it should be, we heard the boom of the surf – and that with no wind. I did not think we could haul the laden dinghy up the beach. The sunlight broke through the fog mid-afternoon and we crept close to the shore, but could see no suitable place to pull out and wait for the fair tide, so Frank finally decided to anchor and wait for daylight. He tied all the available anchor warps together and hoped that the anchor would take hold. We were in deep water.

That was the longest night of my life. 'We've done all we can,' said Frank, and he turned over on the floorboards and slept. Having a vivid imagination, I kept sitting up – seeing the sheer cliffs looming and fading and imagining them coming closer. The mournful moan of the fog horns and Bishop's Rock lighthouse boomed out all night.

Eventually Frank, awake again, decided that the tide had turned in our favour, and we rowed on. 'We must trust the compass' he said, knowing that the coast lost in thick fog was on our immediate right, I was still convinced that I saw looming shadows of cliffs all around us: fog plays the most peculiar tricks on all one's senses. Later that morning, we landed safely on the beach at St Ives and I stretched out thankfully in the sun to dry out and sleep.

Line squalls

These may well cause the unwary sailor to capsize. Squalls are well marked cold fronts. They usually appear in the NW as a line of low, black cloud. Strong wind, squalls, heavy rain, even thunder or water spouts may be experienced. If in doubt the cautious sailor will get his sails down before the front hits him.

Thunderstorms
Air over such surfaces as rock or sand will heat up rapidly and rise. Cooler air will flow in to take its place, and spiral inwards. Violent thermal effects are the basic cause of a thunderstorm, with winds becoming erratic and violent.

Land and sea breezes
All the preceding weather phenomena occur over large land and sea masses. However, thunderstorms and sea breezes are more local and can often override the weather that has been forecast. Once, for a whole week I wanted to sail along the east coast of Britain. Ideal weather was predicted daily, 'SW winds force 3–4'. However, each afternoon easterly winds force 3–5 emerged so *Wanderbug* and I chose to cross the east coast bars at dawn or dusk, when the sea breeze did not cause an onshore wind and rough water at the bar.

Land and sea breezes are important to dinghy sailors as they occur in fine, warm weather inshore – where we tend to be sailing. These local winds, if only a few miles depth, tend to blow at right angles to the coastline, instead of being deflected along it as normal winds are. They are caused by the relative rates at which large land and sea masses heat up as a result of the heat from the sun, and cool down at nights as a result of radiation. Thus during hot cloud-free days, the sailor can expect an onshore or sea breeze because the air over the land will heat up and rise, drawing in cooler air from over the sea to replace it. At night the land cools down by radiation faster than the sea, and the reverse effect occurs, giving rise to a land breeze or offshore wind. When the weather is at its hottest, these breezes will be strongest and most reliable. During cloudy cool weather these breezes are unlikely to occur.

The dinghy sailor can often use the night land breeze to make good coastal passages, and on the Norfolk Broads the narrow reed-lined rivers may more easily be sailed if the local winds are well anticipated. On a hot day, for example, an awareness that sea breezes may build up will be helpful.

Sea state

The state of the sea can be assessed according to the wind strength and direction. Swell, in the open sea, builds up when the wind blows over hundreds of miles of open water. Swell also travels out from the centre of a severe storm, sometimes for thousands of miles. The sea takes time to build up, usually about three hours, so the experienced sailor can plan his cruising accordingly. If well out to sea the dinghy can expect no shelter from the land, and safety lies in having sea room. Should a dinghy sailor be caught out in bad weather offshore, possibly the best action is to lie to a sea anchor.

Forecasting

For serious dinghy sailors, accurate weather forecasting is a highly developed science, on which they rely to keep themselves safe. Everyone putting out to sea, however, should have an up-to-date forecast of the area in which they will be sailing. An understanding of the preceding weather patterns and the likely weather trends to come, should also be considered as they make their plans.

Modern weather forecasting, using a wide network of reports and instruments, gives a very comprehensive picture; the wind direction and force are usually extremely reliable, although occasionally the timing of the moving depressions and anticyclones is less accurate.

The shipping forecast is issued four times daily in the UK by the Meteorological Office. It can be obtained on Radio 4 on 198 kHz/1515 metres Long Wave. Local radio stations also provide local weather reports and an inshore waters forecast is broadcast on BBC radio 3 on 1215 kHz/247 metres daily. Television weather charts and forecasts, based on satellite pictures and computer graphics, give a good overall picture of the weather.

Gale warnings are broadcast before the scheduled forecasts, and bulletins are usually given in three parts:

1 The synopsis This is an account of the pressure systems and fronts likely to affect sea areas. The depth and intensity of the depressions will be given. The terms *vigorous, active* or *weak* will be used, and are self-explanatory to the listener.

2 Forecasts Winds, visibility and precipitation will be given.

3 Reports Weather conditions at the time of the bulletin going out will be given.

Dinghy sailors can obtain these reports on their ordinary radio receivers, or can telephone the British Telecom Marinecall recorded forecast. The Harbour Master's office is also a source of up-to-date information on the weather.

Handheld VHF (Very High Frequency) marine radios in waterproof protective cases can be useful to the dinghy cruiser if he wants to contact the Coastguard, marina or another boat to obtain an update of the weather forecast. Channel 16 is the small boat safety frequency, which you can switch on to in an emergency.

Marinecall from the Met Office, combined with the Telephone Information Service Ltd, update the forecast daily at 0730 and 1930 hrs. These recorded messages can be obtained 24 hrs a day; the Marinecall weather forecast for yachtsmen and fishermen also gives a 3 to 6-day outlook forecast based on the estimated movement of weather systems. Landsmen such as farmers and inland lake sailors are better served by Weathercall Service, as this provides inland weather patterns and predictions.

The following table explains the shipping forecast that is broadcast four times daily on Radio 4.

Weather for Seafarers

Beaufort scale	Wind speed (in knots)	Description	Wave height (in feet)	Sea state
0	< 1	Calm	Calm	Calm
1	1–3	Light airs	< ½ ft	Calm
2	4–6	Light airs	1	Smooth
3	7–10	Breeze	2½	Smooth
4	11–16	Moderate	5	Slight
5	17–21	Fresh	9	Moderate
6	22–27	Strong	13–14	Rough
7	28–33	Near gale	18–19	Very rough
8	34–40	Gale	24	High
9	41–47	Strong gale	30–31	Very high
10	48–55	Storm	36–37	Very high
11	56–63	Violent storm	45	Very rough
12	above 63	Hurricane	over 45	Extremely rough

It is comforting when listening to a weather forecast giving a fresh wind description to know that though the conditions you are experiencing may fill you with trepidation, it is only a force 5, and with sensible planning the moderate sea state and expected wave height of 3 metres (9 feet) are conditions a dinghy can cope with.

After twenty or so years of dinghy cruising, I have yet to find a more satisfying occupation. To judge the weather accurately, make a good landfall – whether it be 1 mile or 100 miles – anchor in some quiet spot, and watch the sun set over a calm sea while the kettle boils for a cup of tea – why, that's the stuff dreams are made of!

9
Sleeping afloat

Tents

With practice you can be as comfortable in your tented dinghy as in the cabin of a yacht. It takes us about twenty minutes to convert our sailing dinghy into a cosy overnight home. Once the dinghy sidedecks, seats, floorboards and stern hatch are mopped and dried out, we sit and drink a cup of tea, relaxing and letting the sun, wind or warmth from the stove further dry out the boat. The tent supports are then erected. There are many basic tent designs, and any dinghy can be adapted to support a tent.

There are several important factors to consider:

- Shape of the tent.
- How will it be fixed to the hull of the dinghy?
- What kind of tent material?
- How long will it take to erect and take down?
- Does the interior of your boat lend itself to sleeping above the bilge water, and is there room to live in your dinghy and provide dry stowage for camping gear.

Ridge tent

This is the easiest tent to make. Using the boom for a ridge pole, the tent material can be draped over the boat and secured around the edges of the hull. Less material is needed for this basic ridge pattern, therefore the tent should cost less. It will be easier to stow than the other styles, because there is less material to pack and unpack. It will be quicker to erect and take down because all that is needed to give the tent its rigid shape is one simple crutch at the stern to support the boom. Moreover, water runs off the

The boom crutch for a ridge tent. It is made of wood so that, should it go overboard, it will float and be easily recovered. Note the double use of all gear on a dinghy; the mainsheet is tightened and tied down to the horse to hold the crutch in position and prevent it jumping out in lumpy water. *Photo: Len Tate*

sloping walls quickly. This tent has only one disadvantage – living beneath it can be cramped, as headroom is very restricted. A sliding gooseneck allows a slightly higher ridge, but if your boat has a fixed gooseneck the boom may have to be secured to the mast above this gooseneck. If you do not want to carry

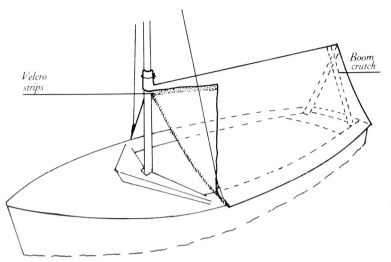

Fig 13 *Ridge tent*
Quick and easy to put up and stow. Minimum fitting required. Lacks headroom except beneath the boom.

Velcro strips

Boom crutch

wooden crutches the aft end of the tent may be held up by the main halyard, which has to be removed from the head of the sail and shackled on to the aft end of the boom. Crutches give a more rigid support to the tent, which is particularly important if people are entering and leaving the tent at the rear, as they will grab at the rear end of the boom if the boat rocks. Some people extend the tent to the front of the bows. While this does give extra space to stow wet oilskins and sails, it adds to the tent's bulk and makes stowage more difficult.

Hooped tent

This tent increases the space inside by using hoops made of flexible plastic pipe or light alloy, but they are a difficult shape to stow when not in use. The hooped tent seems to be the least widely used, mainly because of the difficulty of getting a rigid shape, without which rain collects in the hollows between the hoops. The windage of this shape of tent also seems to cause the dinghy to sit less happily head-to-wind when at anchor.

Walled or frame tent

Frank and I had cruised to the head of Hardanger Fjord in western Norway one wet, windy August. Crouched beneath a

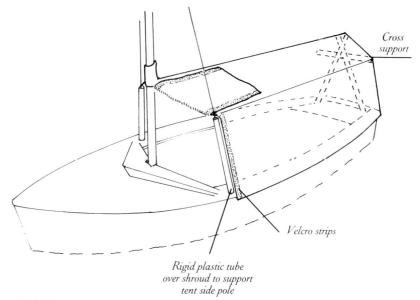

Cross support

Velcro strips

*Rigid plastic tube
over shroud to support
tent side pole*

Fig 14 Frame tent
Much roomier than the ridge type, with full sitting headroom throughout. The sides can be tied up to make a sun lounge or windbreak. Bulky to stow, takes longer to erect and take down, and more fittings have to be carried (jointed side poles and cross support).

wet canvas ridge tent, in constant pain from recent spinal surgery, I said, 'Isn't it time we had a bigger boat?' Frank horrified at the thought of taking up big boat cruising, spent the following winter redesigning the tent to give us sitting headroom throughout. We now call it our Hilton Hotel and it is an enormous improvement. Its design is now widely used by people who want a roomy tent for family dinghy cruising. The stern scissors crutch has an added crossbar to support the rear end of the tent side supports; the shrouds are a convenient place to attach the front end, either clipped or tied on; and by carefully adjusting the height of the boom, the slope of the roof, from the ridge to side walls, can be altered within limits to run the rainwater off quickly. A sliding gooseneck with a longer track than standard allows the tent to have maximum headroom. The sides of the tent can be rolled up to make either a sun awning or a windshield on one side.

All three tent designs should fit snugly around the mast and

The Mark III Wayfarer tent. Frank designed this frame tent in 1970, which gives 76 centimetres (2 feet 6 inches) sitting headroom. The side supports are made of bamboo or light alloy rods which clip on to the shrouds and rest in side supports on the boom crutch at the stern.

shrouds. Windows add to the feeling of spaciousness inside the tent; to make these, panels of melinex or sheet plastic may be sewn into the tent walls.

The framework over which the tent is fixed can be made of a strong flexible hardwood like ash or bamboo, both of which will float in the event of a capsize, or of rigid plastic or aluminium tubing. Doorways are best situated at the bow and stern of the dinghy, but a side door is a great convenience. Openings, round mast and shrouds, and door openings are best sealed with Velcro or ties; zips tend to corrode and jam.

Tent fastenings

I heard of one dinghy sailor who cruised across the Channel from England to France, waited until his dinghy dried out, then draped a roll of bubble plastic over the boat and fastened it to the hull with sticky tape!

It is important that the tent can be secured to the hull from inside, as it is not always possible to land on a firm beach to walk round the outside of your boat. Hooks on the hull beneath the rubbing strake with shockcord on the bottom of the tent are a quick and easy way of attaching the tent. However, hooks can be dangerous, catching clothing or fingers should you capsize, and I think they are better replaced with trumpet cleats, through which lines from the tent skirt can be threaded. This method is quick, reliable and, properly positioned, gives a good lateral pull along the tent wall. If the tent is secured along the hull merely by a series of hooks and not stretched laterally, the tent material will sag and rain will collect in the pockets. Lacing eyes screwed to the hull beneath the gunwhale with a line threaded through them and through eyelets in the tent skirt work well, but this involves bending over the side of the boat to thread the cord through the eyelets and should you be anchored in a swell, this is a certain way of inducing seasickness!

Velcro stitched to the inside bottom edge of the tent walls, and Velcro glued to the underside of the rubbing strake on the hull, allow a quick and easy connection between tent and hull, and has the advantage of being mosquito proof. For those with GRP hulls for whom this glue method is not possible, a girdle of prestretched light Terylene rope should be permanently fixed along the hull beneath the rubbing strake. Then, sitting inside the tent, it is a quick and easy job to secure the tent walls by means of a line of self-locking Velcro tapes sewn perpendicular to the tent edge, passed through the girdle rope, and back to the Velcro strip on the tent. This system has an advantage over the hook and eye method in that if the tent shrinks because of rain it can be re-tensioned by adjusting the Velcro tapes.

Taking lines under the hull to pull down the tent edges is a wet and laborious way of securing the tent to the boat.

Wanderbug uses the fixed girdle method.

To illustrate how important the design of the tent fastenings are, I recall a horrible storm. We were some weeks into our most recent American cruise. It was a calm evening at Beaufort in North Carolina. We had a single Danforth anchor down from the stern with a bowline tied to a nearby wharf, and were just enjoying a slice of fresh pineapple while supper heated. 'What's that?' I asked as a high whine could be heard over the low-lying sandbanks. 'Look at that,' I said, pointing to a line of white water racing towards us. Within seconds the tornado hit us. The anchor dragged and we were swept into the wooden pier. Damage to the mast or tent was imminent. The bright sunny evening had turned into a dark, stormy night in seconds. 'Take down the tent', yelled Frank, his voice nearly drowned out by the wind. he was up on the bows, trying to fend the mast off the wharf. Luckily our latest tent was secured to the boat by Velcro tapes through the bolt rope around the dinghy's hull. It was only a moment's work to rip off each tape. 'Sit on the tent or it'll blow away,' shouted Frank from somewhere outside in the screaming wind and torrential rain, while he rowed the boat furiously away from under the pier and I was buried under the tent.

Half an hour later we rescued the pineapple slices from the floorboards and resumed our supper, now tied to a buoy off the end of the dock – feeling extremely relieved that the tent had come off so quickly.

Tent material

Synthetic fabrics are light and easily stowable, but because many of them are totally waterproof they cannot breathe, and condensation is almost as uncomfortable to live with as a leaking tent. One person's breath in one night produces one pint of water, so a tent made of waterproof plastic needs to be well ventilated. With so many new fabrics and coatings coming on to the market, there is plenty of variety if a synthetic material is your choice. I retired beneath a plastic nylon ridge tent at the Earls Court Boat Show recently, and was too uncomfortable to sleep. Beneath the lights the heat inside the tent was unbearable, yet when the heating in the hall was turned off the tent quickly became cold and very clammy. The condensation inside the tent was high, yet I could not ventilate the tent by opening the door flaps because watchmen patrol the building all night, and I needed privacy.

The advantage of using synthetic material for boat tents is that it does not shrink or rot, neither does it lose its shape. The material is usually cheaper to buy than natural fibre, but should it tear it cannot be sewn or mended with needle and thread – it has to be welded.

Canvas costs more, is more bulky to pack and stow, it shrinks, and will rot if packed away wet. However, it is much more pleasant to sleep under because it breathes and gets rid of condensation. Natural fibre cloth is warm in cold weather and cool if you are cruising in warm latitudes. Sewing, repairing and adapting these tents with a home sewing machine or needle and thread is also a practical proposition; 340 gram (12 ounce) canvas makes a robust but heavy tent – 198 gram (7 ounce) canvas is easier to handle. Cotton tents can be re-proofed satisfactorily using either an aerosol can or liquid applied with a rag or brush, and is a job that only needs doing about every third season. Possibly a mixture of canvas and man-made fibre is a good compromise, but I have not tried it.

When we planned a long cruise in the United States we packed our Mark III canvas tent. It weighs 9 kilograms (20 pounds) and packs down into a parcel approximately 1 metre by 25 centimetres by 12 centimetres (3 feet by 10 inches by 5 inches) and takes twenty minutes to erect and fifteen minutes to take down. We planned to use this tent when stopping more than one night in a place, or when entertaining. We also packed a simple ridge tent made of a breathable nylon-coated material for use when travelling daily.

When single-handing in my own dinghy I use a simple ridge tent made of Ventile cloth. Being olive green in colour it blends inconspicuously into the marshes or reed beds. Blue tents are rather dark inside; light green, beige or white ones give the illusion of space and light.

Sleeping bags

Some people prefer to sling a hammock from the boom, others like to sleep on the flat floorboards and keep their weight low in the boat, and others rig a flat base above the bilges by extending the side seats or extending the main thwart into a bunk. Whichever part of the dinghy you sleep on, a good sleeping bag is essential. Sleeping bags suitable for the climate you are cruising in can be bought from all good camping and outdoor sports shops. You can get bags for all seasons and a loose liner made of insulating material will give extra warmth.

Bags made of duck down are excellent but expensive. Mixtures of down and feather are cheaper, but both lose much of their insulating properties when wet. Bags using natural fibres retain their warmth when wet, are easily washed, they pack into a small space, and are light, but continual compression causes them eventually to lose their insulating airy texture. Since they should not be washed too often, a cotton liner is advisable. When sailing at sea it is important to keep sleeping bags away from salt water because, once wet, the salt causes them to absorb moisture easily, so they remain permanently damp. The better-quality bags have a separate waterproof, and thus saltproof, outer covering.

Sleeping bags made of man-made fibres are the most practical to select for sea sailing in warm climates, as they can be washed, de-salted and dried more easily than down ones. Quilted bags ensure that the insulation is retained within the stitched panels. It is important to check that zips are made of plastic or a material that will not rust or corrode in salty atmospheres. Some bags are designed so that the head and shoulders are enclosed within the bag. These parts of the body are the ones that most rapidly lose heat, and for cold-climate cruising these so-called 'Mummy' bags with a cover for the upper body and tapering towards the feet are a great comfort.

Mattress

As with everything else, the best-quality mattress is also the most expensive one. For several years we have used self-inflating mattresses. We bought them in the United States (the British-made versions are more bulky to stow) for £50 in 1981, but they are excellent value having lasted so well. They are filled with a thin but firm foam pad that expands as soon as the valve is opened, thus drawing the air in. A couple of puffs is all that is required to top up, and the valve is then closed trapping the air. In the morning the air is expelled when they are rolled up, and the valve is closed again. The small salt-resistant valve has never given trouble in five years of hard use. The tough outer covering can be easily sponged down, it dries quickly, and the mattresses deflate into a small roll 61 centimetres (2 feet) long by 13 centimetres (95 inches) in diameter. Frank has recently bought some self-inflating air beds which appear to be good quality and incorporate some improvements. They are only two thirds of the price, being made in Taiwan, but they lasted less than three weeks before needing to be replaced under warranty (twice) – not an economic proposition.

Air beds or lilos are useful and comfortable provided they are not blown up too hard. The extra work of blowing them up by mouth at the end of a hard day makes some people prefer to carry a small pump for inflation.

Kari Mats made of varying thicknesses of closed foam make good firm water-repellent mattresses. I use layers of bubble pack. This is cheap, easily shaped to the size of the cockpit, can be thrown away at the end of the cruise, or used to pack fragile items collected on the holiday. (I always collect a shell from a beach I have enjoyed sleeping on. During the winter, I can look at my collection and re-enjoy nights in the Arctic, those I spent in the Persian Gulf, or the coral rocky Florida Keys.)

Ashore or afloat

If cruising with the family, it heightens the sense of adventure to pull up on a different beach, make camp, and sleep ashore, but there is much more work involved in this system. All the sleeping, cooking and clothing gear has to be unpacked from the boat, taken ashore, then repacked again every twenty-four hours if a cruise along the coastline is planned. This method is therefore best adopted when overnighting for several days at a time. However, it may be impossible to find good land campsites along the waterway you are cruising; and, in any case, to leave

Wanderer 48 cruising the west side of Denmark (see outer ring of reefs to seaward). We pulled up nightly at high water to have an undisturbed night on the dry sands. *Wanderer 48* No 1 is our favourite dinghy; she now lives in the National Maritime Museum, at Greenwich having cruised over 64,300 kilometres some (40,000 miles). *Photo: Frank Dye*

the dinghy and sleep ashore means that if a storm brews up overnight or there is an extra high tide or if burglars visit the dinghy in your absence, damage to your boat may cost you valuable lost sailing time.

We were once cruising round the south coast of the UK and broke off the trip in a delightful little Devon estuary so that Frank could attend to business. While he took a train back to Cheshire I decided to find casual work in a local sailing school. The hotel was noisy and the village B & Bs were all fully booked, so returning to *Wanderer* I decided to sleep in the dinghy park beneath the boat cover. Much later I awoke. Somebody was going from boat to boat. A thief! I had never slept alone in a boat before. As hands pulled the corner of the cover off *Wanderer* I yelled 'Thief!' in an angry, fierce voice. After a horrified silence, there was a scramble of feet over the sand, a bang as somebody tripped over a rope, and then the sputter of an engine. Later the police told me that they had been plagued by local boat thieves all season, but it had stopped suddenly one night in July . . !

When I close the flaps of *Wanderbug*'s tent and nestle into my Norwegian eiderdown sleeping bag, I am happy. If it rains, the patter of raindrops on the tent is an excellent lullaby, and the morning light on the tent is a lovely prelude to the day afloat as I enjoy my mug of tea in bed.

My going to bed routine rarely changes. After supper and before I close up my tent I check the anchor, giving it a tug to see that it is well dug in, as well as visually checking with stationary shore objects that the boat has not dragged. Next I check the mast to see that halyards are frapped (tied away from the mast) so that they will not tap in the night breeze and disturb my sleep. If the genoa is furled I usually tie it to prevent it unwinding or I take it down to store inside the boat. If the mainsail is wet or a storm threatens, I take it off the boom and bag it up. If it is dry I wrap the sail around the boom (taking care to lay the battens straight along the boom and not twist them into the sail) and throw the tent over both sail and boom. Rudder, tiller and heavy food items, like water jars and rucksacks of tinned food, are stowed on the opposite side of the boat to my bed.

I may listen to the radio if there is a good programme on Radio 3 or an interesting talk on Radio 4. I make a flask of hot water last thing and lay out teabag and milk beside it. To awaken by listening to the 0600 hr forecast while sipping tea in bed is a lovely way to enjoy my tented hotel.

Usually I sleep well, but am prepared for the occasional disturbed night when the tide turns violently and the wind against tide means I have to get up to let out more anchor warp, or reposition the centreboard to reduce the boat's roll, or re-tension the wet tent. The compensation is being woken after the next sleep to owls hooting, a ravishing dawn chorus, or the sight of a beautiful daybreak through the tent flaps. Give me a tent afloat rather than a hotel any night!

Several families I know have started their dinghy cruising by day sailing, staying in bed and breakfast accommodation or hotels at night. Others have sailed to campsites. In every case these people have progressed into sleeping afloat. The difficulty in finding good campsites close to the water, then the double work of having to unload the boat (only to have to repack everything before sailing off), as well as the worry of leaving the dinghy unattended while camping some way off, becomes prohibitive. To carry a tent and sleeping gear inside the boat, staying with it overnight, lessens the work and worry. Should a change in weather occur, or vandals visit, you are already aboard to deal with the situation, and your plans can be more flexible.

It is better for the boat to keep it afloat, but often it is nice to come ashore for exercise and exploration. Care must be taken to chock the dinghy chines to support the hull if you are sleeping in it. Shovelling sand under the hull, or using beach driftwood or a fender to support the hull is an easy job, and a level boat ensures a comfortable night. If dragging a dinghy ashore on rollers, care must be taken to inspect the beach first for submerged rocks, coral heads or metal rubbish. The farther up the beach you roll the dinghy the better the protection you will have from swell and storms — and from sea-snakes should your landfall be a tropical island!

Safety

In the early days of cruising, we only met helpfulness and kindness. Today, in times of worldwide mobility and violence it seems sensible to think of safety, especially for the cruising female singlehander.

Nowadays I carry a sheath knife in Wanderbug, well secured but easily available. I also now carry a mobile phone which has the advantage of enabling me to make contact with other people in an emergency and also puts me in touch with weather forecasts and other information, such as lock closure times.

10

First aid – for humans and boats

In more than 25 years afloat, we have never had a serious accident. A dinghy has light gear, so lifting and moving it does not put excessive strain on joints and muscles. Lighter gear is also unlikely to inflict damage by crushing (such as dislocated fingers or broken bones).

To be forewarned is to be forearmed. I wear sailing wellington boots about 60 per cent of my time afloat because dry feet are more likely to keep warm than wet ones. Jumping ashore from a dinghy can cause cut feet from broken glass, or a sprained ankle if you land on an uneven bank or fall into a rabbit hole. Boots safeguard against these possibilities. Quite often you need to walk into the water to pull a dinghy ashore, push it off, or just land to go shopping. Polluted water, sewage outfalls, walking into poison ivy (if you happen to cruise in Canada) or being brushed by highly poisonous sea-snakes or sting-rays (if you cruise in the Middle East) mean that feet need protection. Inside the dinghy we have often spilt boiling water while filling a flask, seen a saucepan boil over, or tipped up a hot drink, as a result of an unexpected severe wash from a passing boat. On every occasion boots have prevented injury to feet and legs.

First aid kit

Every cruising boat should carry a first aid kit. We keep ours in a plastic Tupperware container – clearly labelled. We carry plenty

94

of waterproof plasters, an elastic bandage, medicines for constipation and diarrhoea, lotions for sunburn, a good barrier cream, seasickness tablets (we prefer Stugeron), salt tablets, mosquito repellent, pain-killer tablets (aspirin or paracetamol), a pair of sharp scissors, and tweezers.

Prevention is better than cure, and good sunglasses, a wide-peaked hat, use of lipsalve to prevent chapped lips, and a good sun block cream to protect against sunburn are better than spoiling the holiday afloat by suffering from sunstroke or sunburn.

Before going on an extended cruise, we have a thorough medical check and a dental inspection. All injections for polio, malaria, yellow fever and tetanus should be kept up to date by those planning to take their dinghy farther afield. Increasingly, food poisoning is a problem, and it is wise to treat suspect water with sterilising tablets, and wash and peel all fruit.

Broken glass in a dinghy is highly dangerous, and all personal medicines should be tranferred to small, clearly labelled plastic bottles. Peace of mind helps to keep a person healthy, and I find noisy anchorages and traffic disturbs sleep patterns. Wax ear plugs are carried and used if needed.

The following problems are listed in the order in which you are likely to encounter them.

Dehydration at sea is an insidious complaint because you will perspire a lot as a result of activity, high temperature and humid climates; plenty of water and fruit juices (but not alcohol) should be drunk.

Cramp Salt tablets will reduce attacks of cramp if excessive perspiration has caused you to lose too much salt from the body.

Chafe is another insidious discomfort. Many people wear denim jeans for sailing, but I find these too hard on the skin, tight and cold when wet, and too constricting to allow free air flow around the legs. Loose light baggy trousers or corduroys, cotton tops or sweatshirts, and well-fitting oilies, particularly at neck and wrists, prevent chafe.

As mentioned earlier, embarking on an extended time afloat, I rub methylated spirits on my buttocks, knees and hands. This hardens the skin and prevents boils on the behind and blisters on the hands, and checks rope burn from the jib sheets. Neutrogena is an excellent skin cream.

Seasickness   Seasickness in a small open boat is generally not so much of a problem as on a big vessel. The action of the boat is quicker in a dinghy, you are in the open air all the time, and you do not need to go below to cook or be affected by the smell of the engine. Helming the boat also concentrates the mind, enables you to keep your head up, eyes on the horizon, and usually these things help alleviate the sickness. If you do suffer it is better to keep eating. Fruit juices, dry or non-greasy food, and glucose sweets all help if you are fighting seasickness. There are also many types of seasickness cures on the market. Tablets that cause least side effects, like drowsiness and a dry mouth, have to be found by trial and error. If women taking contraceptive pills are seasick, they may be unprotected from an unwanted pregnancy; thus other precautions should be taken.

Cuts   Deep cuts that will not stop bleeding with the application of a waterproof plaster should be covered with a sterile pad, handkerchief or clean towel, and held firmly in place with a bandage. No attempt should be made to clean the wound. Training oneself to use a knife carefully and to cut away from the body should lessen the risk of deep wounds. Check also that there are no sharp or jagged projections around the boat before you step overboard. Wood or GRP splinters should be removed with tweezers or a sterilised needle.

Burns and scalds   If scalds and burns do still occur during your dinghy cruise, despite wearing wellington boots and oilskin trousers while cooking, the best course of action is to plunge the damaged limb overboard immediately. Water will ease the pain and keep out the air. This is a brutal remedy, but an effective one. No oil or cream should be put on burns; they should be kept dry and protected from the air. Cover with a sterile dressing or a clean towel. Blisters should not be broken lest infection gets into the wound.

Sunstroke   must be treated by keeping the affected person in the shade, which is difficult in an open dinghy. The symptoms are a hot, dry skin, a confused attitude, and vomiting is likely. Sponging the skin (even using seawater) helps and plenty of fluids must be drunk.

Heat exhaustion   shows itself when the person's skin is pale and moist. Sometimes the sufferer is sick. They must keep drinking, take in extra salt, and rest in the shade.

Shock   Being knocked overboard by a gybing boom, continuous seasickness, or a serious accident can all cause shock. This is easily recognised as the victim's skin will be pale and clammy, breathing may be shallow and quick, his pulse may be rapid, and he may become restless and apprehensive. Treatment for shock on a dinghy may be difficult. If possible, one should beach the boat or make for harbour. The best treatment is to keep the sufferer quiet, warm and reassured. Tight clothing should be loosened and no alcohol should be administered – only sips of water.

Drowning   Drowning from a dinghy is quite a remote possibility. The boat is low enough in the water to allow you to get a crew member back on board quickly and, unlike a large yacht, you know immediately if someone falls overboard. Man overboard drill is a skill every dinghy sailor should practise. Everyone owning a dinghy or going afloat should also know how to resuscitate a drowned person by the mouth-to-mouth method (see *Artificial respiration* p. 98).

Recovering a waterlogged shocked crew member may be difficult even in a low-lying dinghy. The easiest method is to ask him to lie alongside and roll into the boat using an arm and leg to hook himself inboard, while the skipper pulls the boat over to scoop him in. Another way of recovering someone is to make a loop with a sheet, and let the person in the water use the loop as a ladder to hoist himself back into the dinghy.

Hypothermia   is a much more likely condition for a dinghy sailor to find himself in. Both Frank and I have experienced this as a result of prolonged cold, wet and exposed sailing conditions. The onset of the attack is very gradual. The person will become listless and appear not to care for the boat or themselves. A very pale skin and the inability to shiver reveal that a person is losing deep body heat.

Wrapping them in a spare sail, forcing them to put on more clothes (particularly on the head where heat loss is most rapid), keeping them out of the wind, and providing them with sips of warm sweet fluids (but no alcohol) will help the slow safe return of heat to the body core. If a person falls overboard, there will be a faster loss of heat from the body if he or she tries to swim; instead, the victim should curl up in the water and keep still while the man overboard drill is successfully performed.

Concussion   If this occurs, possibly as a result of being hit on the head by the boom, it is important to get the sufferer ashore as soon as possible. Until that can be done, the casualty should be kept quiet, warm and reassured.

Constipation is often caused by the change in diet or environment or by lack of exercise, and can be relieved with fresh fruit and vegetables and more exercise. Brown rice, dried fruit and bran all act as mild laxatives. Senokot or Laxoberal can be bought at chemists and are reliable laxatives.

Diarrhoea   This can be helped by eating bananas, cheese and apple juice. Alcohol and coffee should be avoided, but plenty of liquids should be drunk. Imodium is an effective drug for this condition.

Fatigue   has symptoms like forgetfulness, lack of concentration and a tendency to hallucinate. Ordinary tiredness after a good sail is easily repaired by sleep, but the insidious creeping tiredness of fatigue is more difficult to recognise. The long-distance sailor should be aware of its early symptoms. Eating quick energy giving foods like honey or boiled sweets, and putting on extra clothing, helps recovery.

Jellyfish stings   can be very painful. The tentacles should be removed from the affected area, using gloved hands, then the skin should be bathed in copious amounts of fresh water. A paste of bicarbonate of soda relieves the pain.

Artificial respiration   If the person is not breathing, action must be immediate. The following steps must be followed:

1 Clear the mouth and throat of foreign matter.

2 Tilt the unconscious person's head backwards. Press down on their forehead, and push the lower jaw upwards to open the airway.

3 Seal your lips around their mouth, holding their nostrils closed with your fingers. Blow air into their mouth.

4 Remove your face after each breath to check that you are managing to inflate the chest then allow the patient to breathe out normally.

5 Inflate the lungs of your patient 3–5 times, watching for chest movement.

6 Maintain a steady rhythm of 10-12 breaths per minute until the patient's own breathing pattern is restored.

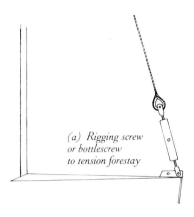

(a) *Rigging screw or bottlescrew to tension forestay*

Fig 15 Forestay adaptations
a Standard fitting.
b Fitted with rope tail to enable the mast to be lowered when standing inside the boat. A second block may be fitted to the forestay eye if space permits.

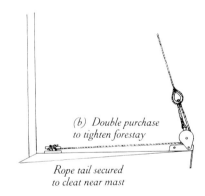

(b) *Double purchase to tighten forestay*

Rope tail secured to cleat near mast

Running repairs to the boat

The important aspect of running repairs is that they can be done while afloat or even underway, so that the cruise does not have to be aborted or interrupted.

All cruising boats, whether of wood or GRP construction, should carry spare marine plywood. If the hull is holed, an article of clothing can be stuffed in the hole and a wood patch screwed over it on the outside of the hull to effect a temporary repair.

Cleats may break off, hooks pull out, and booms split; a wood block screwed beneath or over the damaged area to lend support can be effected while underway. Battens or seat supports may be trodden on and broken, rudder blades may be damaged or centreboards split; by carrying spare wood and carefully chosen tools in the bosun's box, you can patch up the majority of accidents likely to occur while sailing.

It is a sensible exercise to think of all the likely weaknesses in your boat. Carrying a spare centreboard or rudder can take up valuable space and overload the dinghy. Twice we have used part of a floorboard to substitute for a damaged centreboard, and an oar was onced pressed into service when our rudder blade snapped. If a bowspirit or mizzen mast breaks, again an oar can be used as a temporary substitute or you can go ashore and cut off a like-shaped branch from a tree!

Both Frank and I have worn our jib sheet cleats until they no longer hold the sheets. If they are unscrewed and the teeth filed or the unit reversed they will serve until the end of the cruise, with no lost time or need for change of cruising plan.

All boats should carry spare lashings, warps and lengths of Terylene line. If a bottlescrew breaks while sailing and the shroud parts company with the boat, the mast can be saved if the boat is put on the opposite tack while a repair is made, using lashings to bring the damaged shroud back into use. If shackles or splitpins break, Terylene lanyards can often act as a substitute. My husband broke his wooden mast in the North Sea on the way to Norway; he and his crew scarfed the damaged mast and lashed wood splints into position. This mast of reduced length served another 320 kilometres (some 200 miles), enabling them to make a safe landfall.

Carrying a car glassfibre repair kit, tubes of waterproof glue and mastic can take care of accidental damage to the boat, but a strongly constructed boat should in any case stand up to the reasonable wear and tear that cruising demands of it.

Possibly the weakest part of any dinghy (and incidentally the part where damage is most difficult to repair afloat) is the transom fittings. If, for example after drying out, the tide returns and swings the dinghy, with the rudder and tiller lashed in position, the rudder blade may jam and put enormous leverage on the pintle. Likewise, the rudder may be jammed and difficult to raise to reduce the strain on transom fittings. I usually remove rudder and tiller when not sailing, tying them into the boat in anticipation of such likely damage, because even clamping the rudder in the up position does not necessarily prevent damage of this type.

Finally sails, in particular around the sail battens, can very easily tear while sailing. Carrying needles, thread and sail patches means that you can stitch and repair afloat. After all, who wants to return to base once a cruise has begun!

Hull repairs

Wooden hulls   If there is a crack or hole to repair, the damaged area should be cut into a square hole. A marine plywood patch should be cut to fit, preferably of the same thickness. A backing patch of wood, larger than the square hole, should be glued, nailed or screwed inside the hull over the damaged area and the wood patch then fixed into place on the outside of the hull. Extra strength may be provided by a layer of glassfibre mat moulded over the inside.

GRP hulls   Cracks should be cleaned of dirt and dust and filled with the mixed gel coat, resin, hardener and mat fragments worked into a paste. The area should be covered with a plastic sheet or taped down to allow the gel coat to cure. In a warm climate this can take less than an hour, but in damp humid conditions you may have to leave it overnight. Care should be taken that no air bubbles are allowed to form or be trapped within the crack.

Holes should be cut into a square, the edges bevelled inwards with a file, and all dust removed carefully. A thin patch of marine plywood 10 centimetres (approximately 3¾ inches) larger all round than the hole, should be taped to the outside of the hole. Glassfibre mat should be cut 6 centimetres (approximately 2¼ inches) larger than the hole, laid over it, and criss-crossed in several layers, each being saturated with resin and hardener, until the required strength and thickness is built up. Care must be taken to eliminate the introduction of air bubbles.

11

Gaining experience

There is a great deal of difference between the dinghy sailor and the seaman. The former enjoys owning, maintaining and sailing his boat to the best of his ability. The seaman gains his experiences, skills and boat handling over a long period of apprenticeship and ends up as someone who respects the sea.

Punching into heavy seas off the east coast of the United States under reefed main and small jib. Note the neatly coiled reefing lines. Heavy-weather sailing often demands that sails are reefed and unreefed several times a day, and ropes must never snarl up in these situations. Washboards on the Wayfarer ensure a dry cockpit. *Photo: Frank Dye*

Dinghy cruising is safe, provided those who enjoy it learn from each experience and are prepared to learn slowly.

Good seamanship involves an enormous number of skills. While gaining this experience and these skills, remember to plan coastal cruises so that there is always shelter available if the weather turns bad. However, lee shores (shores on to which the wind is blowing) should be given a wide berth if your cruise carries you past an 'iron-bound' rocky coastline where no landing is possible.

For offshore dinghy cruising the biggest danger is really heavy weather, when the land can become dangerous. No dinghy and crew should run for shelter to escape onshore weather that is brewing up, unless certain that an entrance can be made safely; harbours, rivers, creeks or coves frequently have bars that become impassable in heavy onshore weather. A better choice is to make for a lee under a prominent headland or behind an island. Closing the land is the most dangerous part of any cruise, and it may be a more prudent seaman who stands off to await better weather.

Beating

When beating into confused seas, it may be necessary to luff into the breaking crest of a wave. Watch out for the squalls and be prepared to luff, letting the main free a little if there is a danger of being overpowered. To avoid losing speed, and therefore control, it is vital to pay off or bear away to gain speed before tacking. Wait for a quiet patch of water and a lull in the wind before pulling the mainsheet in hard, and spinning the bows of the boat round by positive action with the tiller to leeward. If the dinghy is caught 'in irons', the crew may back the jib momentarily to bring the bows round. The helmsman can reverse the tiller if the boat loses way and starts to drift astern.

The height of waves is governed by the strength of the wind, the length of time it has been blowing, and the fetch (which is the distance across open water that the wind can blow). You may experience rough sea conditions other than deep water waves, however, around headlands seas may be confused; uneven bottoms can cause this also. Short breaking seas can develop in wind-against-tide conditions, especially if both are strong. Early reefing is sensible, and even in winds of force 6 a well-reefed boat

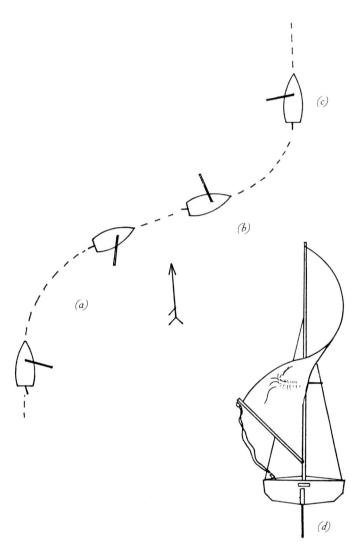

Fig 16 A safe way of gybing (when there is plenty of sea room) Sail more and more by the lee *(a)* until the boom blows over *(b)* when the sail will be empty of wind, and the boat can be brought back on course *(c)*. This method was first suggested by Uffa Fox in his book *Crest of the Wave.*

A Chinese gybe is caused when the wind gets behind the mainsail on a dead run, resulting in the lower part of the sail gybing while the top half remains filled with wind. *(d)* It usually results in a capsize and the sail being torn on the spreader. This can be prevented by the used of a kicking strap to prevent the boom 'skying' during an unexpected gybe.

does not need to spill wind, and can therefore carry on beating with only a deep-reefed mainsail and no foresail.

If you are sailing where there is a big swell you may lose the wind as you slide down into the trough of one wave before climbing up the next one. It is important to allow for this wind loss by not reefing too deeply, otherwise the dinghy may lose all her wind in the troughs and be unmanoeuvrable when she is hit by the wind as she rises on to the next crest. We experienced these conditions when attempting to cross the Gulf Stream from Florida to the Bahamas. The waves probably measured 6 metres (20 feet) and we were becalmed in the troughs.

Gybing

Gybing is sometimes the safer way to come about in heavy winds providing you are not carrying too much sail. It is quicker and more positive than tacking, and you do not risk losing steerage way if the boat comes head to wind and refuses to come about. Make sure that the centreboard is raised so that the dinghy can slip sideways through the water, without tripping over it. Ensure that the boom is fully out, with the mainsheet holding it just away from the shroud. Sail more and more 'by the lee' until the wind is almost on the beam and the sail will blow over. There will be no wind in it and no restraining mainsheet to cause severe heeling as it comes across. Straighten up on course again. Such a free-standing gybe in heavy weather is safer than pulling in the mainsheet to centre the sail before letting it run again.

When the wind increases, a dinghy will run easily before the wind in surprisingly bad conditions under genoa or jib only. On our return across the Outer Minches after visiting St Kilda we had a SW force 7. In such conditions a broach would have been highly likely even with a deep-reefed mainsail. We took down the main and sailed with the genoa and jib hoisted on the forestay, boomed out either side with a whisker pole. We sat back and planed down the front faces of the hissing waves for several hours until we rounded Cape Wrath. There was no tendency to broach at all.

Sail balance

This is important because it improves a boat's handling, increases speed, saves unnecessary correction of the helm, and

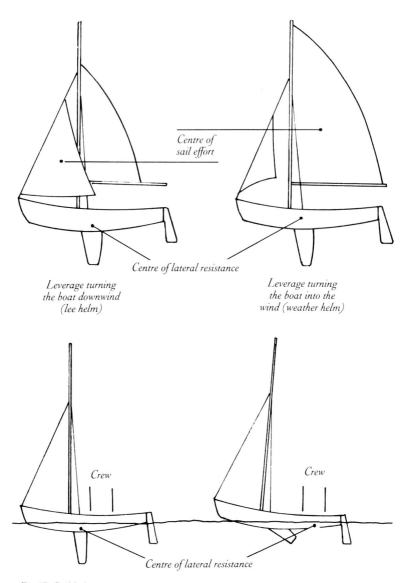

Centre of
sail effort

Centre of lateral resistance

Leverage turning
the boat downwind
(lee helm)

Leverage turning
the boat into the
wind (weather helm)

Crew

Crew

Centre of lateral resistance

Fig 17 Sail balance

a If the centre of effort (C of E) of the sails is forward of the centre of lateral resistance (CLR) of the hull, it will force the boat's head downwind ('lee helm').

b If the sail area is too far aft of the centre of lateral resistance of the hull, it will force the boat up into the wind ('weather helm'). Correct balance will cause the boat to gently round up into the wind if the tiller is released.

c Adjusting the centre of lateral resistance of the hull.

Moving the crew aft will immerse the stern and lift the bow. Raising the centreboard also moves the CLR further aft.

reduces drag from the rudder blade. The centre of effort of the sails should be a little behind the centre of lateral resistance of the hull, ensuring the dinghy will always round up into the wind if the tiller is let go. The most frequent cause of a broken rudder is fighting excessive weather helm in heavy weather or in shallow water. To prevent this you need to move the centre of sail effort forward by increasing the foresail area or reefing; or moving the point of lateral resistance aft by raising the centreboard slightly, lowering the rudder blade, or moving one's weight aft. Should lee helm be a problem when sailing, it may be reduced by moving the centre of sail area aft by reducing the foresail or increasing the mainsail area, or moving the centre of lateral resistance forward by putting the centreboard fully down. The dinghy should be controlled mainly by the balance of her sails and not by excessive use of her helm.

Reefing

Reefing the sails is something that racing people rarely contemplate, for speed is their main consideration and they generally have a safety boat in attendance. To a seaman, safety is more important than speed and he must be prepared to reef promptly. There are two methods of doing this:

Roller reefing   This involves lowering the mainsail as much as is needed to reef. Take the boom off the gooseneck and neatly and tightly roll the sagging main around the boom. A pleat has to be taken in the leech of the sail to prevent the boom sagging. A separate kicking strap has also to be rolled into the folds of the rolled-up sail, or a reefing claw used, because the rolled-up sail will prevent you from using the fixed kicking strap on the boom. Usually two reefing lines are fitted to the mainsail, one below the lower batten, and the second just below the second batten pocket. It is advisable to remove the batten from its pocket if using the roller reefing method, as a twist in the sail may tear the pocket's stitching. Another roll can be made over these around the boom to further reduce the sail.

Slab reefing   This is the method more generally adopted by cruising people because it is simple and can be done more easily singlehanded. Reefing lines are fitted through the sails ready for instant use throughout the cruise. It only takes a few minutes to lower the sail to the tack cringle, pulling the reefing line tight and

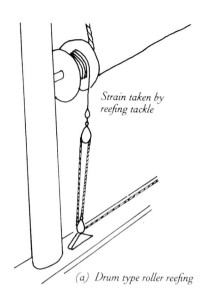

Strain taken by reefing tackle

(a) Drum type roller reefing

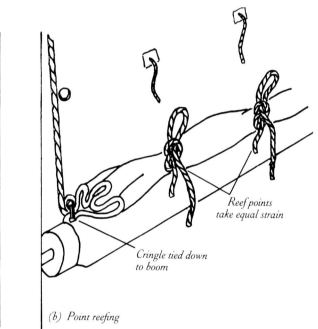

Reef points take equal strain

Cringle tied down to boom

(b) Point reefing

Fig 18 Reefing

a Drum type roller reefing Rarely seen except on older dinghies. It is reliable and quick. If the halyard and drum line are taken aft through a block it enables the helmsman to put in a reef from the sailing position.

108

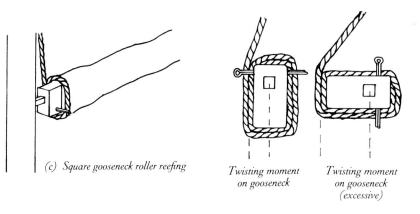

(c) Square gooseneck roller reefing

Twisting moment on gooseneck

Twisting moment on gooseneck (excessive)

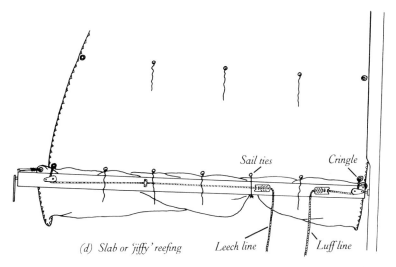

Sail ties

Cringle

(d) Slab or 'jiffy' reefing

Leech line

Luff line

b Point reefing An old system of reefing often combined with reefing pendants on working sail boats. Also found on reefing jibs. The reef points should be tied under the foot of the sail (not under the boom) and adjusted to take an equal portion of the sail.

c Square gooseneck roller reefing A reliable means of reefing but it puts a considerable twisting strain on the gooseneck. Packing is required on the boom under the leech of the mainsail to prevent the boom dropping. Not as quick or easy as slab reefing. This can be used to gain an additional reef when both slab reefs are already pulled down.

d Slab or 'jiffy' reefing A quick and easy method of reefing. The sail is lowered until the cringle is against the boom, and the luff and leech reefing lines are pulled in and cleated (sometimes the luff cringle is hooked on to a hook fitted on the boom). These lines take the weight of the boom and the ties serve to keep the slack sail tidy. Note that the reefing lines are permanently rigged at the luff and leech, so that reefing can be done instantaneously and when underway.

109

securing it to the cleat on the boom. The line pulling down the leech of the sail should pull back along the boom as it runs through a block, which should then tighten and flatten the sail against the boom. Tightening up the kicking strap, tidying the extra main halyard, and tying in the excess sail can be done by the crew, once back on course. Slab reefing ensures a flatter sail shape with no distortion to it.

Heaving-to

This is done when you want to slow down and stop the boat in order to reef, cook, 'spend a penny' or navigate. It is easier to heave-to while awaiting daylight or a fair tide rather than anchoring. The dinghy should lie quietly, lifting easily over the waves, and drifting slowly to leeward. The method involves bringing the dinghy head to wind until she stops, freeing off the mainsheet, lashing the tiller to leeward, backing and cleating the jib, and partly raising the centreboard.

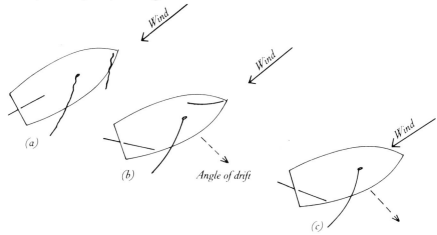

Fig 19 Stopping the dinghy
a Losing speed by luffing into the wind or freeing the sheets until the dinghy is just jilling along, usually in order to reef. Not very satisfactory as the boat is not under control and it is only too easy to lose steerage way.
b Heaving-to in order to reef, navigate or eat. By freeing the main, backing the jib, and tying the tiller to leeward, a boat will heave-to comfortably, looking after herself and drifting slowly across the wind. The centreboard may have to be adjusted, but it should be partly down to reduce the rate of drift.
c A boat will also heave-to under mainsail only, but it takes a surprisingly long time to lose all steerage way (there is no backed jib to prevent her tacking).

110

Capsizing

Seamen rarely capsize because they keep an eye on the weather to windward and reef in good time. If such an event does occur, stay with the boat; never try to swim to the shore. Avoid all unnecessary movement, as this causes heat loss.

To right the capsized dinghy, the skipper should stand on the centreboard near the hull, and by leaning backwards, holding a jib sheet, pull the boat upright. The crew waiting at the bows, holding the dinghy head to wind, should let the skipper bail some water from the unstable waterlogged dinghy before rolling themselves in by the shrouds. The person inside the dinghy can help scoop the crew aboard by tilting the dinghy towards the person in the water. The dinghy is less likely to re-capsize if the crew comes in over the stern of the dinghy. A loop in the mainsheet may assist them stepping aboard.

Man overboard

This can happen when least expected, often in the calmest of conditions. A bobbing head is easily lost from view, and the skipper needs to keep his eyes on the man overboard. The best method of collecting the crew is to sail off on a broad reach, turn, and approach the man in the water on a reciprocal reach. With foresail flying and boat speed reduced, the boat should have stopped as the helmsman comes forward of the shrouds, leaving the tiller as he picks up the man in the water on the windward side of the stationary dinghy.

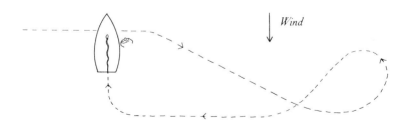

Fig 20 Man overboard drill
The helmsman sails away from the victim without panicking keeping the person in the water in view. If the wind is gusty it is better to tack round rather than gybe and risk a capsize. Reach back and luff up so that the boat will be stationary with the man overboard by the shrouds. A loop of rope hung over the side enables the person to use it as a ladder to get back aboard.

111

Being Towed

For a long tow the sails should be taken down and lashed in the dinghy, and the centreboard be pulled up. Crew weight should be at the stern of the dinghy, and the helmsman should steer straight into the line of pull. The towing warp should run through the fairlead on your bows. A capsize may occur if the tow rope is allowed to jump out of the fairlead. To control the situation you should not cleat the warp, but merely take a turn round a strong part of the boat like a samson post, thwart or mast, and keep the free end of the warp in your hand so that you can instantly release the dinghy should need arise.

Jury Rig

A cruising person should have the imagination and the ability always to remain self-sufficient and be able to effect repairs to his dinghy while at sea, sailing home under jury rig if necessary. If a rudder blade breaks, an oar can be lashed in position, which is an effective if heavy substitute for steering. We once broke a rudder fitting before lying to a sea anchor north of Orkney waiting for a gale to blow out before landing on Fair Isle. This method got us 19 kilometres (12 miles) to windward and we landed safely.

If the mast breaks, the boom could be utilised to support a loose-footed sail. If the dismasted boat has a wooden mast, this could be splinted and lashed, possibly using a paddle to strengthen it. Part of a floorboard could act as a substitute for a broken centreboard. If a shroud parts — with a quick tack to take the strain off the mast — a lashing can be made to replace the broken bottlescrew or shackle.

Sea anchors

I have only laid to a sea anchor once. We had successfully crossed the Pentland Firth — one of the most fearsome areas around the UK coastline where tides run at 12 knots in places — then worked our way through the Orkneys, and started the crossing to Fair Isle. The following log records the experience.

A GALE APPROACHING FAIR ISLE

Just before the 1745 forecast, Frank took over the boat, put up more sail and decided to make for shelter and sail in to Fair Isle. The forecast spoke of NW gales all around but not in our area. The

112

Pentland Firth is a place of fearsome repute, and is treated with great respect by all seamen. At 1900 hrs we were 6 kilometres [4 miles] off Fair Isle. Through the murky light I could see lights on the island. As I busied about with supper preparations I heard a loud crash, and the dinghy seemed to go inert, lying helpless in a deep breaking wave trough. Frank yelled instructions, but his voice was lost in the noisy sea. Sensing something had broken, I unlashed an oar. Frank pushed it through the transom and, with both arms straining, got the boat under control using the oar to steer with. We were very cold having sailed more than twelve hours in taxing conditions. The force 6 wind rose to near gale force. Wind and tide were now in opposition.

An hour later above the screaming wind Frank said that he was going to lay out the drogue. I felt helpless; I had never done this before. The dinghy was bucking like a crazy horse – to stand up would probably mean being thrown out. Somehow, crawling around the dinghy and holding on with one arm, we got a routine worked out. The lashing wind was icy and the noise was shattering.

Frank told me to hold the boom crutches in position on the transom, while he lowered the mast in its tabernacle, using the extended forestay to control its descent. We lashed the mast down, tied up the shrouds, laid out the drogue and then lay on the floorboards with the spray dodger pulled over the cockpit area. We felt rather than saw that the dinghy was held head-to-wind by the canvas drogue. It was 2100 hrs, the wind was now only force 6, but much of the North Atlantic pours through the gap between the Orkneys and the Shetlands, reversing every six hours, and together with a spring tide running into the wind the whole seascape was worse than gale conditions.

Every few minutes the boat seemed to pull tight on its warp, hover, shudder, and then plunge downwards. After a second's halt, the sea would hiss past and the dinghy would lie limp in the wake of the foamy waves before gathering to face and climb up another wall of water. We were both very seasick. I knew that Frank was also very angry with himself, because he muttered, 'I am sorry I brought you out here. I always swore that I would try never to be in the wrong place at the wrong time.'

I tried not to think about the dinghy rolling over with us trapped beneath the canvas cover, and I found myself tensing to listen for the next hissing roar of water thundering past, because this meant that the next wave had broken correctly. Frank listened to the midnight forecast but, as he removed his headphones, I did not ask what it said. I think we both thought there was nothing we could do. 'What's that?' I asked, sitting up from the floorboards. We both strained our ears, because I thought I had heard muttered human voices. We flashed our torches to announce our presence, and then lay down again, almost relieved to be alone. Each time I lay down I heard the undertones of long conversations, but each time I sat up to identify the position of the sounds they disappeared. We were later told that the wooden boat had acted as a sounding board for whales or other sea creatures 'talking' below us.

I thought daylight would never come and it seemed too cold to sleep, but I must have dozed because I was woken by Frank saying in quiet excitement, 'Margaret you should take a look at this'. I blinked, expecting to see at least a beautiful sunrise or a ship close by. Instead, I was horrified to see an endless mass of foam flecked white water all around and breaking seas dashing at us from all directions. I retreated ostrich-like under the cover again, and marvelled at our dinghy and the effect of the drogue. By midmorning the seas seemed less mountainous, and the wind had stopped that dreadful whining sound. Frank thought it had dropped a little. He outlined his plan. It would be slack water in one hour's time, and he thought that with the tide flooding with the wind the seas might die sufficiently for us to sail into the lee of Fair Isle.

It was a relief to do something positive. We ate, and then rolled back the cover and raised the mast. Immediately, the boat seemed to roll in an arc of over 40°. We crawled about the boat, working with one hand, holding on with the other. Once the reefed sail was up and the oar in position, I hauled in the drogue, controlled the sail with the mainsheet and was ready to bail. Frank had both hands on the long steering oar; this was very tiring work because if a wave hit the hull wrongly, Frank had to reverse the oar to avoid a broach. We were fine reaching into very big seas, and the boat was swamped often. If I stopped bailing to be sick, the water rose above the centreboard case; we were knee-deep in water. Slowly we reached the lee of the island and the seas flattened. The wind now only screamed over a bright blue sea. Fair Isle South Harbour, by contrast, was green and peaceful. We grounded, jumped out, and pulled Wanderer ashore.

(a)

(b) Parachute-type sea anchor

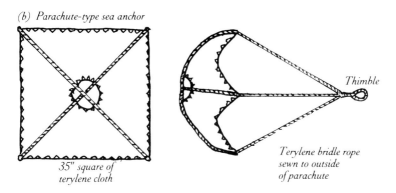

35" square of
terylene cloth

Thimble

Terylene bridle rope
sewn to outside
of parachute

Fig 21 Using a sea anchor

Fig 21 Using a sea anchor

a If it is not possible to reach shelter or a beach before conditions become impossible, the only alternative may be to stand out to sea and lie to a sea anchor util the weather moderates. It is essential to gain sufficient sea room before lying to the drogue to allow for drift. The sea anchor should be streamed out on a long warp made fast to a strong part of the boat (ie the thwart) and tied down to the bow fairlead so it can't jump out, so that it lies in the back of the second wave to windward when it will be in solid water. The length of warp can be adjusted as conditions change.

An emergency sea anchor can be made from a bucket (with a strong handle) or a sail tied to form a bag, or placing any spare clothes into a sail bag.

When the conditions are too bad to continue sailing, the boat should lie to sea anchor. This is usually made of canvas sewed into a cone, open at either end, with the mouth strengthened with rope or metal to hold it open so that the dinghy is held head on to the wind and sea. Alternatively, a small parachute type can be used which is easier to stow. It may be necessary to take down the mast, lashing it securely to the boat in a boom crutch. Since the boat will be drifting astern, the rudder and tiller should be shipped and centreboard lifted.

Night sailing

Sometimes night passages are quite restful because offshore breezes may be gentle and steady. Towns and coastal buildings can be identified by their lights, and lighthouse flashes are easy to identify, but it is possible to confuse moving headlights from coastal traffic with navigation lights.

A dinghy sailing at night should carry battery-operated lights as high as it is possible to secure them, and a bright torch may be shone on your sails to warn approaching boats of your presence. A white flare may be let off in the event of you fearing collision with another boat. The skipper should know the main light configuration carried by larger boats. (Almanacs have useful quick reference illustrations of boat lights.) The greatest safety for dinghies, of course, is that they can sail in shallow waters where there is little danger from big boats. All sailing boats at anchor should carry a white light at their masthead. When night sailing, lifejackets and lifelines should be worn.

(See also *Light signals*, p. 153-4)

Fog

A folding radar reflector should be slung from the shrouds as high as possible when night sailing in commercial waters or when sailing in fog. When assembled, it is essential that the three reflecting planes of metal stay exactly at right angles to one another. It should be flown in the oblique position. The minimum recomended size is 400 mm (16 inches) from one corner to another, and surfaces should be kept clean and corrosion free. It is important that the reflector is as high on the shrouds as possible – a minimum of 4.6 metres (15 feet) is recommended. It should be secured in a stable position and not blanketed by metal spares. (But a 400 mm reflector is too big, and 4.6 metres too high, to rig in a dinghy without chafing the sails, you say. *Wanderer* carries an 18 centimetre (7 inch) collapsible reflector hoisted under the mast spreader; this seems to show up well in any conditions that she is likely to be out in.)

A mouth-operated fog horn should be carried and used regularly in fog, bearing in mind that motor boats are unlikely to hear a hand fog horn above their own engine noise.

A dinghy should sail or anchor in the shallows if caught out in fog, but small fishing craft can be a particular hazard in dense fog as they sometimes fish in the shallows, often travelling fast between hauling pots as they know the area. They do not expect to come across sailing boats so close to the shore.

(See also *Fog horns*, p. 154)

Flares

There are three types of coloured flares. Red is only to be used in a dire emergency, to ask for help; orange flares are more easily seen than red flares if the emergency happens during daylight hours, and white flares indicate your presence, warning that a collision is impending. Flares burn for about two minutes and can be seen for 5 kilometres (3 miles) in good visibility. All handheld flares should be pointed downwind and away from other people.

Each cruising dinghy should carry several of each colour. They should be stowed in a waterproof container, and kept within easy reach in the boat. The drill for using and striking them should be learned before they will be needed at sea. Out-of-date flares should be discarded.

Frank's attitude to using red flares is absolute. In a bad sea, I nervously asked if he wanted the flare box got out in case it should be needed later. 'Nobody asked us to come out here,' he replied quietly. As his new crew I soon learned to think more positively, to become more self-reliant, and to plan more carefully!

A flare is only of use if somebody by chance happens to notice the light; do not rely on them.

Approaching a bar

Great care should be taken to approach bars by knowing the state of the tide. Conditions are usually most favourable just before high water. If a capsize happens, or the boat is swamped by a breaking wave, the flood tide will carry you inshore. As the tide ebbs, however, the channel becomes shallower, the water runs faster, and kicks up a heavier sea. Never approach bars in bad weather or when a strong ebb tide is running. With wind against tide it is sometimes safer to creep in across the shallows at the end of the bar where there is often a little shallow channel.

When crossing a bar it is important to hold the boat true to each wave. Looking backwards you can visually check each run

117

of waves, and a sharp correction on the tiller will keep the dinghy transom parallel with each cresting wave. Great concentration will be needed by the helmsman during this time. It is important to choose a good wave and plane in on it; it is not nice to lose a weak wave which will leave you to wallow, possibly allowing the next breaking sea to roll the dinghy or swamp it, so keep oars ready to provide a quick pull. When there is too little wind it may be more practical to take down the sails and row in over the bar, because with oars you can choose which wave to come in on.

If conditions are suspect, certainly if the waves are more than twice the height of the freeboard of your dinghy, it may be better to take the boat in stern first, towing a bucket from the bow. Occasionally it is better to sail away from the bar, realising it is too marginal to risk entry. Finding a beach farther on or a windward drying sandbank to await better conditions are advantages a dinghy has over a cruising yacht, which has no choice but to anchor off if conditions on the bar deter it from approaching.

Landing on open beaches

This is a major advantage dinghies have over keel boats. With an offshore wind the sea should be flat, so approaching slowly the crew can visually check for rocks or underwater hazards. The centreboard and rudder blade should be raised to avoid damage as the dinghy glides on to the shore. Often taking down the main and sailing in under jib only is a sensible approach.

With an onshore wind, a prudent skipper may wish to sail along the beach, watching for a place where the surf appears to break more gently. If the surf is higher than he wishes to sail through, it may be better to anchor outside the breaking waves, take down the sails and then row in, towing a bucket over the stern to slow down. Alternatively, the dinghy can be anchored from the bows and backed in. With the rudder removed and stowed inside the dinghy, the oars must be used to keep the boat heading into each sea as the anchor warp is carefully paid out by the crew. As the boat touches land, the person leaping out with painter or anchor line and to steady the boat – preventing it grinding into the shingle – should be aware that breakers produce undertow. To lose balance or allow the dinghy to swing and roll on to your body could result in a dangerous situation.

On exposed coasts such as north Cornwall, there is little margin for error as so many of the sands are surf beaches. Frank's log records that on one trip we got in through the surf only just in time.

NORTH CORNISH COAST: A SURF BEACH

We row out of Boscastle harbour between sheer cliffs on either side one August day at 0800 hrs. What an impressive entrance! The wind settles dead ahead, force 2. We have a fair tide until 1230 hrs and HW at Bude is 1330 hrs. I don't want to be later than HW at Bude as it is a surf beach and I imagine the ebb out of the estuary into the Atlantic swell could be nasty. If the wind does not get us there we can beach at Millhook at HW which will be sheltered, or return to Boscastle. The wind settles into NE force 3 and we brew tea. It's hazy; we are offshore about 1 1/2 kilometres [approximately 1 mile].

Visibility decreases to about 1 1/2 kilometres and the two farthest headlands disappear. We stand out for twenty minutes to get help from the tide, and then tack and stand in. This is an open, exposed coast, but the small islands and ridges running out into the sea help to identify it positively. The land is hazy in the mist and it gets lower and beaches appear; it must be Widemouth Bay. There is surf a long way out all along this beach. We can now see the cliffs up to the coastguard and then the flagstaff marking Bude entrance. The winds become gusty so we turn down a small reef. By this time we are close enough to see the features of Bude entrance; from the cliff, a reef made up with a wall extending to a rock about 9 metres [approximately 30 feet] high with a beacon on top. On the far side of the estuary is sand with a long line of heavy surf. We can hear the surf; it sounds like an express train. The channel must be close under the rock with a sharp turn behind it into shelter. While we hang back and watch, a big swell breaks right across the entrance; we can hear it roar, and see its foam-flecked, back dark brown with stirred up sand. Another roars in immediately, and Margaret mutters, 'Where on earth are you taking us this time?' There is a smooth run of sea and we close haul in almost to where the swell begins breaking. A very fast tack until we are almost touching the rock, another for 18 metres [approximately 20 yards], and an even quicker one behind the rock. Looking back I can see the next line of heavy seas breaking, but we are safely inside. Margaret dares not look back; she had thought we would end up as matchsticks on the surf beach. It's a very nice spot. We chat to the local boatmen who said we came in just right. The shallower channel was now a seething white mass.

Rolling up a beach

Inflatable rollers are available in reinforced rubber or plastic, other types are pneumatic and rigid. They may be carried in the boat as extra buoyancy, toggled in position and put out of the way beneath the side seats. To roll a heavily laden dinghy up a beach it may be necessary to unload the heavy gear before doing so. Placing a roller under the bow of the boat, she may be rolled up the beach. By placing a second roller under the bow as the first reaches the point of balance, she may be walked up a gently sloping shore, but two rollers and two people are required. Three of each is better. It is useful to leave the last roller under the stern of the boat, so that an easy start next morning is assured. The boat rollers, being expensive, should be tied to the boat, and washed to remove sand and grit before they are returned to the cockpit. Lanyards on the rollers allow for easy recovery from under the dinghy. Sand is easier to roll up than shingle. Avoid mud.

Berthing

Berthing next to another boat or to a pontoon or quayside will require fenders or inflated boat rollers to protect the hull. (Squeaking fenders can be cured by the application of washing up liquid, or even saliva!). Remember to tie up only alongside another boat that is bigger than you (and one that is leaving after you next morning!). It also saves embarassment if you can tie up and detach yourself from a neighbouring boat correctly.

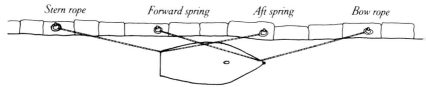

Stern rope   Forward spring   Aft spring   Bow rope

Fig 22 Using springs alongside a quay
If staying overnight at a quay or pontoon the use of springs will permit the boat to lie quietly on the tide.

Knots

The only knots I remember are the ones that I constantly use.

Bowline forms a loop in the end of a rope. It is easily undone, and will not slip or jam, and can be tied and untied with one hand. It can be used whenever a loop is needed, but should not be used to join ropes together as it reduces their strength by nearly 50 per cent.

Sheet bend is useful for joining two ropes of unequal size, or for attaching a rope to an eye splice or to a ring.

Anchor bend is used to connect a warp to a ring or to an anchor.

Round turn and two half hitches is a good knot to use when securing the dinghy to a buoy, post or mooring.

Reef knot is useful for joining the two ends of a single rope, or two ropes of equal size. It is easy to undo and will not slip.

Figure of eight is used as a stopper knot – for example, to prevent the ends of a rope escaping through a block. Unlike an overhand knot it does not jam.

Clove hitch is useful for attaching a rope to a spar, post or another rope where the pull is more or less at right angles to the object which is attached.

Rolling hitch is used where the pull on the rope is in the direction of the length of the fixed object.

Every sailor needs to care for his ropes, checking for chafe or rot, as they are used to control the sails and for berthing and anchoring the boat; you can never carry too much rope.

Synthetic rope has advantages over the cheaper vegetable fibre rope, such as sisal and manila, because it is stronger, will not rot or grow mould, and will not normally kink or swell when wet. Nylon is subject to elastic stretch, which makes it good for anchor warps but poor for sheets and halyards. Terylene has very little stretch and thus is good for halyards and sheets.

A correctly coiled halyard on its cleat is a sign of a careful seaman. All warps should be correctly coiled so they do not foul, kink or knot when needed.

12

Navigation and pilotage
for dinghies

One advantage dinghies have over larger yachts is that the dinghy skipper can always land on a friendly looking beach if his dead reckoning is suspect! Also, with a lifting centreboard he can be less worried about going aground.

Offshore navigation is an enormous subject and largely outside the scope of the average dinghy sailor. For coastal cruising continuous checks on wind direction and speed, times when the winds change, the boat's estimated speed and the speed over the ground, are the most important aspects to keep a note of.

Leeway in a dinghy can generally be ignored as a factor, since most helmsmen unconsciously steer higher than the correct course. A dinghy sailing to windward in good conditions with the centreboard down will make little leeway, but when reaching into a breaking sea, with the centreboard lifted to diminish the risk of a capsize, leeway may be considerably greater. Experienced helmsmen can estimate leeway by looking astern and calculating the angle of the boat's wake in relation to the dinghy's heading. In other words, navigation is a combination of common sense, practice and experience.

Pilotage or 'coastal navigation' is more widely practised by dinghy sailors. This involves piloting the dinghy from one harbour to another, using the buoyage system as the sea's signposts, and largely navigating by eye, using charts, binoculars, compass and pilot books or cruising guides. Dead reckoning along a planned route also plays an important part. The navigation buoyage system is mainly established to help commercial shipping and deep-draught yachts, yet dinghies too need to be aware that, particularly in new and unexplored estuaries and coastlines, the buoys and the information they give cannot be ignored.

Reading charts and tide tables, and using navigation instruments is not an easy task in a small open dinghy on passage. A firm chart table and a sheltered corner of a cockpit are not benefits available to the dinghy navigator, therefore all the navigation homework needs to be done before setting off on the cruise. We buy the charts of the area we plan to cruise many months before the setting-off date. They are laid out, pored over, and discussed and memorised. Time must be allowed, however, to get the charts updated before setting off, should they be very out of date. Charts may be updated at any recognised chart agents. Corrections are also detailed in Admiralty Notices to Mariners if you wish to make your own corrections.

Buoyage

The coasts and tidal estuaries of the UK and the continent are buoyed, the width and direction of navigation channels being marked by port and starboard buoys. A good deal of information is given on the buoy itself; its shape, colour and number all convey certain details. As you enter a harbour with a fair tide, or sail on a flood tide into an estuary from seaward, the right-hand side of the channel is marked with black or black-and-white starboard hand buoys. These are conical shaped and may carry conical or diamond-shaped topmarks on them. The left-hand side of the channel is marked by red port hand cylindrical or can-shaped buoys, which may carry can or 'T'-shaped topmarks to aid identification. Leaving red or red-and-white chequered buoys to port, and you may see even numbers painted on them; uneven numbers usually identify the starboard hand buoys.

Spherical buoys painted in stripes of black and white or red and white indicate where the main channel runs. These middle ground buoys are placed at channel junctions. Red striped ones indicate that the main stream runs to starboard, while black striped spherical buoys indicate that the channel bears to port.

Special feature marks can be conical, can shaped or pillars. They are painted yellow and may carry a yellow flashing light. A green buoy always indicates a wreck and may carry a green light. Its shape will indicate on which side you should pass.

In many places this lateral buoyage system (also known as Trinity House buoyage) is what you will meet. Where in force, the International Association of Lighthouse Authorities (IALA) buoyage system gives standardised instructions. This Cardinal system places the buoys according to their bearings from the danger or channel. The name of the Cardinal mark indicates that it should be passed on the *named* side – that is, a West Cardinal buoy should be passed to the west. The Cardinal buoys are colour coded as follows for easy identification:

North mark is black above yellow
South mark is yellow above black
East mark is black with a yellow band
West mark is yellow with a black band

Each mark is supplemented with two black arrows as topmarks to indicate further the type of mark it is.

On charts, navigation lights on buoys, lighthouses etc. are represented by a tear-shaped symbol with a dot at its end; the dot itself marks the buoy's exact position. These lights are marked on the chart using abbreviations:

F   – fixed, meaning a continuous steady light
FL   – flashing, meaning the light is repeated at regular
            intervals
GpFl   – group flashing, meaning the flashes are combined in
            groups
Iso   – isophase, meaning the light and dark intervals are of
            equal length
Occ   – occulting, meaning a light in which the periods of
            dark are less than periods of light
Qkfl   – Quick flash, meaning continuous flashes

Minor channels, in estuaries for example, are often marked with withies or spars or even broom heads. If they carry a red flag or colour they should be left to port when going up river; green ones should be left to starboard. Naturally, all buoyage information reverses as you sail out of harbour.

In the Admiralty booklet 5011, *Symbols and Abbreviations*,

Fig 23 Beacons and withies
Many different types of beacons and withies are used to mark shallow channels for creek crawlers.

much information on buoys, beacons and lights is given, plus much chart information relating to coastal features, lights, fog signals, radio and radar, tides and currents and small craft facilities.

Charts

Charts are expensive to buy and bulky to stow. The one in current use on the cruise should be housed in a waterproof clear plastic chart case. Before setting off the chart should be folded so that the complete area in use is visible. All the work on the chart should have been done before setting sail: distances, courses to be steered, suitable sheltered anchorages along the proposed route, and all relevant details on pilotage information should be marked on the chart. Some people like to note these details with a waterproof pen or soft pencil on a small pocket pad for easy reference while sailing. Others like to mark up on the chart case. This can be washed clean at the end of each day.

Nautical charts can be bought from boat chandlers or obtained from chart agents. They provide a wealth of information to all sailors, like the quality of the sea bottom, navigation hazards, tide rips, wrecks, overfalls or underwater obstructions. The abbreviations and symbols are all listed in Admiralty booklet 5011 *Symbols and Abbreviations* available from most chandlers. The main ones should be memorised before starting the cruise. Depths are marked in either metres or fathoms and feet. Metric charts can be distinguished from the older fathom charts, which still remain in use, by their use of colour and the marginal 'Depths in metres' printed clearly on them. On metric charts the depth soundings are placed in the centre of the sea area and they are shown in metres and decimetres. Bearings are given from the seaward and refer to the true compass bearing.

The number of an Admiralty chart is printed outside the lower and upper right-hand border of the chart and is prefixed with BA (British Admiralty). Other charts widely used are Imrays and Stanfords. For dinghies, the Standfords editions are good as they are clearly coloured and have bearings and distances already marked on them. Their 'Allweather' version is printed on waterproof tear-resistant material. It is better to keep to one make of chart so that you become familiar with the format. Large- medium- or small-scale charts can be chosen, depending on whether you want a lot of detail over a small charted area, or whether you want to make a long passage and so need less detail over a large area.

Charts show lines of latitude and longitude which provide a grid on which the navigator can identify the boat's position. One minute of latitude represents (measured from the side of the chart) 1 nautical mile. A nautical mile is approximately 1852 metres (6076 feet) rather longer than a land mile. A cable is one-tenth of a nautical mile. The scales at the top and bottom of the chart should not be used for reading off distance. They are longitude lines, and their relative distances change according to how far from the Equator they happen to be. You should always read off the *distance* from the *latitude* scale at the side of the chart closest to your own position on the chart.

On each chart there will be at least one compass rose. The outer ring gives the true compass bearing, and the inner rose (or an arrow) gives the magnetic one. In the UK the compass variation is decreasing by a few minutes annually, so to convert the chart bearings from true to magnetic for your compass course you have to add the magnetic variation to the true course calculations. On the east–west line of the magnetic rose is written the magnetic variation, the year for which it is correct, and the annual rate of change.

Small craft facilities are shown on the enlarged harbour

insets on Imray charts, and are useful to the dinghy cruiser. Slipways, telephones, post boxes, sailing clubs, camp sites, water taps and restaurants and toilets are all extremely useful details. Tides and currents are also marked on charts.

Tides

When coast hopping from one harbour to another, or estuary sailing, the dinghy sailor needs to keep a careful check on tides.

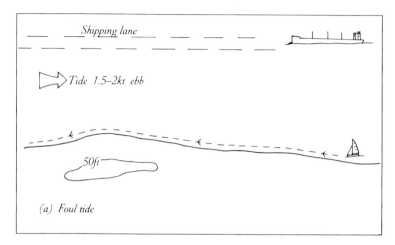

(a) Foul tide

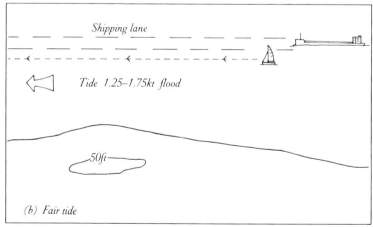

(b) Fair tide

Fig 24 Using the tide
a Foul tide Stay close inshore to 'cheat' the tide (the current runs slower in the shallows).
b Fair tide Stand well out to gain the full benefit of the current.

Since tides run strongest in the middle of the channel and fastest off headlands, the skipper can plan whether to cheat the tide by sailing in shallow water, keeping close inshore, or sailing farther out to make the best use of the tidal conditions. Often it is sensible to set off on a cruise an hour or two before the tide turns in your favour, because the tidal flow is weakest in the first and sixth hour of its run, and strongest in the middle two hours of the tide (the Twelfths Rule).

From HW or LW

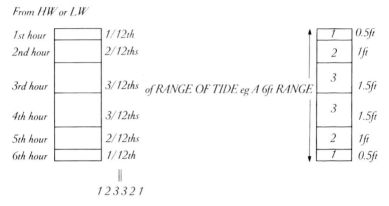

1st hour	1/12th
2nd hour	2/12ths
3rd hour	3/12ths
4th hour	3/12ths
5th hour	2/12ths
6th hour	1/12th

of RANGE OF TIDE eg A 6ft RANGE

1	0.5ft
2	1ft
3	1.5ft
3	1.5ft
2	1ft
1	0.5ft

‖
1 2 3 3 2 1

Fig 25 The 'Twelfths Rule'; rise and fall of tide
Having applied this rule you can prepare the length of your anchor warps to allow for the range of tide.

When the tide changes, a different wave pattern on the surface can be detected, with practice. As the tide begins to run into the wind it produces short, square, sloppy waves. When the wind and tide are together, the water should be smoother.

Rough water may be expected over an uneven bottom, or where two tides converge. Local knowledge will always tell you where to expect a strong tidal stream and where eddies will form. Tide rips and overfalls, caused when a line of rock juts out from the shoreline beneath the water, are often found around headlands, and the chart will indicate where to expect these. Tidal streams are strongest on the outer edges of a curved channel, and slower over shoals. Tidal flow in restricted channels will be strongest in mid-channel, and weakest in the shallows at the edge. The tidal stream turns first inshore and is less strong than offshore. If you know these facts, you can plan

128

to pilot your boat in waters that will give you the safest water, the greatest speed, and the best shelter.

Periodic vertical movements of the sea level as a result of gravitational forces of sun and moon on the Earth's surfaces produce tides. Around the coasts of Europe and the UK, tides are semi-diurnal – that is, approximately two high and two low tides daily in the period of 24 hours 50 minutes. Therefore high water is a little later on each successive tide. The Solent is the exception to this rule, as there is double high water at each tide or a 'stand', when the tide remains at its high water level for an hour or more. This is because of the configuration of the land in the area.

The *range* gives the difference in height between high and low tide, and the *tidal stream* produces the horizontal flow of water around the land.

Spring tides are caused when the sun and moon's gravitational forces are most powerful – that is, a couple of days after each new and full moon. Neap tides are to be expected a couple a days after the first and third quarters of the moon. (ie higher high tides and lower low tides). Tidal range is greatest at springs and least at neaps. I try to cruise new waters at neap tides because it gives me more time either side of high water to explore tidal harbours and beaches, and because the tidal flow will also be less fierce.

Charts give depths or soundings from chart datum which, by international agreement, is now the level of the Lowest Astrological Tide (LAT). This is the lowest tide that is likely to be experienced during the year. Previously British charts were to a datum near or below Mean Low Water Springs (MLWS) in the area, so a small correction is needed. Area tide tables or almanacs provide all the tidal information required. An up-to-date publication must always be used.

When the tide is rising or entering harbours, rivers and estuaries it is known as the flood tide. The ebb tide is when the water level is dropping and retreating from the river.

Currents

This is the horizontal flow of water. On a non-tidal river it always moves in the same direction. On tidal rivers the current will generally run upstream with the flood tide and downstream (and faster) with the ebb tide. Water currents are deflected by obstructions and bottom friction, therefore water flows strongest

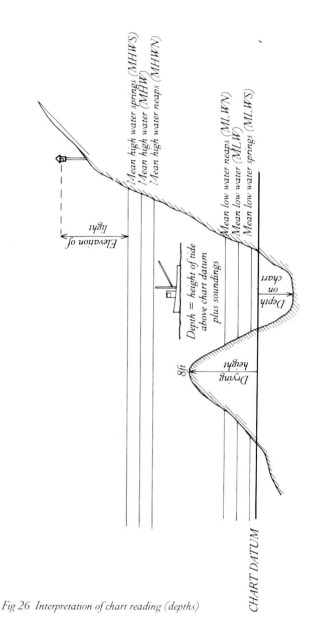

Fig 26 Interpretation of chart reading (depths)

in deep channels, and slower over shallows and near river banks where there is more friction from both the river bottom and the bank. By watching the swirl of water around buoys, moored

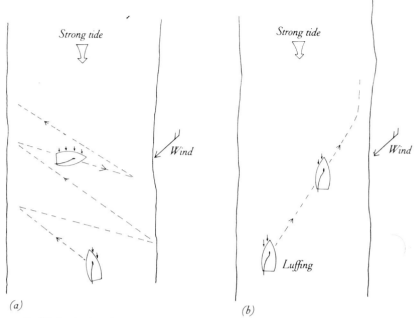

Fig 27 Lee bowing the current

a The current acting on the lee bow causes the boat to be set sideways, losing ground.

b By hardening in the sheets and pointing a few degrees higher into the wind, it is possible to bring the current under the lee bow and use it to push the boat up to windward. With the sails 'lifting', the boat speed may drop, but the gain to windward is considerable. (Beware of losing steerage way and losing all the distance gained.)

boats, posts and withies, the sailor can estimate the speed and direction of the current. Like the Twelfths Rule of tides, currents vary in rate according to the 123321 system.

Favourable currents can add greatly to a boat's speed, and the experienced skipper will hug the banks and sail in the shallows to cheat a foul tide. A current from dead on the beam will not effect the forward progress of a boat, but it will push it to one side or the other. A current on the lee bow of your boat will help to push you to windward; you can make positive use of this effect (Fig 27). Wind against current will produce larger waves where the current is strongest, and conversely when the wind is with the current the waves will be smaller. An experienced dinghy sailor passing through crowded anchorages or moorings will always be aware of the tides and currents for safety.

131

Navigation instruments

You will need dividers for measuring off distance, a Perspex parallel rule for laying off bearings from the compass rose, a soft rubber and a hexagonal HB pencil (round ones roll into the bilges), a reliable compass and a watch. A Douglas protractor (a square of transparent perspex with edges graduated from 0-360° with vertical and horizontal lines to align the protractor to the lines of latitude and longitude) is a good dinghy navigation aid. Plotting in a dinghy, using the chart efficiently with no stable chart table, calls for speed, and using the instruments, laying off courses, converting bearings from true to compass (magnetic) all require a steady hand and eye. Time spent in the winter practicing using plotters and compass at RYA navigation evening classes will be time well spent.

Since I wrote the first edition of this book there has been a great leap forward in position finding — GPS (Global Positioning System). In any weather condition it is possible to find the boat's latitude and longitude by merely pressing a button, and in fog particularly the GPS is a Godsend! The modern handheld sets are eminently practical in an open dinghy. It is commonsense to update your GPS position on the chart on a regular basis in case you need to go back to traditional navigation. Most cruisers feed in the waypoints they need while ashore and sometimes feel they need to do nothing more. It is a mistake to rely on it solely. In Canada Frank came across a party of power boaters on a social cruise who did just that for a 25 mile open water passage in Georgian Bay. They fed in departure and arrival waypoints the night before. No one realised there was a reef half way across. It was only when a local fisherman asked where they were headed that a multiple shipwreck was prevented!

Everybody has their own opinion about which kind of chart, tidal information tables and compass best suit their own needs. Compass choice is very wide. The hand-bearing ones are of two types: eye level and arm's length. If you wear reading glasses it is easier to take bearings using an arm's length compass, but this type is often bulky and more difficult to keep steady in a rough sea. Bearings are read directly from the side of the compass card, or off the top through a prism which also magnifies the scale. Compasses that read directly from the card have the added advantage of doubling as a steering compass. The Sestrel Junior compass can be used to take bearings and then be positioned on the boat in its bracket to be used as a steering compass. We have used this type for many years.

Over the course of time we have experimented with where to house the compass in its steering position so that the person steering can use it easily. One should, in theory, have the compass gimballed nearly a metre (3 feet) away from all iron and steel as this could cause magnetic deviation. In dinghies, though, what with stowed tinned food, anchors, camera, rims of glasses, torch batteries and even a pocket knife, it is impossible to meet this rule. We used to mount the compass on the stern locker, but now we sink one into each side bench just ahead of the helmsman. From whichever side of the boat we are steering we can read off the course without twisting the body. In an earlier experiment we used a grid steering compass in a box placed on the floorboards against the rear locker. It worked well, but too often it got kicked or trodden on and it was too easy to put items into the stern locker for dry safekeeping, forgetting that they were magnetic and that the compass was immediately the other side of the thin bulkhead.

Whatever type of compass you choose and however you use it, a good fix depends on your speed and accuracy in sighting. This is largely a result of how quickly the card settles on to its target and how easy it is to read the card. A card marked at 10° and 5° intervals makes for the easiest reading. Good choices of compass are: Solva 70 UN, which doubles as hand bearing and steering compass; Sestrel Junior, which can also be used as a hand bearing compass with the addition of a sighting ring: the Sestrel Suresight; Rigel Capstan; Plastimo Mini HB; Silva 70 UN; Sunto Commando; Weems and Plath mini compass. Electronic compasses though excellent, may well be beyond the pocket of the average dinghy cruiser.

Reading a chart and using navigation instruments is obviously a well-defined science, but navigation is also an art. On many occasions I have seen Frank picking his way through narrow shallow swatchways between the sandbanks of The Wash, navigating mainly by the 'look' of the water, using the spread of his fingers to measure distance from the chart, and with only an occasional glance at his watch to establish distance run.

Boat speed

Distance run through the water may be read off a patent log, which consists of a rotator over the stern of the dinghy with the revolutions registered on a dial. An impeller can be fitted outside the hull which works much like a speedometer in a car. Unfortunately both these logs tend to pick up weed as the boat sails into shallow water, which causes under-readings at slow speeds.

Quite effectively, skipper and crew can cross-check each other's estimate of their boat speed. With practice, by watching your progress past a floating object (a buoy or withie, for example) you can estimate your speed quite accurately. A quick walking pace may be about 4 knots and a leisurely ramble about 1½ knots. However, when the skipper and crew are tired or seasick, or the light is poor, this method is inefficient. More reliable is the method known as the Dutchman's Log (or a chip log). A plywood triangle on a long string, knotted in pre-measured lengths, is dropped off the boat's bows. When it passes the stern of the dinghy the skipper notes the time. Then, by counting the number of knots that run out in a set time, it is a simple calculation to express the boat speed in 'knots', remembering that 1 knot is 1 nautical mile (not statute mile) per hour. A Dutchman's log is too cumbersome for us, but there is a quick simple variation.

Many years ago I remember hearing Peter Grainger, who organised the Wayfarer Winter Weekends at Frank's marina, propounding the use of a Tennis Ball Log. An old tennis ball (an inverted small plastic funnel works just as well) is threaded on to a cord (length 10.2 metres (33 feet 9 inches), tied to the helmsman's finger and dropped overboard. It will jerk the helmsman's finger in 20 seconds at a speed of 1 knot, in 10 seconds at 2 knots, and so on.

Deviation

Deviation is the error caused by having metal objects, such as iron or steel close to the compass. It is impossible to keep all metal objects in exactly the same place in a dinghy, so a permanent deviation card recording the errors cannot be worked out. It is therefore better to keep metal away from the compass altogether. If you suspect that there is a compass error you can check by placing two compasses in different positions in the boat. However, in rough conditions even a very good helmsman cannot steer a light, quick-moving dinghy to an accuracy greater than 2°–4° either side of the desired course. After a 17 kilometre (11 mile) sail, a difference of 5° in course gives a 1.6 kilometre (1 mile) error, so a visual correction of your landfall must be made. In poor visibility it may be better to anchor off and await better conditions before committing yourself to a landfall.

Leeway

Leeway is caused by the wind pushing the boat to leeward. Leeway can largely be discounted when sailing on a beam reach or when running. However, when beating in a heavy sea, sailing an accurate compass course is difficult and you must expect leeway to be greater. What is more, if the sea is breaking it is almost impossible to judge the angle of leeway by looking at the wake astern. If the expected landfall does not turn up at the estimated time you need to watch out closely to windward.

Navigation lights

A masthead light visible through 360° is the ideal, but in practice it is difficult in a cruising dinghy when you may need to lower the mast. The regulations state that a white light shown in time to prevent collision is adequate for a sailing boat under 7 metres (nearly 23 feet) in length. It is prudent to carry white magnesium hand flares, since these are sufficiently brilliant to announce your presence unmistakably to big ships on a collision course. To be realistic, small sailing boats are not easily seen from the bridge of a ship, which is high above the water level and a long way from the bow, where the ship's lookout is probably concentrating on vessels showing on radar. It takes time for a ship to alter course, and her forward visibility is greatly restricted by her bows, so it is essential to indicate your presence in good time.

Navigation lights are of most practical use to a dinghy when travelling at night in flat water, such as on a river or lake. It is difficult to mount the lights high enough from the deck to make them of real use when sea sailing. Port and starboard lights can be clamped to the dinghy handles, fixed to the bows, or fitted as high as possible up the shrouds. They are operated by six volt dry cell batteries rigged in tandem. Masthead lights can be run off a dry cell battery with an on/off switch. A cable can be run down the mast and brought out through the spinnaker sheave, or the cable can be run down the outside of the mast.

We tend to carry a powerful torch to shine on to the sails to warn other boats of our presence, keep in shallow water where larger vessels cannot go, cross shipping lanes speedily at right angles, and choose cruising waters where we can expect little commercial traffic.

Sailing guides and tables

Pilots and sailing guides, tidal atlases and tide tables are bulky but essential reading if you plan serious dinghy cruising. They make good wintertime study for anybody interested in navigation. Admiralty Pilots are written for commercial ships, but there are excellent guides published for cruising folk available from local chandlers. Some are available only from the cruising clubs who publish them, such as the Clyde Cruising Club guides to the west coast of Scotland, Royal Northumberland Yacht Club's guide to the north east coast.

Log book

A log book should be written up daily on a cruise. Notes from the chart such as courses steered, times and bearings should be transferred to the log before the chart is cleaned up and the next day's cruise worked out.

Plotting a course

1 Note carefully on the chart the dangers, such as rocks, tide rips or overfalls, since they may cause you to vary your course to avoid them.

2 Lay off each leg of the course on the chart with a pencil, and find the compass bearing by 'walking' the parallel rule or plotter over to the compass rose. To set this on the chart you need the magnetic bearing, which can be obtained by reading the magnetic compass rose. (Alternatively, you can work in true bearings taken from the grid and add the magnetic variation obtained from the compass rose, but we find it easier to work in magnetic all the time.)

3 Work out the time of high water that day and consult the tidal atlas. Check the tidal stream diagrams hour by hour and calculate their cumulative effect on your course during the hours it will take you to complete the course.

4 Work out the new course to allow for the tidal offset.

136

Dinghies can go where other cruising boats can't. *Wanderer* floats in inches of water in the upper reaches of the river off Plymouth Sound. *Photo: Frank Dye*

5 Be prepared to continually update and adapt this plan as conditions demand (eg if the wind drops, the tide turns early, or if you suffer gear failure and have to anchor).

Fixes

Using the hand bearing compass, take a bearing on some easily identifiable object on the shore like a church tower or a lighthouse. (This can be quite a difficult job in a small lively dinghy.) When drawing this bearing on the chart you can assume that your dinghy is somewhere along the line. Take a second bearing on another object, if possible at the angle of 60° or more from the first, and where the lines cross is roughly your position. A bearing of a third object, again at as wide an angle as possible from the other two, should give you three lines on the chart that create a triangle or 'cocked hat' which gives a closer estimate of your position. It is not possible to take an accurate bearing, especially from a light boat jumping in a seaway; errors can amount to 5° or more, so never forget that positions are always approximate.

13
Passage planning

Racing is about exercising competitive skills, about boat speed and handling, and making use of your knowledge of the rules to win races. Cruising in a dinghy involves having a curiosity about what lies beyond the next headland and in the next estuary. It is a lonelier sport, involving leaving your home base and the social life of the sailing club and going from point A to point B. What to do with a dinghy at the end of a cruise is thus an exercise in pre-planning. Sometimes you can leave the dinghy with a friendly sailing club, travelling home by local transport or taxi and then collecting car and trailer, or you can continue the cruise another weekend. On one occasion we left our home base in north Norfolk and in six separate Sunday sails reached Windsor. We were able to leave the dinghy in a convenient mud berth, friendly sailing club or in a friend's waterside garden, returning home each Sunday evening by coach, bus or rail, ready for work on Monday.

A cruise can be enormous fun even with very little planning, given experience and good luck, as the following log shows.

THE TALE OF A TOOTHBRUSH

In early November, Frank remarked over supper that the tides were just right to cross the Wash 'It might be our last chance this year,' he said. Grabbing food, thermal clothes and sleeping bags, we turned off the central heating and just caught the tide. 'Be home tomorrow,' I thought, 'Can't stay out long in November, so it won't matter that I've forgotten the toilet bags.'

The Wash in winter is a mysterious place, and sailing there always leaves one feeling refreshed. The wind was south-easterly, and it was very cold so we were glad to be sailing downwind.

Next afternoon, just as the wind died, the flood tide carried us to King's Lynn. 'Might as well carry on to Denver,' said Frank. Shooting bridges and railway connections was easy with a fair tide, and by dusk we had floated many miles into the quiet Fenland river system. Downham Market Bridge was shot in darkness, and we just avoided scaffolding stretched across the arches. It was very dark by the time we got to Denver Sluice, but the obliging lock keeper put on all the lights and locked us into the non-tidal Ouse. The light of a riverside pub gave us sufficient illumination to erect our boat tent, and later we ate there royally, being the only customers. It was a lovely meal; the only thing spoiling it was that I couldn't clean my teeth afterwards.

Next day the mild stern winds encouraged us to go farther. We made Ely just before darkness fell, enjoyed choral evensong in Ely Cathedral, and finished off the evening watching a fantastic firework display.

The following day we planned to reach Cambridge by midday, which would give us time to shop for a toothbrush. But on reaching Linton locks we found the river full of racing skiffs. We heard that there was a fair at the Meadows where we had intended to camp, so decided to moor Wanderer some way off Cambridge centre where we should be safe and peaceful. We caught the local bus into the city and arrived just in time to enjoy choral evensong at King's College. 'D'you think we're too dirty to go in?' asked Frank at the entrance of the superb chapel.

Ignoring his unshaven face, muddy wellington boots and damp oilskins and forgetting my unwashed face and gritty teeth, I was deeply moved by the glorious singing of the King's College choir. It was when we were walking out at the end that I realised that everybody else was dressed as befits a solemn Remembrance Day service, in silk blouses, smart suits and elegant hats. We walked tall and tried to feel clean!

We had left Wanderer at the friendly Cambridge sailing club and on our return we found the remains of a huge bonfire still burning – they had been clearing up after the October gale. We cooked chicken legs in the embers and enjoyed our supper in the mild darkness, with owls hooting in nearby copses.

A mini-cruise in November is a great treat, but for once I was glad to get home – where my toothbrush. awaited me!

Arranging for a member of the family or a friend to meet dinghy and crew at the end of the cruise with car and trailer is a more convenient way of getting home, but it does involve careful pre-planning if one or other party is not kept waiting – or even waiting at the wrong place if the wind and tide do not co-operate. Some means of contact should be arranged to communicate a change of plan. The telephone number of a friend who is known to be at home is the easiest plan. An alternative is to carry a handheld VHF radio in the boat, which makes it possible to connect with the telephone system and phone an hour or so before landing.

Whether sailing alone or in company, whether planning a few hours, a few days or several weeks, certain basics should be observed:

1 Obtain charts and maps of the area to be visited.
2 Identify good launching sites and places where the car and trailer may be left.
3 Use an Ordance Survey map of the area to identify villages, towns and places of interest. Food, fresh water and fuel may need replenishing, and occasionally it is pleasant to go ashore for a coffee or to explore.
4 From the pilot books that supplement chart information find out details about local harbours, ports, lights, buoys and significant coastal features like offshore rocks, steep-to cliffs and bolt-holes which you may need in the event of bad weather. Charts give a wealth of information, including depth of water, and local hazards such as rocks, reefs, sandbanks, tide rips and spoil grounds. A tidal atlas provides information on the direction and speed of the current for each hour of the flood and ebb tides, and times of high and low water are provided by the local tide tables. *Reeds* or the *Macmillan Silk Cut Almanacs* include a vast amount of information, such as tidal atlases, tide tables and chartlets of popular harbours. However, they are expensive and bulky and need replacing each year.
5 Find out about the local weather patterns for the area. Start by talking to the locals before you start the cruise to see the pattern of fronts.

6 Go through your checklist of equipment for the boat, car trolley/trailer and your own personal gear. Check tyres and tyre pressures, lighting board, and attend to fuel and water for the car.

7 On the day of the cruise, check the latest weather forecast, then load heavy stores into the car and light gear in the boat. Secure the dinghy and check a few miles along the route for any sign of chafe, whether anything has moved, or if lashings have come undone.

8 On arrival, rig the dinghy and obtain as much local knowledge of weather as you can. For example, local fishermen and coastguards can tell you when commercial traffic is likely to enter or leave harbour, where there are inside passages along the coast, particular local hazards such as uncharted wrecks and good landing places, and when the local gunnery range will be firing out to sea.

9 After launching into salt water, wash down the trailer/trolley with fresh water if possible, before parking it for your return.

10 Take time to relax after the journey and have a meal or at least a hot drink before setting off.

11 If in doubt about the weather or sea conditions it is always best to sail out to take a look. If conditions are marginal, the experienced sailor is more able to say, 'No. I don't like it; we are going back,' than the novice. It takes courage born of experience to go back and face the good-humoured banter from the bystanders who so recently waved you goodbye and wished you luck.

If the forecast indicates that the weather is moderating, it may be worth continuing, but if it deteriorates it is better to do some local sailing or wait for an improvement.

Some people fill in a 'Yacht and boat safety scheme' form so that coast guards know of your route. In this case, it is essential to telephone in should you have to change or abort your planned itinerary otherwise a sea search may result. It is not obligatory to fill in this form, however. The freedom to change one's plans, exercise total self-sufficiency, and the difficulty of keeping in contact with the coastguard if you land on some remote island, make this impractical. However, it is sensible to leave details of your passage plans, however varied or flexible with friends or family.

It is a logical step to progress from day sailing to weekends afloat to a week exploring. Whether cruising tidal or non-tidal water, it is warmer, drier and faster to sail down wind, but is easier, and therefore safer, for the inexperienced to judge a deterioration in the weather when beating. When sailing 'on the wind' it is obvious when a boat is being overpressed and in need of a reef. Running before the wind takes experience to judge when it is necessary to round up and reef, or possibly even to take down the main and carry on under genoa. The rule is: *if in doubt, reef early*.

Sailing from one harbour to another, or even across a bay, can present two quite different types of sea according to the state of the tide. Wind against tide will produce short, steep or even breaking seas, whereas when the tide turns and runs with the wind, a pleasant flatter sea is presented to the dinghy sailor.

Before setting off on each leg of the cruise it is essential to work out the times of high and low water. Sailing with the tidal stream in your favour, or alternatively keeping in shallower water closer inshore to cheat a foul tide, makes for an easier and faster passage. Arriving at a beach at low water and having to roll the boat a long way up the beach to camp above high water, or trying to enter a harbour that is already drying out or cross a bar at the wrong side of the tide, are all frustrating and even dangerous exercises.

Considering the daylight hours and what time you will be making your landfall is important when planning a longer cruise. It is difficult to approach a strange place in the dark, so it is best to plan to arrive with as many hours of daylight as possible. For example, when we planned to sail to St Kilda, an uninhabited island off Scotland, we estimated that it would take approximately twelve hours' sailing to complete the passage. Setting out from the Outer Hebrides in the evening we aimed to arrive the following morning with many hours of daylight in hand. Closing the land, whether it is from a short day sail in an estuary or after crossing the sea out of sight of land, is the time to be most vigilant as it is the most dangerous part of the cruise, and you will need all the daylight and information you can get to make a satisfactory landfall.

By using fair tides and planning the cruise with these things in mind, you can cover large distances across tidal water. If fog closes in and visibility becomes bad, the dinghy sailor should hug the coast, keep out of big boat channels, and cross shipping lanes at right angles as quickly as possible. When sailing along estuaries you will make the best passage if you use flood tides, and you can cheat the ebb by sailing over the shallows where the tide is not so strong.

Being aware that hot weather will create afternoon onshore breezes and that early morning will produce an offshore breeze gives speed to your sailing performance if these conditions can be utilised. When cruising along rivers or creek crawling, dinghy sailors can gain the best speed by reading the local currents. Close inshore the current often runs at a different speed and direction from what is experienced in midstream. The current flows fastest around the outsides of bends, and so good distances can be achieved if you study the geography of the river. For the inexperienced, landing on lee shore banks should be avoided, because the wind will pin you on them.

Nowhere is farther from the water in the UK than a few hours' driving. Beautiful unspoiled cruising grounds are to be found in Poole Harbour, Milford Haven, the Plymouth rivers, Chichester and Falmouth, the rivers Dart, Salcombe and Helford, the Thames and Dee estuary, the Clyde, the Firth of Fourth, Menai Straits and the Essex and Suffolk rivers. But for loneliness, space, and lack of development you may need to go farther afield as we did – to Norway and the United States.

FOREIGNERS IN FLORIDA

Wanderer, *our 4.7 metre [15 feet 8 inches] wooden Wayfarer, was stored in Gilbert's Marina on Key Largo last year. December 14 saw us again leaving Heathrow Airport on a snowy, bleak, winter day. This was our third winter cruise in Florida. On this trip, we planned either to attempt to cross the Gulf Stream or visit the Marquesas Keys, depending on weather conditions.* Wanderer *looked immaculate with her varnished decks and blue-grey painted hull, exactly as we had left her eleven months before.*

Anchoring overnight in Angel Fish Creek, we enjoyed subtropical paradise. The creek between the mangroves was empty of traffic and the 28°C temperature and sparkling starry sky emerging from a radiant sunset had been panoramic as we cooked supper. In the quiet tropical evening blue, white and grey herons

Wanderer V on the east coast of the United States, sheltering from a gale blowing outside. We find a beige-coloured canvas tent better than dark green or blue canvas. In strong sunshine it creates an illusion of more space and coolness, and on darker days it affords more light. The tent fits neatly to the hull of the dinghy. Velcro strips fasten back on themselves, through and over a bolt rope on the hull.

Note that the foresail is furled. The main is rolled tightly around the boom and is tidy beneath the tent. Should a wind switch necessitate a quick move, the sails are ready for instant use. *Photo: Frank Dye*

145

glided over our mast on their homeward flight, and two roseate ibis rose up from the mangroves while we rested at anchor.

It seemed too beautiful to put up the tent that night so, rolling out our sleeping bags on the floorboards, we sat drinking coffee, chins flush with the decks, absorbing the wonderful night. A cloud of luminous balls just below the surface of the water seemed to be approaching us from the Gulf Stream. These waving, streaming, yellow and green luminous swirling circles, some half a metre in diameter, surrounded us. 'UFOs?' I said, as I grabbed the bucket and tried to catch one. On closer inspection they turned out to be jellyfish swimming along the pathway of the moon.

We left Angel Fish Creek on a sunny morning with southeast winds of 5 to 10 knots and made preparations to cross the Gulf Stream if the wind freshened. Passing whistling Buoy 4 marking the edge of the Gulf Stream, the sea colour changed dramatically. The turquoise waters of the shallows of the limestone shelf ringing Florida turned an instant indigo blue. 'Will we see sharks or whales?' I thought as I prepared lunch. Instantly the wind dropped, so we sat sweating and willing the dinghy to sail and make way against the southerly current. Checking our speed and our leeway from the buoys marking the channel we sat helplessly watching as we were swept sideways. On our horizon were a continuous string of tankers and cargo boats using the current to their advantage. At dusk we rowed back towards the low-lying smudge of mangrove trees off the Florida mainland.

The next dawn saw us rowing back towards the Gulf Stream. The forecast promised southeast winds of 10 to 15 knots; it also warned of a strong northerly front moving in. We hoped to be across the Stream before this arrived, but it wasn't to be. There is nothing more frustrating than watching the wind die. We knew of several big boats that had waited for weeks to get just the right conditions to cross to the Bahamas; we did not want to spend our precious three weeks waiting, so we turned around for a second time and returned to Florida. I was weak enough to wish for an engine as we rowed for four long hot hours!

Two days later, we had one of those sails that come once or twice in a lifetime. At 2 am Frank woke me. 'Weather was right for a good sail south,' he said. In happy silence we brewed tea, packed sleeping bags and checked the charts. The moon and starlight were bright as day. These were soon blotted out by a fiery, spectacular *dawn. The wind was 20 knots from the north west so we set off on a broad reach just off Rodrigues Key. The land sheltered us and there was no fetch; the sea was calm and flat and the sailing was good.*

By midday we had sore backsides. Wanting to unkink our backs and stretch our legs, we sailed in close to a beach, threw the anchor overboard and waded ashore. Australian pines sang in the wind and the palm trees swayed as the northerly swept in, but on the beach all was quiet. For an hour we walked on Long Key beach, fascinated by all we saw: hermit crabs of bright pink, a black snake, horseshoe crab shells, mauve jellyfish and beautiful shells and lumps of brain coral. Being a biologist, beachcombing is my hobby and Frank had a hard job persuading me to leave handfuls of my findings behind.

The sun shone brightly, the sea was vivid blue, the wind was increasing and soon we weighed anchor and were storming along with two reefs in the main about half a mile off the beach. Sightseeing this way amused us; the coastline was interspersed with bridges linking up the Keys, some of which were little more than clumps of mangroves, while others like Key Vaca and Marathon had holiday villas, hotels, marinas and airstrips.

'We'll spend Christmas Day in Key West,' said Frank, as we stormed past Saddlebunch harbour. This was one of the nicest Christmas Eves I had ever spent. No basting turkey or rushing about doing last-minute shopping – just a wonderful twelve-hour downwind sail in brilliant sunshine.

As we closed the last low-lying headland of the mainland and close reached around the tip of Florida we were flung about into very steep seas. Water was thrown at us from all directions and we were blinded as the salt water smeared our glasses and stung our eyes. The dinghy moved slowly and was heavy with water.

I leapt inboard and began pumping hard; I heard Frank yell above the howling wind, 'Sit her up.' A full gale was blowing and we continued to beat into a tumble of green frothing breaking seas; the waves were probably about 4 metres [12 feet] high, short, steep and breaking, and there was a long fetch. Warm green shelves of water poured on to us from from every direction. Once Wanderer *hung back and we held our breath as she refused to come through the wind and on to the next tack. The smack of the waves on the rocky white shore barely 3 metres [10 feet] away was not a nice sound.* Wanderer *seemed literally to claw her way through the* walls of water and, as so many times before, I marvelled at the stability and seaworthiness of our little boat.

Two tacks later, spilling wind in the huge gusts as we were overpowered, Frank said, 'Watch the next wave. I'm going to turn back – we have too much sail up.'

'Let me take in another reef,' I yelled. As I stood up, a wave nearly lifted me out of the boat. Fear got the adrenalin pumping so effectively that even Frank was surprised how quickly I grabbed in another reef with wet, slippery fingers. With a third reef tied in, we settled down to beat up the channel towards Christmas Island.

Seeing all the big boats stagger and snub their moorings in the lee of Christmas Island, we felt this was no place to spend Christmas, so we pressed on. Instead of tacking around the next headland up to windward, Frank decided to take a short cut beneath a bridge linking two islands. Knees trembling with tiredness, I steered while Frank took down the main, lowered the mast and rowed through the bridge. Luckily nobody was about to listen to us yelling as we rowed like madmen to get through the bridge before the headwind and tide swept us back on to it.

An hour later we were snugged down in Key West marina. We had sailed 112 kilometres [70 miles] in the 13 hours since we left Rodrigues Key. It was lucky that Wanderer, by American standards, was so small – because the marina was full. However, we were snugged into a crack between two larger boats.

While I showered, Frank dried out the boat and put up our tent. And while he showered, I decorated the tent and prepared for Christmas. Cards, balloons, tinsel, Christmas roses, iced cake, nuts and wine set out on the thwarts greeted Frank when he stepped back into our tent. It was a marvellous Christmas Day.

The northerly turned out to be a bad one. All the weather bulletins kept telling us it was the worst weather since 1892. The palm trees whipped and whined in the wind and that night the temperature dropped to 4°C. The rain was torrential, the wind rose to 35 knots, and we were amazed that our tent remained on the boat and did not leak. Many people living in large yachts in Key West marina came to visit us and admire Wanderer. We were offered charts, given boxes of biscuits, and told how free we were in our little centreboard boat. We began to wonder if the dinghy cruising era was about to break in Florida!

Our next sail had to wait until the vicious string of northerlies *had passed. Stormbound for three days, we happily explored Key West. The old harbour was full of history, as was the town with its beautiful conch houses and subtropical gardens blooming with colourful blossoms.*

When the northerlies had passed, we set out from Key West with a freshly washed and provisioned dinghy. The first night out we were treated to a magnificent display of fireworks organised from Mallory Square. The sky was rent with curtains of red, blue, silver, gold and green patterns of sparkling stars and fiery tailed comets. Anchored off Christmas Island we had a grandstand view.

The next day we broad reached southward and were glad to find that the scattered low-lying keys on the horizon served to break up the swell. As we pulled down a reef, the reefing blocks on the boom flew off, so we hove-to while Frank dug out his tools and repaired the damaged boom. An hour later, the block flew off the traveller and the mainsheet lost its position. Once more Frank took out fretsaw, glue and screwdriver and made repairs.

Over the next two days, we sailed right around the Marquesas Keys. But three weeks had passed too quickly. South Florida and the Keys had more wonders to offer than we could absorb in so short an adventure. Our last glimpse of the roseate ibis was on our final sail along the mangrove channels leading into Barnes Sound. We had only encountered two cruising dinghies and, at most, a dozen cruising yachts on passage, a wonderful change from the overcrowded waters around our home harbours in England.

Taking a dinghy abroad for a foreign cruise is a great thrill. In addition to all the information needed for home cruising, extra information and items have to be collected: passport, visa, vaccination updates, travellers' cheques and local currency, etc. A bill of sale, evidence of ownership of your dinghy may be useful in some countries. It is also a good idea to take along your local sailing club membership card. Finding out about customs regulations is necessary, and quarantine rules must be noted. Try to land at the official Port of Entry of a country. Carry a yellow 'Q' flag asking for 'pratique' (clearance to land) and a courtesy ensign of the country you are visiting. Check that your insurance covers you to cruise abroad. It is essential to take out medical insurance when planning to cruise either home or foreign waters and dinghy insurance is also important.

We have always enjoyed wonderful hospitality and genuine offers of help from sailing club members in countries as far apart as Ireland, the Persian Gulf, Scandinavia, the United States and Canada. Lasting friendships have been built up from these contacts. The only foreign waters that have disappointed me were the Mediterranean. For dinghy cruising I found the oily calm of the mornings and the reliable force 5–7 winds of the afternoon rather difficult for engineless passage making.

After months of planning and anticipation, it is disappointing to find that conditions, very far away from home support, make the proposed route impossible. It is a good idea, therefore, to plan alternatives:

Cruise A when all conditions are ideal, making for good, safe, easy passages and all objectives can be achieved in the time available.

Cruise B allows for indifferent weather or slight bureaucratic hold ups, allowing part of the cruise to be completed only.

Cruise C is put into operation when major problems force a total change in plan – even sailing from a different area or with a different crew.

Adaptability is what dingy cruising is all about.

14

Communication

Self-sufficiency is the hallmark of successful dinghy cruising. Uneventful landfalls rarely make the headlines, but the satisfaction for those who achieve them is enormous. One of the first cruises I was privileged to make in *Wanderer* we were off Fair Isle, an isolated island between Orkney and Shetland, and a vicious squall was overpowering us. Shivering, wet cold and frightened, I asked Frank if he wanted me to get out a flare.

'Nobody asked us to come here,' was the reply.

Later he explained, 'It's wrong to expect other people to hazard their lives to rescue us. It's best to rely on yourself. Anyway, it's unlikely that anyone would see us and probably it would be too late by the time they found us.'

Twenty years on Frank has spent three summers cruising the east coast of America and Canada, covering about 4800 kilometres (3000 miles) as the crow flies; he carries no ship to shore radio or sophisticated navigation devices. In some remote places charts cannot be bought, so he has successfully used road maps. A seaworthy well-found dinghy and an experienced seaman should cause no danger to other people.

Communication with the land

Once you have left your base, communication with the British mainland can be maintained easily. A Long Wave radio tuned to 1500 metres will give you the shipping forecasts, and a VHF handheld marine radio can keep you in contact with the Coastguard and other boats. (Channel 67 and 16 are reserved for small boat safety.)

The Yacht and Boat Safety Scheme is maintained by the Coastguard. By sending in a card obtainable from the shore authorities (Coastguard Harbour Office etc) detailing your proposed cruise itinerary, your boat details, home address and contact telephone number, overdue boats or boats in distress can be more easily identified and helped. It is important to realise that should you wish or need to alter your plans while away sailing as a result of bad weather or other unforeseen emergencies, you need to let the shore-based contact know immediately to prevent a search being instigated.

For those venturing offshore, emergency position indicating radio beacons (EPIRBs) can be used as homing devices, in conjunction with satellites and rescue aircraft fitted with direction-finding equipment. This is a high-tech system and very accurate. The rescue services are automatically alerted once the device is activated, so a false alarm is very expensive; EPIRBs must therefore be stored out of reach of children. I remember reading of an international search and rescue operation which eventually located the transmitter in a bedroom of a house in Glasgow where the children had been playing with it.

For inshore emergency (up to 4.8 kilometres (3 miles) use red hand flares or an orange smoke signal to indicate your positions and your need for help. In coastal waters, two star red flares or red parachute rockets should be used for distress. The flares should be held away from your body on the downwind side. (See also *Flares*, p. 117). Other recognised distress signals are slowly and repeatedly raising and lowering outstretched arms simultaneously, flying an article of clothing on an oar, flying signal flag 'NC', or flying a square flag with anything resembling a ball above or below it. The ensign flown upsidedown or tied in the rigging, or the continuous sounding of a whistle, will all be recognised by anyone looking out that you need to communicate or require assistance. At night, white flares or white star rockets can indicate your position to those looking for you.

Communication between a fleet

While some dinghy cruisers prefer to travel alone or with a crew, others like the safety and friendship of fleet cruises. Fleets composed of several classes tend not to be successful, since speed and performance and the point at which they need to reef all vary so widely between classes that the fleet spreads out to the point of disintegration. Dinghies of the same design and performance, in particular, can more easily stay within visual contact of one another, but some amount of control is necessary – and intercommunication can be preplanned – by flying flags on either shroud, for example. The lead boat in a fleet should have an easily identifiable shaped or coloured flag, and any signal from that boat should be instantly responded to. Racing within a fleet cruise is not sensible, and the speed of the least experienced skipper or the slowest boat should set the progress of everyone on the cruise.

Another system is for boats to pair up. If a nightly rendezvous or a weekly meet up is planned between a fleet of boats, a shore telephone number should be established to relay messages from any of the boats. If a dinghy should get separated from the others, forced to abort plans, or suffer gear failure, then the rest of the fleet need not waste time or money looking for the missing boat. If bad weather threatens, the boats should try to sail within visual distance of the rest of the fleet.

Sound signals between the fleet should not invade the peace and privacy of the area. Shouting is intrusive, but a quick blast on a fog horn, or banging a spoon on a metal plate, may serve to attract the attention of the other dinghies and bring them within speaking range. Some skippers like to communicate with one another or with those ashore by CB radio.

Light signals

It is important to know what other boats are signalling as you sail in their vicinity. A boat at anchor hoists a black ball in the rigging in the fore part of the boat by day, and at night should display a white light visible for 3.2 kilometres (2 miles) with 360° visibility in the fore rigging. Boats more than 50 metres (164 feet) long at anchor should show an afterlight lower than the forward one. Oil rigs must have an all-round white light visible for 16 kilometres (10 miles) with a red light at each corner of the rig visible for 3.2 kilometres (2 miles). A vessel constrained by her draught, such as a supertanker, should show three red lights in addition to normal steaming lights. Fishing boats over 50 metres (164 feet) when trawling should show a white all-round light and a green over white light forward. Fishing boats over 20 metres (65 feet), but not engaged in trawling, should exhibit a red over white light.

A vessel that is towing another displays a diamond shape in its rigging, as does the towed boat. At night they show two masthead lights in vertical line. Sometimes the towrope sinks below the surface and it is only too easy to sail between them, so it is important to know this signal.

Hovercraft display a flashing yellow light (120 flashes per minute).

See also light characteristics given on p. 124.

When night sailing, your own dinghy should display a green starboard and red port light. In practice this is difficult for a dinghy because of the need for battery power. A combination red and green light can be mounted on the bows, but the height of the lights is frequently too low to give warning to other craft since it tends to be hidden in the wave troughs. Fortunately the regulations permit a sailing boat under 7 metres (approximately 23 feet) to have a white light ready to exhibit in time to prevent collision, and we have found that a paraffin lantern to hang in the rigging and a powerful torch to shine on the sails to warn approaching boats works well enough. (We hoist our lantern using the jib halyard, and toggle it to the forestay as high as we can reach, by standing on the deck.) Better still, arrange to night sail outside shipping lanes and anchor in quiet corners and in shallows where big boats will not disturb you. (You should display a white riding light on the forestay if anchored in or near a channel, fairway or where vessels normally navigate.)

Fog horns

In fog it is difficult to identify sound or direction or distance with any accuracy. Usually a boat at anchor or aground uses a bell signal, while a fog horn or whistle indicates that a boat is underway. Sound signals from other boats given by fog horn or by siren are as follows:

- ● 1 blast – 'I am turning to starboard'
- ●● 2 blasts – 'I am turning to port'
- ●●● 3 blasts – 'Engines going astern'
- ●●●● 5 blasts – 'Look out' or 'Your intentions are unclear'

(See also *Fog*, p. 116.)

Steering and sailing rules

Applying the rules of the road mean that you effectively keep out of trouble when cruising among other moving boats. The important rules to observe are:

1 The overtaking boat keeps clear of other boats.
2 If on port tack give way to boats closehauled or on starboard tack.
3 The windward boat keeps clear of other boats sailing in the same direction.
4 When running before the wind keep clear of closehauled boats.
5 Expect boats under power to give way to those under sail, but don't rely on it.
6 Never expect a deep-draught boat or a commercial vessel such as a ferry or fishing boat to give way to you.

You should always show your intentions to other boats in good time if you are required to change course.

Flags

Flag etiquette should always be observed when sailing your own boat. A sailing boat should fly the correct burgee; a square one indicates that you are racing and a triangular one (usually showing details of the owners yacht club) shows that you are cruising. The burgee is flown at the masthead.

The red ensign (for British boats) should be flown from the prime position aft. We have a light bamboo flagstaff that slips through two eyes screwed to the rudder stock low enough to prevent the mainsheet catching on every gybe. The courtesy flag of the country you are visiting is flown from the second position on the starboard spreader, while your club flag is flown from the third position on the port shroud. A yellow flag requesting customs clearance when arriving from a foreign country is also necessary, and should be flown from a prominent place on the boat, usually below the courtesy flag.

Weather forecast communication

At night, storm warnings are shown in harbours or at Coastguard lookouts as follows:

White light over green – gale expected from NW
White light over white – gale expected from SW

155

Red light over white   – gale expected from NE
White light over red   – gale expected from SE
Lights red, green, red   – hurricane expected

The visibility scale used in weather forecasts is as follows:

Fog   – visibility less than 1000 metres
Mist   – visibility less than 1000–2000 metres
Poor   – visibility less than 2000 metres – 2 nautical miles
Moderate – visibility of 5 nautical miles
Good   – visibility over 5 nautical miles

Reunions

Arranging to meet up with another boat during a cruise can be quite difficult because of the problem of communication.

On one occasion Frank and I were sailing round Denmark to meet the Danish Wayfarers at their annual rally. Bad weather caused us to snatch passages between gales whenever we could; we arrived on the last day of their rally just in time to say 'Goodbye'. On another occasion we planned to meet two Canadian friends Dr Alan and Joy Phillips, in Florida. After shipping our boat to Miami we aimed to sail up the coast and across Florida to meet them in Fort Myers on Florida's west coast, while they trailed their boat from Ontario, Canada. We made excellent time up the Intracoastal Waterway to St Lucie Inlet, through the canal to Lake Okeechobee, then down the Caloosatchee River as we had several gales from astern. On the day we had arranged to join our friends we still had 19 kilometres 12 miles to travel and there was no wind. Rowing our hearts out, we kept going in temperatures of over 32°C, and then across the wide river we saw the unmistakable hull shape of another Wayfarer. *Wanderer* was only 20 minutes late in her tryst with *Kingfisher*. That Alan and Joy had trailed 3200 kilometres (2000 miles) through snow and slush and we had travelled across the Atlantic and sailed 240 kilometres (150 miles) across Florida since we spoke gaily on the telephone in the UK saying, 'See you in Fort Myers on 5 January at 1030 am', was a quite remarkable feat of communication and preplanning.

Some people say that when a boat reaches the end of its life and is retired there is no communication left. They are wrong. When we sailed *Wanderer 1*, No W48, to the National Maritime

156

Museum at Greenwich, she had cruised over 64,300 kilometres (some 40,000 miles) and parts of her hull were soft. But each spring the museum brings her out to enjoy the Wooden Boat Show. I promised *Wanderer* that I would never forget her, so each June I take our boat tent and cruising gear back to her, and make my home aboard her overlooking the Thames where she last sailed. When all the crowds go home at night *Wanderer* and I share wonderful memories as supper steams on the boat stove.

15
Singlehanded cruising

I think you have to be a little in love with your boat. No ugly, badly maintained or unpredictable dinghy would tempt me to spend hours afloat her. If you always have to be careful to balance a dinghy, take care where you walk, and cannot relax in her, then you will always be looking enviously at other boats.

I find *Wanderbug* lovable. Some 4.2 metres (14 feet) in length, bermudian rig, with lifting rudder and centreboard and two-piece floorboards, she is my perfect sailing partner. Her beam is generous, thus she is stable enough for me to use her as my floating home; and as the marine plywood floorboards fit over the entire length of 2.3 metre (7 feet 7 inch) cockpit, there is plenty of flat space for storage buckets and for me to move about. The upward curved wooden thwart not only enhances the elegant lines of her GRP hull, but the slight curve allows plenty of room to sleep beneath on the floorboards – while also being in the right position for comfortable seating when rowing. Her hull is moulded in three separate units which makes her a strong boat. I find her lively and stimulating to sail either on my own or with friends; she will carry three. The moulded side seats are exactly the right height off the floor for a comfortable leg position when helming or crewing, and her lifting rudder with detachable tiller extension can easily be stored on the floorboards.

Considerations for singlehanding

My Wanderer MD has been redesigned for me by her designer, with singlehanded sailing in mind. Her buoyancy has been redistributed from beneath the aft side seats to both ends of the dinghy; she will now float lower in the water should I capsize, which makes climbing back into her singlehanded much easier. Inversion is much less likely as I use an inflatable pad in the top of the sail (see Fig 2) and a foam filled boom, both of which prevent the mast and mainsail from sinking.

I like to get up at dawn on a fine summer day, and either get ready to sail before the rest of the world wakes up or else turn over in my sleeping bag, enjoying an early morning cup of tea in bed and sleep on. Sometimes, lifting a flap of the tent, the sun shines on my face, and I listen and watch nature very intimately. Without a crew all these pleasures are a personal whim, and I don't have to feel guilty or selfish. Naturally there is twice the amount of work, worry and energy output if you travel alone, so singlehanding is about making life easy for one pair of hands and looking ahead to avoid getting into an awkward situation.

Becoming cold or tired too quickly can spoil a good day afloat. This is best avoided by having readily available a hot drink and carbohydrate foods. Extra clothing also needs to be at hand. Stowage for the singlehander can be easier since there is only one person's gear to carry, but with only one pair of hands to do everything, stowage needs to be straightforward, with easy access to everything without having to lift and rearrange gear to get at it. In any case, with or without crew, successful dinghy cruising is best achieved by adopting a very disciplined attitude to stowage. Scrabbling about to find a box of matches with wet hands, or a clean jumper with muddy ones, makes for disorganisation and bad temper. I am happiest in *Wanderbug* when everything is in its right place and instantly available when I need it.

Freedom to set sail for an hour, a day or a week is an excellent tonic and a good discipline in self-reliance. With nobody to blame except oneself if things go wrong, and with little but the bare necessities, a better harmony can be established with oneself. I love to wake beneath my tent. A dawn chorus, the sounds of weather, the sight of a sunset, the smell of honeysuckle or clean salt air are so immediate. If one has had a cold, wet sail or an exposed dark night at anchor in a storm, to see the dawn emerge, brew up tea and relax and get warm in the morning sunshine are memorable moments.

A bonus in sailing singlehanded is that you are only alone if you want to be. Couples or groups afloat are often considered self-sufficient, but the singlehander is available to accept all kinds of invitations. 'Come aboard for coffee', 'Would you like to see my boat?' 'Would you like a shower?' 'Come and join us for dinner', are all offers I have happily accepted on many occasions.

Safety when alone

Sleeping afloat alone can occasionally be worrying now that we live in a more violent society. With no door to lock, and only tented protection, I keep a whistle and sheath knife beside me at nights. Also, I tend to tie up or anchor at nights within shouting distance of other boats or, alternatively, well away from river banks close to cities, or quays leading to the undesirable ends of ports. On the whole, people are expected to sleep in cabin yachts, so that a small tented dinghy is not ostensibly attractive to the casual burglar. My olive green cotton tent merges easily into the countryside background, and so is not at all conspicuous. However, twice I have been approached while sleeping out. In each case I had the advantage of surprise. The prospective burglar was probably looking for gear, or maybe dry shelter for the night, and when I made a great deal of noise, using language I didn't realise I knew, the surprised feet pelting off meant that I did not need to fear another visitation that night.

If I am staying more than one night in any place I strip the main sail off the boom, dry it, and stow it away. However, if I plan to move on each day I roll the sail around the boom. The tent fits over the bulkier ridge quite well. Should there be a switch in the wind or unexpectedly violent weather and I have to move quickly, the sail is ready on the boom to get me off a lee shore in a hurry.

Wanderbug's hull has a continuous line tied around her just below the rubbing strake. This serves the dual purpose of acting as a grab rope should I go overboard, and for the tent attachment girdle. Self-locking Velcro strips sewn on to the tent edge quickly secure the tent to the hull as they easily lace over the girdle line. Being singlehanded, erecting a tent needs to be as simple as possible. I used to have hooks on the hull to which my tent was secured with elastic shockcord. This method caused a

Sleeping arrangements on *Wanderbug*. For the singlehander it is practical to load gear on the opposite side to one's sleeping bag. Note the flask prepared for early morning tea and a torch beside it. *Photo: Len Tate*

minor disaster once. When landing on a sandy beach I leapt out of the boat sideways, both to use the momentum of the dinghy to pull her farther up the beach and to check her impact with the land. Running my hand along the hull to keep contact as I prepared to run through the water I was stopped, pulled backwards, and I lost my balance. The hook beneath the rubbing strake had hooked into my wedding ring. Had I been sailing faster, damage to boat and my hand could have been serious. Replacing hooks with trumpet cleats worked well for a season, as I secured the tent to the hull by ropes that threaded through the trumpet cleats positioned laterally along the hull. The advantage of my present system of using a girdle rope for attachment is that I can quickly fasten the tent from inside the boat without having to lean out to thread the ropes through the trumpet cleats as previously. Also, should it rain and the tent shrinks and needs to be slackened, a quick adjustment to the Velcro strips from inside the boat – again without needing to lean out of the boat – is a simple task.

Solo techniques

All shackles, for example on the main halyard and on the kicking strap, have been replaced by snap shackles, enabling them to be operated by one hand. If, for example, I want to run ashore or sail down a dyke to my mooring and there is not room to turn head to wind to take down the main before continuing under jib, I like to be able to release the kicking strap with one hand while keeping the other on the tiller to steer. The main can be run down, and hardly a change in direction is necessary.

With the control line of the jib furling gear running back to a cleat on the back end of the centreboard, I can furl the jib while still steering. I often reduce sail; running before the wind under genoa only, or beating with main only. For the singlehanded cruising sailor safety is more important than speed and, with no crew to sit out the boat, reducing sail early is sensible. In any case, with a well-balanced boat like the Wayfarer or the Wanderer I find I can sail well enough with the main, or even a reefed main, only. Good visibility is also achieved with no genoa or jib to block my view. Some people prefer sails with windows for improved visibility, but I dislike plastic windows because I find they make stowage of the sails more difficult also the plastic appears to deteriorate quicker than the sail material.

To reduce wind pressure on the sails which results in heeling, the solo sailor can sail broader on the wind, or luff in the gusts. To avoid getting caught in irons when tacking, particularly if sailing on mainsail only, the solo helmsman needs to harden in the mainsheet very positively to pull the boat through the wind. It is not sensible to have to grope for the jib sheets every time you tack, so a continuous jib sheet (or just tying their ends together) enables the singlehander to control the foresail from the helming position. Reefing the main by means of jiffing reefing is described in Chapter 11. It is an ideal and safe reefing system, since the singlehander can work from the centre of the dinghy where the boat is most stable.

If you need to wait for a tide to make a quick snack, 'spend a penny', do any task afloat, or just want a few minutes' rest from sailing, heaving-to (Fig 19) is a good manoeuvre to practise. This needs a little sea room, as the dinghy will lie quietly on the water drifting slowly sideways and forwards at less than 1 knot. Until experienced, it is best to heave-to before reefing. The

162

technique involves bringing the boat on to the wind, freeing the mainsheet and jib sheet until she has lost way, and lashing the tiller hard down to leeward. The centreboard is brought half up, and the jib is 'backed' and cleated to the windward side. The dinghy will be stable in this position, but beware of strong gusts; be prepared to let the jib sheet fly if the sails are caught aback in a strong wind.

Using oars of the greatest length that is practical (lashed down on the flat floorboards, when not in use) is a technique worth practising. I often row at dawn or in windless conditions for several hours or miles with no real fatigue. My oars are 2 metres (7 feet 6 inches) in length, and the rowlock sockets are situated towards the outside of the deck hull so that the oars enter the water without chafing the edge of the deck. Sockets and the rowlocks can be chrome on brass or stainless steel. Plastic ones are to be avoided because they are not as strong, and they tend to flex when pressure is put on them. The claws of the rowlock are a close fit on the sleeve of the oars so that the oars remain in postition even if I lose hold of them. The rowlock sockets are positioned 8 centimetres (3 inches) aft of the centreline of the thwarts so that rowing is not over strenuous; the trick is just to lean back on the oars as they sweep through their stroke.

In restricted waters where there is insufficient room for rowing, a paddle comes into its own to move the boat. My paddle is 1.2 metres (4 feet) in length with the shaft in one piece of wood for greater strength. Paddling is not an efficient way to propel a dinghy of *Wanderbug*'s size, and it is very tiring because you have to bend over and out of the dinghy to make a stroke through the water. My method is to sit on the stern near the tiller, make one paddle stroke, and then correct the direction with a hard push of the tiller away from me. With this rhythm of one push with the paddle through the water then one push against the tiller, I find *Wanderbug* will keep a straight course. Sculling with one oar over the stern is a more efficient way of propelling a boat with one oar or paddle, but few people have learned this art – including me.

Usually after a sail I prefer to sleep afloat. If I choose a bank side to overnight on, I look for a tree stump, post or other firm base to attach the bow line. This I run through a fairlead on the bows to ensure the dinghy does not sheer about. A stern line/

warp ashore is taken from a ring bolt, bolted through the transom for strength. Checking that the warps allow sufficiently for a rise and fall in water level, I may put out a spring to ensure the dinghy lies quietly overnight, and use fenders to protect the hull. In any case I have a specially strong and big rubbing strake fitted around *Wanderbug*'s hull. Alternatively, it is a simple matter to pick up a vacant mooring for the night if you can be sure the owner does not want to return to it.

Staying afloat while camping is easier on both boat and crew, but occasionally I will pull up on a gently shelving beach if I think there are no stones beneath me to damage the hull gel coat. Levelling the hull by shovelling sand under the chines or placing a long roller under one side keeps the boat stable enough to sleep and live aboard her. I have had a pulling-out ring through-bolted to the bow of *Wanderbug* which enables me to attach a three part block and rope tackle to it; if no help is at hand, I can pull *Wanderbug* above high water (see Fig 4). In calm settled weather, good planning allows you to land at high water on an evening tide of a coastal hop and have a whole tide to explore the area, leaving the beach with the assistance of the next high tide. Remember not to do this on a dropping tide though, or where the wash of passing boats will cause you inconvenience before the dinghy dries out. Also check most carefully the ground on which you are drying out for rocks, stakes or glass. Beaching a dinghy using rollers singlehanded is not really possible.

Launching and leaving the shore

Managing a boat singlehanded when it is afloat and sailing is a straightforward matter. However, there are problems to overcome when the dinghy has to leave the land and take to the water. On a gentle slope I give the boat a lifeboat launch, ensuring I have a long painter to control her as she runs into the water off her trolley. If the launching ramp is too long or too steep I may walk the trolley across the slope at angles of 45° and zig-zag my way down the slope (see Fig 5(c)). Once launched, it is simply a matter of getting the boat head to wind, hoisting the sail, pushing down the rudder blade and centreboard if the depth of water allows, in a co-ordinated series of movements, and sailing away from the shore. If there is limited space I push out hard from the bank, and by backing the jib the bows of the boat blow quickly off the wind; I free off and am sailing away.

Stern boarding is another method of getting away from the shore. A crew makes the manoeuvre simple, but with practice it can be done satisfactorily singlehanded. With the boat head to wind, you need to stand in the stern of your boat facing backwards. One hand or a shoulder should pin the boom hard out against the shroud; the other needs to keep the tiller central. Once the painter had been released from the shore the boat should drift backwards. As the mainsail catches the wind you should release your hold on the boom and direct the tiller so that the rudder blade points in the direction you wish the stern to go. The mainsheet now needs to be pulled in to get the boat sailing away from the land. Lastly, the jib sheets can be dealt with.

Returning to land

Coming back into land demands careful judging of the weather. With the wind behind, I run in under jib only. If the wind is light and there is plenty of room, I sail straight in, turning head to wind to lose way before jumping out with the painter in my hand to restrain the dinghy. I always aim for a gentle landing!

If the wind falls light, or the tide turns early, getting home may take much longer than planned. I never carry an engine because I know from experience that generally they are more trouble than they are worth. They can be useful in a calm when short of time to get home, and especially when stemming a strong foul tide in light airs, but most of the time they are not needed and are smelly, bulky things to share one's boat with. The odd tow along a narrow tree-lined canal or river, or along an estuary, is a real enjoyment anyway. I carry a long light warp which I can offer to a suitable boat, though generally they have their own. I prefer to wrap the towing line once round the mast and hold it, ready for quick release should anything happen that would make me want to separate from the towing boat (such as the boat going too fast, or if there is danger of collision).

Sliding back in the dinghy with the towline in one hand, and putting the centreboard up, one can sit well back in the boat, steer straight into the stern of the tow boat, and enjoy the ride. The sails should be doused and loosely tied to prevent them being caught by the wind and blowing into the water thus affecting your visibility or the boat's stability.

16
Laying up and fitting out

Even the most enthusiastic dinghy cruiser will expect to be out of the water some time between November and February. The odd day sail or even a club race may be enjoyed throughout the winter, but passage making and sleeping afloat are more enjoyable from late spring until early autumn in northern climes.

Laying up consists of removing and storing all gear from the boat, and protecting the hull from the elements. Fitting out involves putting everything back on the boat so that she is ready for the keenly anticipated new season afloat.

Since work of any kind on the dinghy is not an attractive occupation in January or February unless you have the luxury of a heated boat shed, garage or a dry undercover shed, we like to do a major refit on the boat in the summer, just before our annual cruise. The evening light is longer, the weather warmer, the humidity usually lower, and often the task of washing off, rubbing down, varnishing and painting is the more enjoyable because holiday plans can be discussed, worked out and anticipated while attending to the boat jobs.

Every dinghy, like any other vessel, needs annual maintenance. Sensible lay-up procedures should enable the following year's cruising to be trouble free. The following checklist should provide the basis for winter maintenance.

Sails Strip the sails off the boom. Wash thoroughly in fresh water, using mild detergent if there are stains on them. Once they are completely dried and aired, examine them with care. Broken stitches, weakened seams, tiny chafe patches or holes

166

can be repaired. The areas that usually show wear quickest are the batten pockets in the mainsail and the wire luff seam in the foresail.

If two edges of sails have to be stitched, herringbone stitch will hold the two edges flat without distortion. Before any kind of stitching is done, however, old seams need to be cleaned and the old thread removed. Some seams can be repaired with the careful application of waterproof glue, and patches can be glued or sewn over small holes or chafed areas.

If the sails have been left damp or in badly ventilated conditions all season, they may show fungus spores as tiny black spots. On a warm day the sails can be laid out on a dry area, scrubbed with water and a mild detergent, and then throughly rinsed. Sails should be stored over the winter in a well-ventilated place and in as uncreased a state as space permits. Storing them in rolls and hung up in waterproof protective sacks prevents damage occurring during the off season.

Floorboards, centreboard, rudder, tiller, hatch cover, mast and *boom* must be removed from the boat and thoroughly washed in fresh water. If they need varnishing or painting, these tasks are better done early rather than waiting until the weather is snowy or frosty. A couple of coats annually should be sufficient to keep the boat parts well protected. If the tips of centreboard and rudder have been damaged by a grounding or contact with rocks during the season, these tips should be repaired before painting or varnishing. Oars and paddles should also be treated in a similar manner, and stored blades uppermost.

Floorboards should be stored in such a way that air can circulate round them and so that they cannot warp. Wooden masts and booms need to be stowed in a frost-free place and supported evenly along their entire length to prevent them warping. Alloy spars, on the other hand, may be stored out of doors, but still need to be supported. If they are wrapped in plastic no pollution or dirt will collect on them.

The dinghy hull should be carefully washed in fresh water and then checked for damage. Any repairs or alterations should be done as soon as possible after the end of the sailing season. Ensure that self-bailers are free of sand, grit and grease. Occasionally a bad launching may have bent them; if this is the case, carefully tap them back into shape. Bung holes need to be cleaned, and the bungs examined for signs of wear. I have had *Wanderbug* built with no drainage bung holes. On a dark night at anchor, it is all too easy to imagine they are leaking, and a friend once had his bungs torn out of their drain holes as the tide turned and the stern anchor warp fouled them. He returned from a pleasant meal and walk to find his dinghy very waterlogged.

The dinghy hull needs to spend the winter upside down where water cannot collect in it, then freeze, expand, and split the hull. A wooden hull needs to be evenly supported above the ground on tyres, chocks or trestles so that air can circulate – and under cover if possible. If it does have to winter outside, a tarpaulin should be wrapped over it. GRP hulls can be upturned and kept outside, providing rainwater is not allowed to collect in any part of them. Once inverted, the keel band can be checked for signs of wear or damage. If the boat has been frequently launched over stony ground or pulled up a concrete ramp, the screws may need to be replaced or fresh mastic used to bed them back into position to keep the hull watertight.

All hull fittings should be checked too. The chain plates, bow fittings and horse fittings should all be firm. The transom fittings in particular may have worked loose after a hard summer's sailing and will need to be secured. The rudder hangings (the upper gudgeon and lower pintle) should be especially carefully examined. Sometimes the screws may have worked loose and just need to be tightened. If, however, the screws need to be replaced, longer ones used or the wood around them repaired, these jobs are best done in covered comfortable working conditions.

All rigging needs to be washed to remove salt residue and examined for signs of fraying, rusting or corrosion. Shrouds and forestay may stay attached to the mast for the winter but, if they are removed, wipe them with an oily rag, coil and tie them several times around their circumference, and then hang them up.

All shackles, pins and bottlescrews should be checked to see that they move freely, rinsed free of salt, and then oiled.

Boat covers need to be washed, whether made of canvas or plastic. Ties need to be mended and split seams or torn corners repaired before they are folded, bagged up and stored in a well ventilated place.

Laying up on a trolley. If wintering the dinghy on the trolley or trailer, remove the wheels and chock up the frame. This ensures that the suspension units in the trailer are not kept under continuous tension, and that damp does not wick up the rubber wheels of trailer or trolley.

Laying up outside. Circumstances may force the dinghy owner to lay up the boat outside, perhaps in a boatyard or in the back garden. If the boat is to sit on its own trolley or trailer, great care must be taken to see that the hull and mast are well supported and that the bailers are left open to allow rain water or snow to drain out of the boat. A well-fitting cover (and possibly a tarpaulin over that as well) should ensure that the dinghy stays dry. Any pockets of water collecting in a badly draped cover or tarpaulin can easily freeze and weigh heavily on the boat.

Regular checks If kept outside over the winter, make regular checks on the boat. I once had friends who wintered their cherished dinghy in a friendly farmer's field, many miles away from their home. Periodic visits were made by the farmer to sweep away snow or scoop water off the cover. Come spring, my friends journeyed to their dinghy and found the cover well drained and snug over the boat, but a family of mice had spent the winter inside the hull. Sheets, sail bags, even the burgee, had been chewed into warm fluffy rags to line their nest!

Fitting out is usually an expensive time. Renewal of boat licences and club membership fees, and payment of berthing fees and river tolls, are some of the details to be attended to, but they are also a pleasant anticipatory reminder of the joys afloat as a new season approaches.

If sails have been taken to a sailmaker for valeting or professional repair they need to be collected before the sail loft reaches its busy time, usually just before Easter. New charts may have been ordered, new pilot books and tide tables bought (if not received as Christmas presents!) and new oilskins tried on if last season's set won't do. Everything has to be eased back into the old routine.

Lists made when laying up are of great benefit during the fitting-out period. Every part that was removed from the boat now needs to be collected, laid out, checked, and put back on the boat. Some people like to paint and varnish in the spring, but remember that good marine products and good brushes (ones that do not shed whiskers over the newly coated hull) should always be used; it is definitely a false economy to buy cheaper products. Toe straps need to be refitted, and all fittings put back on to the dinghy hull and mast. Care must be taken not to overtighten the centreboard bolt when fitting it back into its casing, and it is a good idea to check that the pin securing tiller to rudder head still fits.

Trolley and trailer, especially if they have spent the winter outside, need a careful overhaul. Wheel bearings should be greased, screws, nuts and bolts checked, and rubbers for the cradle supports seen to be still flexible, not cracked or unable to support the dinghy hull. Check also the trailer lights and ball bearing hitch on the trailer.

One short-cut to a trouble-free fitting-out time is to tape together each boat fitting with its screw in position when removing each one from the boat. This prevents the panic of having to play hide and seek with the wrong sized screws during fitting-out sessions. Too often, if this precaution has not been taken, a worrying heap of washers, nuts or bolts, clevis pins or screws remain oddly unaccounted for after the dinghy appears ready for her first launch.

17
Quality time with a Gull Spirit

———

Dinghy cruising is generally enjoyed by younger sailors, and the Victorians actually believed that you should have a foot of boat for every year of your life! Certainly, over the years I have watched several of my sailing friends with creaky knees and aching backs sell their dinghies, and then buy small yachts. Invariably though, they then seem to sail less and less and they are dependent on having crew; they also seem to be more restricted in their choice of sailing areas as available moorings or marina locations become major considerations.

Since physical stamina and a sense of adventure and independence are necessary ingredients to successful dinghy cruising, and full enjoyment of it often requires considerable effort, not too many people sail dinghies into retirement. Indeed, since *Dinghy Cruising* was first published, people from all over the world have written to me wanting to discuss a variety of subjects relating to dinghies and 90 per cent of the letters have come from youngish men.

One memorable conversation I had was at the Greenwich Wooden Boat Show. I was standing beside our Wayfarer, resplendent with all her cruising gear, when a lady came up to our stand. 'I'm going to buy a Wanderer, trail to Venice, and then sail around the canals and lagoons,' she announced. 'That's one of my dreams too,' I replied, and we talked long into that sunny afternoon overlooking the Thames, discussing tent designs, cookers and sailing rigs. 'Send me a postcard when you arrive,' I said as we parted. I have waited eight years for the postcard, hoping to hear that a dinghy cruise around Venice was as good as we had both dreamed it would be. It was only last year that I partly achieved that dream when I borrowed a boat and explored a little bit of the lagoon and lesser known canal system of Venice. It was a wonderful trip.

Since that conversation at the Greenwich Wooden Boat Show I have down-sized from a Wayfarer to a Wanderer. For singlehanding, the Wanderer — being lighter and smaller — should have been an advantage, but in actual fact both dinghies are two-man boats if mobility is to be fully achieved. Pulling these dinghies laden with cruising gear up beaches and steep slipways is not easy for the ageing singlehander. Increasingly, at the end of a cruise I would find myself wondering, 'Will there be someone around to give me a pull out?' Sometimes I cruised one area over much simply because there was a winch near the slipway. All too often, I felt I was losing my freedom afloat.

Over the following two years I experimented with various types of craft. The fold-away Sea Hopper and a sailing canoe both caught my attention. I wanted to sail in a greater variety of sea areas and to achieve more mobility and flexibility. I then wrote to *Classic Boat*, explaining that I wanted to be able to portage, sail, row and manipulate a craft over land and water, and also be able to sleep afloat. To my amazement, letters came in from boatbuilders in Germany, Norway and Canada, as well as several in the UK. I had some especially helpful and stimulating conversations with the Suffolk Canoe Company, and their pretty wooden craft won my heart. I suppose the appeal was the yearning for the simplicity of an earlier era. However, to be able to sleep afloat on these craft, leeboards or outriggers would be needed to achieve the necessary stability.

I also rediscovered my need to actually *sail*. The 30-year-old buzz I experienced when a dinghy danced over a sun-drenched sea, or the rush of adrenaline when a dinghy punched into waves and performed well in a rising wind, were still necessary ingredients to my happiness in our increasingly crowded and urbanised society.

That very same month, a new dinghy came onto the market — the Gull Spirit. By coincidence, I'd had a Gull in the 1950s:

My first encounter with the Gull dinghy was in the 1950s; she was the original hard chine plywood boat. Ian Proctor had designed her to teach his children the joys of sailing. You are never too old to enjoy the Swallows and Amazons experience: here we are making a drift wood fire on the shore of a Scottish loch; I am sharing an evening with Wayfarer friends.

Ian Proctor's 3.3 metre (11 foot) double-chine gunter-rigged dinghy, which he designed in order to teach his children to sail, and which was on his drawing board just before the birth of the Wayfarer. My Gull had been constructed from a wooden kit and built by that great craftsman Jack Chippendale, and together we had dinghy cruised around Scotland in the 1950s.

By the early 1970s, the Gull dinghy had developed a round bilge hull that was better suited to the GRP material now popular with many dinghy designs. Many years later, Joan Palmer, secretary to the large class of Gull Mark II and III dinghies sailing from Megham Rythe Sailing Club on the south coast, asked Ian Proctor to bring back the original Gull double-chine design. Sadly, in 1992 Ian died, before making a decision about Joan's request. However, the Proctor Partnership agreed to the request, and gave Anglo Marine Services the sole right to relaunch the Gull.

The Gull Spirit, as she was now known, retained her original double-chine hull, but her interior was cloned from the Wanderer dinghy. Nevill Towler, managing director of Anglo Marine (the firm that had also built my three Wanderer dinghies), suggested that I borrow the Gull Spirit prototype to see what I thought of the design. This sounded an excellent idea, so the prototype dinghy was towed to Norfolk and I experimented with her for several weeks during the spring of 1998.

I found her to be well built, lightweight, robust and fuss-free, with a good sailing performance. Most important of all, though, I rediscovered my sailing freedom with her, in that I could launch and recover and sail her in most conditions. Because she had been designed before the Wayfarer, with a redesigned interior based on the Wanderer, I felt I knew her intimately and respected her pedigree. At 3.3 metres (11 feet) long, with a beam of 1.6 metres (5 feet 3 inches), a weight of 88

I found the Gull Spirit to be well-built, robust and fuss-free with a good sailing performance; however her small light hull with short waterline makes for a lively sail – less forgiving than the Wayfarer.

For a small dinghy, the Gull Spirit has plenty of stowage space as can be seen from this neat stern locker which can house a folding bicycle and holdall (above).

Here you can see the anchor safely stowed (right) but ready to use quickly and easily when a good anchorage has been found.

kilograms (195 pounds), a draft of 0.9 metres (3 feet), and a Portsmouth number RN 1361, she proved to be a robust and stable sailing boat with sufficient space to live and sleep aboard. There was ample dry stowage and a well-constructed outboard bracket and rowlock fittings. This boat has a Bemudian rig. Ian Proctor originally designed the Gull for family sailing, and now – some 50 years on – she is back on the market as the Gull Spirit.

Having down-sized from a 4.8 metre (16 foot) Wayfarer to a 4.2 metre (14 foot) Wanderer, and now to a 3.3 metre (11 foot) Gull, it seems that Ian Proctor provided the means for me to continue dinghy sailing into my retirement years. Quality time is all about choices, and the independence to achieve what one chooses to do with one's leisure time.

Of course, a smaller, lighter dinghy, while affording greater freedom of mobility from shore to sea, also imposes various restrictions. Consequently, my new dinghy was the impetus for fresh ideas and she forced me to revise my sailing techniques. I realised that the stable Wayfarer and the beamy Wanderer had both allowed me to make mistakes while afloat and to get away with them. In contrast, the Gull Spirit smartened up my physical and mental movements. Many of my friends and acquaintances in the 'glad to be grey' brigade had taken up short tennis and aerobics in an effort to stay fit. I have just kept sailing, and found that I have become leaner, fitter and more agile. The smaller the dinghy, the faster she responds, and the singlehander has to react and think ahead more – or run the risk of capsizing.

Space and weight are at a premium in the Gull Spirit, so I began to revise both stowage patterns and weight distribution in my miniature cruiser. To my delight, I discovered modern technology had greatly increased the comfort and safety of the dinghy sailor since Frank first introduced me to the delights of dinghy cruising more than 30 years ago. I have also found that many other people approaching retirement and planning to enjoy quality time have shortlisted the Gull Spirit as a practical dinghy in which to teach the grandchildren to sail, or to give themselves the opportunity to singlehand and sail in new areas. To be able to share one's passions with the world at large is an even greater and unexpected bonus.

Clothing for the 2000s

In our early days afloat, our sailing clothes were pretty basic. Frank had an army gas cape and oilskin trousers; both were heavy, bulky and clammy. As an inexperienced crew, I was given a roll of quilted fabric and told to make myself a tunic and trousers. After wearing seven layers of cotton, and wool and silk beneath these, I always felt uncomfortable. Coming back from our first cruise, I took all these garments to a laundrette. 'Do you work in a submarine?' asked a sympathetic attendant. On our second cruise I took all our oldest sailing clothes, then threw them away as we changed into clean layers. We travelled back to the UK in the clothes we stood up in, rejoicing in no luggage to haul home. However, being offloaded from a warm aeroplane into an icy open-air car park with snow drifts round our van, after winter cruising round Florida, was rather a shock!

Developments in clothing technology have revolutionised the comfort and safety of all outdoor enthusiasts; and dinghy cruisers in particular have benefited – no longer having to endure cold, clammy wet-weather gear, leaking and stiff at collar and cuffs in PVC, or heavy wool garments that take an age to dry. Modern fleeces and thermal undergarments create a layered system which keeps the body warm and dry. They dry easily when wet, and take little space to stow. The trick is to layer one's sailing garments to maximise the efficiency and endurance of the body. The outer layer of clothing needs to be waterproof to prevent water entering from the outside. The inner layers must be breathable to prevent the build-up of perspiration, yet be capable of trapping warm air. A windproof layer will stop the wind chill factor.

I now use a High Polartech fleece, which has a lined collar and hood, with double cuffs. I find Gill Key West jacket and dungarees foul-weather gear are soft, flexible and easy to stow, with reinforced and breathable seats and knees.

Cold feet are a problem with dinghy cruising. Faster movement in a small boat demands good mobility with a good grip on wet GRP surfaces. I have now discarded Wellington boots in favour of soft polyurethane or neoprene bootlets. They have an insulating sole with a soft, removable cushioned inner sole, and have a soft ankle cuff with non-slip reinforced heel and toe.

One's head takes a lot of punishment when sailing, and heat is lost from around the skull in cold and windy weather. I have now discarded my itchy wool helmet in favour of a hood with a polartech fleece lining with ear flaps. In hot weather, a baseball-type cap with a large peak to protect the eyes from glare, and spectacles to give protection from driving rain, is a popular choice, but in Canada last year I was given a canvas hat used by the uniformed lock keepers. It keeps the back of the neck and ear lobes protected, which the popular peaked cap does not. Keeping the face, ears, hands and legs protected from wind and sun as well as wet and cold conditions is important, when long days enjoying the elements in a dinghy can expose the body to harmful ultraviolet rays. Skin cancer today is on the increase due to the depletion of the protective ozone layer surrounding the earth. Therefore protective sun creams with a high protection factor need to be used.

Sunglasses are another area benefiting from advanced technology in lens construction. I find Serengeti sunglasses give excellent results and good glare protection. Polarised lens are essential when afloat because they cut out a high proportion of reflected glare from the water.

Years ago we used to carry kapok or foam-filled lifejackets. We rarely used them, except in stormy weather, and found them bulky and restrictive of movement; they chafed at the neck, soaked up water and salt, and never dried out. In contrast, modern air-only lifejackets can be worn all day long while working in a dinghy as they do not restrict movement and are lightweight, flexible and dry easily. I now use a Crewsaver. This lifejacket carries a CE Mark of Approval and meets CEN standards. Should you fall overboard, it has high visibility retro reflective tape at key points to ensure all-round night recognition. The lightweight polyurethane-coated nylon inflation chamber is tough and enduring, and there is a non-clog whistle and lifting beckets for ease of rescue, while the teflon-coated abrasion-resistant outer cover protects the inflation chamber.

When both gardening and sailing I try to wear gloves to protect my violin-playing fingers, but in fact I find I tear off my gloves when I need to work. However, if just crewing, neoprene gloves or Amara leather ones protect the hands from the wind chill factor, and stay soft and supple even when the gloves have dried out.

Drysuits and wetsuits have greatly improved over the years, both in terms of comfort and materials used. However, the dinghy cruiser does not expect to capsize or work in the water too often. Dinghy racing sailors who expect to capsize, and who also can have a hot shower in the local sailing club at the end of the race, gain most benefit from these garments.

Food

Food for the outdoor enthusiast has improved in variety, availability and quality. Yet dinghy sailors cannot carry vast quantities of fresh or bulky foods, and ice boxes are only practical if going ashore daily. I still use Tupperware containers; they provide the flexibility needed for the small dinghy explorer, because they are easy to clean and to stow, and remain watertight and flexible.

The new high-energy bars, if carefully chosen, are easy to stow; many however, have little real flavour, only sweetness. Oats deteriorate quickly, artificial banana, chocolate and coconut flavours have a short shelf life, and sugary carbohydrate foods have little flavour. For cold snacks I most enjoy Jordan's cereal and fruit bars, such as Tangy Citrus Frusli: raisins, nuts and all dried fruits remain a good stand-by.

There are many hot snack foods produced now such as dried

soups, noodle and rice mixtures that only require the addition of hot water. They come in plastic containers and often with plastic spoons; sachets of cheese or garlic-flavoured croutons are sometimes added (which bulk out the meal). My favourites are Asda's Quick Snack (because the hot, spicy curry-flavoured noodles contain less additives than most) and Knorr's Tastebreaks of tomato and mozzarella pasta (because they really do taste of fresh tomato). Obviously, no washing-up is required; and if stowage space is at a premium, the contents of these containers can be stowed in small plastic 'press 'n' seal' bags.

Cookers

There is much choice in cooking appliances these days. Size and weight are the deciding factors, with safety and availability of fuel also being important considerations. Available fuels are paraffin, butane, propane, white gas (gasoline), diesel, and methylated spirits. Some stoves are multi-fuel – where a change of jet allows a choice of fuels to be used. Whatever the choice of cooker, quick, simple efficient and safe are the main criteria. Stowage in a small dinghy is also an important factor. Gas is simple to use, being easy assembly, and the flame is easily controllable. One tends to go ashore frequently when cruising a small dinghy, so replacing gas canisters, and the disposal of them, is easy to organise. A good windshield and stable canisters are things to check out. Methylated spirits cookers are good in wind. Petrol fuel is widely available; one needs to use 'unleaded' petrol and to remember that it is highly volatile. Paraffin is efficient, but it needs priming. Methylated spirits is widely available, but has the disadvantage that it is invisible and quiet when burning so a meths-fed fire passes unnoticed until out of control. White gas has similar properties to petrol, but is cleaner and more cost effective, and is widely used in the USA.

Choice of lightweight cookers is wide. Camping Gaz, Coleman, Primus, Go-Go Systems, Sunngas Camping Stove and the Vango Trangia Storm cooker (methylated spirit based) are some of the most often used afloat in small boats.

For those who like to sail to a marina or stop overnight on an isolated beach and cook ashore, two new, slightly bulkier, stoves are now on the market which can be carried ashore for use; the compact, lightweight and ultra-stable EuroGT Gas range is constructed in steel with an efficient alloy burner and is powered by a butane gas cartridge. Ignition does not require matches, and if the gas cartridge is wrongly inserted the gas will not be allowed to flow. A simple dial ignites the gas and controls the flame. The slightly larger AutoCube is an alternative cooker. This is a revolutionary new British invention combining a self-contained portable unit including a two-burner gas hob, and an electric hot/cool box, fresh and waste water tanks and storage for food, utensils and a gas bottle. If plugged into a conventional 12 volt system, the power is provided to cook a meal and wash up in hot water afterwards.

Small kettles and billy cans with folding handles are a good choice for small spaces, and if weight of gear is not too critical, plastic flasks and mugs should be replaced with unbreakable metal ones. Stainless steel flasks and vacuum insulated mugs ensure that the early morning cup of tea in bed – one of the joys in the dinghy cruiser's day – remains hot to the very last drop.

Radio and shipping forecast

There is a fairly new radio on the market which can be useful to the sailor. It has an inbuilt clock and can be timed to record the Inshore Shipping Forecast, which saves getting up to listen at various unsocial hours during the night, possibly dozing off before it is finished, and going back to sleep before the tide floods hours later and forgetting the content. Being mains or battery operated, it can be used in the dinghy, uses a standard cassette, has a headphone socket to avoid annoying neighbouring boats (sound carries far over water), and costs little more than an ordinary household radio. It is made by Roberts Radio, is LW/MW/FM (model RC9907 (mono), SC9908 (stereo)) and currently costs under £40. They produce a unit which includes Short Wave for worldwide reception, but it is much more expensive.

Living aboard

Down-sizing from a Wayfarer to a Wanderer, and then to a Gull, demanded a drastic rethinking of the stowage of camping gear. I used to have a down-filled sleeping bag and a cotton liner. These were bulky and difficult to clean; down readily absorbs salt, then takes a very long time to dry. Modern fabrics make going to bed afloat a joy. I now use a Coleman's

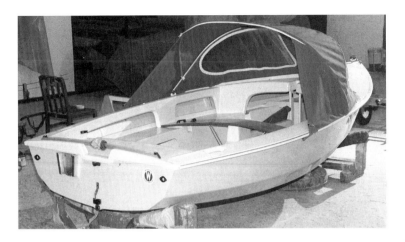

Instead of using a cumbersome tent which, on such a small dinghy would be claustrophobic, I use a spray dodger similar to the one on this Wanderer dinghy (above).

You could use the boom to support a simple ridge tent which makes a very snug sleeping compartment (right).

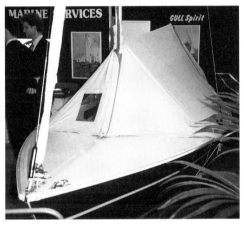

'Bambusa'. It packs into a bag that is 28 centimetres (11 inches) long, and weighs 900 grams (32 ounces). It is filled with Thermolite Micro fibre. It is resistant to squashing and retains heat. I carry a modern bivvy bag to protect my sleeping bag. Condensation is greatly reduced because the bivvy bag has a waterproof, breathable top with a water-resistant bottom. Insulation of the sleeping bag is greatly enhanced by the use of this bag, because it is windproof and water-repellent. There is a head space propped up by means of a short hoop with mosquito netting over my face.

As an emergency protection, I carry a space bag. It weighs just 100 grams (4 ounces). It can be used over a sleeping bag and acts as a lightweight blanket which reflects 80 per cent of radiated body heat. It is waterproof and wind resistant.

On a balmy night I often sleep afloat without using a tent. To fall asleep with water lapping the hull chines and shooting stars or a full moon overhead is indeed quality time. Who wants to be shut away from the dawn chorus in a bedroom or a cabin?

Our inflatable airbeds that we used to blow up by mouth have also been discarded in favour of modern self-inflating sleeping mats. They give maximum non-slip resistance between the body and the mat. Being rot proof, they also have a long life.

A fixed tent to such a small hull would be too claustrophobic, so I now use a spray dodger. The canvas cuff is tied to the mast and the material pulled taut behind the shrouds, and made secure at the jib sheet cleats. It pulls snugly around the washboards and acts as a windbreak as the dinghy lies head to wind. It also has other uses. Sometimes I like to tie up to a reed bed and listen to the birds and watch them unobserved: the spray dodger acts as a bird hide. Sometimes, tied to a jetty, I while away hours alone listening to my radio, or snoozing in the sun. Life afloat is not always about sailing; sometimes quality time means a recital or quartet concert in the open air, or a nice meal afloat.

When I want to spend nights afloat, the spray dodger can be extended over the rest of the boat, by Velcroing a simple ventile cloth to it, and securing it backwards over the cockpit of the dinghy. This eliminates the chore of erecting a framed tent over such a tiny boat. Two hoops made of plastic flexible water pipe fit into the side decks of the *Gull Spirit* and keep the material off my face.

At a recent Wanderer rally, I met a friend who had bought a tent for his dinghy. It was made of heavy canvas, and it took three of us to lift and unroll the material over the boat's frame. After a hard sail, putting up such a heavy tent would have been an enormous endurance test before one could get shelter and make a hot meal afloat. Also, if it rained hard during the night, the wet bulky tent would not be easy to pack and stow before the next day's sail.

Quality time is all about dodging the hardships of life afloat in a small dinghy. Enjoying the challenge of a hard sail, followed by a cosy night alone with nature, away from the bustling world, is very therapeutic. Obviously a radio is essential for weather forecasts, but Radio 3 and 4 offer a wealth of talks, plays and concerts, and a means of keeping in touch with the outside world. A new radio on the market, Miniature Freeplay S.360, is very useful; there is no need to carry batteries as the radio is powered by a tiny solar panel. If the weather is too dull for solar power, then winding the radio will maintain its power; two seconds of winding gives half-an-hour's playing time.

Hurricane lanterns and candle lanterns are too bulky for a small dinghy. A solar-charging hand lamp that is waterproof and floats beam upwards, should it go overboard, is now available. It has a battery back-up. Similarly, old heavy torches have been replaced with magnalite flashlights. They have a high-intensity beam, are water- and shock-resistant, and are very small.

Mobility

All the dinghies I now sail conform to the EU recreational directive. As I have explained, my only reason for down-sizing to a Gull Spirit from a Wayfarer and a Wanderer was because I could not haul the larger dinghies into and out of the water single-handed, and independence is vital for a dinghy cruiser.

Although the lighter Gull Spirit was easy to pull ashore, I found the lightness of the hull caused me other problems. The slightest beam wind or tide seemed to deflect her from her position as I lined her up on the trolley. Small arms welded to the trolley cradle effectively solved that difficulty, and the dinghy can now be pulled on to the trolley cradle in the correct position by one effortless movement.

Once afloat, sailing is obviously the normal means of travelling; however, there are plenty of other ways to explore one's chosen waterways, should the wind fail. Rowing is a pleasant exercise, and takes virtually no energy, providing one just leans on the oars and does not attempt to pull them through the water. Choose the longest oars that are practical to stow in the dinghy. You can also buy two-piece oars, which makes stowage in small dinghies an easier option. Ian Proctor's 'Praddle' has recently been reintroduced into the market. Weighing only 215 grams (8 ounces), it is floatable and easy to stow, and it enables you to paddle with one hand while steering with the other. The advantage of paddle or 'Praddle' is that you look forward, the direction in which you are travelling. If one is a naturalist, there are many visual and auditory delights as the boat glides through waterways, creeks and lagoons.

If you want to explore creeks and narrow waterways, the best way to do this is by sculling with one oar. You can attach a rowlock to the outboard bracket as shown here. Using a simple wrist movement you can propel the dinghy forward with little effort.

Wrist movement
(Diagramatic)

Fig 1 Sculling technique

Many people visiting Thailand remember best the golden jewel-encrusted temples of Bangkok, but my lasting memory of that smiling country is of hiring an ancient boatman and bamboo raft and exploring deep into the lush jungle-fringed waterways. Here I experienced how village people lived in their stilted houses lining the silent, green rivers. My boatman used a peculiar means of propulsion, using a long pole and a slow circular movement. I have tried to learn this sculling art in my dinghy. With a long oar resting in a rowlock fastened on to the outboard bracket (or a wooden block that fits over the transom or a crutch fitted to the gudgeon and pintle and using a simple wrist movement), it is possible to travel forward in a straight line with very little effort. This is an almost forgotten skill in European waters, yet the ancient Chinese employed a *yulah* to move sampans along their waterways. The *yulah* was a single, indigenous oar pivoted on a peg at the stern of the vessel. To use the *yulah* the loom of the oar was pushed from side to side and the shape of it, plus the constraint from the transom lanyard, controlled the action of the blade which twisted, performing a similar motion to the blade of the sculling oar.

184

The majority of sailors carry an engine. I have a small petrol outboard, a 2hp Mariner, but I dislike its noise and pollution, and find it a little too heavy to lift on and off the transom bracket when afloat. Experimenting with the eco-friendly electric engine, with its silent propulsion, was a pleasure, but the batteries were too heavy to stow in a light sailing dinghy, and the infrequency of electric charging points along the waterway made it a doubtful option for long days afloat. Also, I was surprised to find the electric engine not efficient if the wind piped up.

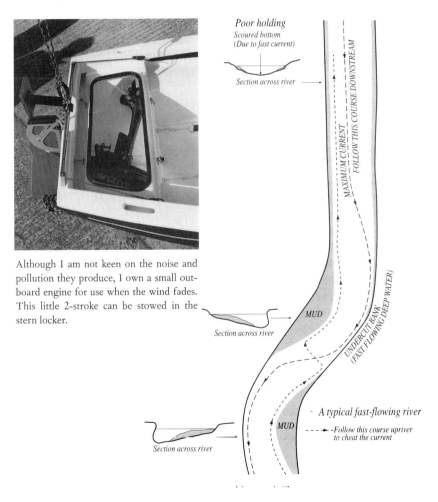

Although I am not keen on the noise and pollution they produce, I own a small outboard engine for use when the wind fades. This little 2-stroke can be stowed in the stern locker.

Fig 2 A typical fast-flowing river

If you are planning to drop anchor in an estuary, check the tide times beforehand to avoid spending several hours surrounded by a sea of mud.

Here you can see the results of my impatience to walk ashore, captured by a highly amused photographer! If you do get caught out, it is essential not to fall over, to take small steps and to keep moving. You can use an oar, as shown, or even try to walk along a warp, if you can get somebody to throw a rope.

On your return you may be horrified to find that the dinghy has capsized, leaving the mast stuck in the mud. Attempting to dig it out will not be successful because the mud will simply flow back into the hole. The trick is to release the shrouds, slide the dinghy backwards in the mud – then the mast can be drawn out of the capsized hull rather like slipping a sword out of its scabbard; then you can right the hull.

A boat roaming round a single anchor can be uncomfortable

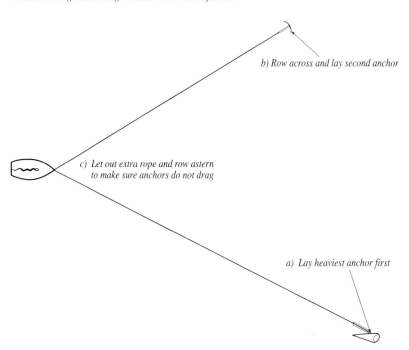

b) Row across and lay second anchor

c) Let out extra rope and row astern to make sure anchors do not drag

a) Lay heaviest anchor first

Fig 3 Anchors laid in a 'v' towards the current or towards an expected wind shift. Note: The Danforth anchor is an excellent burying anchor but in small sizes it is suspect on stone and kelp, as it is possible for pebbles or stems or seaweed to jam the pivotting flukes so that when the anchor capsizes as the tide turns the anchor can no longer penetrate and will drag. It is preferable to carry two anchors of differing type.

In the introduction to Frank's book *Sailing to the Edge of Fear* I said, 'Luckily one soon forgets the terrors, hardships and boredom of long sea passages, and the memories of wonderful landfalls remain most vivid.' These days, enjoying quality time afloat means that it is possible for me to prolong the enjoyable sailing experiences, and eliminate the miseries. There is no longer the urgency to rush back to work each Monday morning or to feel guilty if one lets down a team; nowadays there is time to savour the unexpected – the pleasure of exploring new places.

As I have indicated, happiness for me now lies in exploring afloat, and being close to nature. It is a perfect escape, affording a simple, but rich, lifestyle away from our materialistic, noisy society. Meeting people who have known real wilderness and stillness is always a tonic, and there remain many areas in the world that afford reasonably sheltered sailing conditions. In this new millennium most of us expect to live longer and more active lives, and some would say that nothing prolongs life expectancy more than tackling a new challenge. Sheltered estuaries like the Medway, Crouch, Blackwater; and Solent, Minches and Scandinavian areas protected by islands and close to the UK; abroad the Ijsselmeer and lakes in Holland, the Intracoastal Waterway of the United States, the Canadian Lakes, the Continental lakes; all give one the dreams and desires to travel and dinghy sail into the sunset.

Taking one's dinghy as a travelling home is something we have always done, and foreign destinations are so much more memorable when experienced afloat. The paperwork for travel abroad is minimal; just a certificate of Small Boat Registry, although some countries also require a certificate of competence.

Renting a container on a cargo ship, many years ago we transported our Wayfarer to Miami. With her we have seen life throughout the eastern shores of the USA and Canada. Other forms of transport abroad can be as deck cargo, and by this method I once took my Wanderer to sail in Holland. The lighter Gull Spirit can also be carried in the davits of any sailing ship, or upturned on the deck of a large yacht. The two-piece mast and oars are an advantage here.

If the dinghy is to be carried on a large motorboat or yacht, it has an advantage over the inflatable which is so light that it can easily blow over in a strong wind, losing gear. The hard dinghy is a safer tender. It is safer for getting to and from the large vessel. Also, inflatables degenerate in strong sunlight, are easier to steal, and more easily damaged. In addition, they have to be inflated and deflated – a time-consuming job. A small sailing dinghy can provide safe and enjoyable sailing, and also provide a stable platform from which to go ashore, swim or improve sailing skills, and can be more safely and easily rowed than the usual inflatable tender. Towing from the mother boat is also safer and easier using a small stable dinghy. An inflatable can easily be holed, or even swamped, but a dinghy such as the Gull Spirit has a large skeg which improves directional stability when rowing, sailing or towing. In comparison, flat-bottomed inflatables yaw from side to side, and are a heavy load to tow; for this reason, they are usually brought aboard and deflated.

Most people trail their dinghies behind their car or van. A good combination of trailer/trolley, lighting board, and discipline in stowing gear well is important. Frequent checks to ensure that chafe or movement of gear is not a problem must be made along the journey. Just as when moving a dinghy abroad in a crate, container or aboard another yacht, homework must be done well in advance of the trip to ensure that conditions concerning EC regulations are known and conformed with; also, when trailing, the necessary paperwork must be completed. Sites and launch places should be planned ahead.

Useful publications

There are some excellent books to help with this, some of which are listed below:

Where to Launch Around the Coast by Diana van der Klugt. A new edition of this title provides information on each site and its suitability for particular types of craft and activity, restrictions in force, approximate charge for facilities, and nearby facilities such as car and trailer park, fuel, food and chandlery outlets.

Trailing Down Channel by Bill McDonald. This book provides a guide to launching sites for trailed craft up to 6.7 metres (22 feet) on the Channel and Brittany coasts of France, and the Loire and Western Rivers. Information on each site includes location, access, type of slipway and nearby facilities. Each of the six regional areas is headed by a map that shows location sites. An introductory section covers French towing regulations and emergency services.

The Norfolk Broads and Fens by Derek Bowskill. This book gives details on location of locks, bridges, boatyards and mooring places and other leisure activities in the area.

Planning a Foreign Cruise gives the rules and regulations for the Baltic, North Sea, and Atlantic coasts of Europe and the Azores. *Planning a Foreign Cruise* also deals with rules and regulations for the Mediterranean.

Also useful is PBO's *Boat Owners Highway Code*, which gives the rules of the road, lights, shapes, buoys and signals in everyday use.

HM Customs and Excise publish clear, free pamphlets giving up-to-date guidance on situations the owner of a dinghy wishing to travel abroad may encounter, such as immigration requirements on departure and arrival at a port, responsibilities when leaving the EC, duty-free stores, making a report when arriving from an EC member state, goods to be declared, prohibited and restricted goods, selling a temporarily imported boat, and proof of ownership and proof of VAT status of used vessels.

Rules and regulations

We were once off Dover, hove-to in stormy conditions, awaiting permission to enter the port. We were not happy to be approached by a small official vessel whose personnel requested that we open our stern locker – our main buoyancy compartment! They were looking for people smuggling immigrants into Britain. We were sailing our 4.8 metre (16 foot) dinghy!

One can never know all the regulations when sailing into and out of foreign waters, so thorough homework on all the relevant subjects brings peace of mind and a problem-free voyage.

Frank got into great trouble with the immigration officials recently. Crossing from the States into Canada by water, he landed and went to church before clearing Customs and Immigration. Unfortunately, he was spotted by a Customs and Immigration official who was a regular churchgoer. Frank was lucky not to be deported as this is a serious offence. Yet in Florida a few years before, when we were refused a cruising permit because our paperwork was incomplete, we asked the help of the officer, who after a bit of thought cleared our 4.9 metre (16 foot) Wayfarer as a foreign merchant ship trading along the coast! This illustrates the point that Immigration Officers should never be taken for granted – they will always 'go by the book' no matter how nonsensical. However, if you politely ask for their advice, they can sometimes suggest ways round a problem.

An air bag slipped into the the head of the sail provides mast head buoyancy and should prevent the dinghy from inverting in the event of a capsize.

Heavy weather sailing for small dinghies

Now that I sail smaller dinghies, heavy weather has to be taken really seriously. The stable Wayfarer is an amazingly seaworthy design, because she looks after you when you make mistakes. My 3.3 metre (11 foot) Gull Spirit is not quite so tolerant and demands a lot from her skipper, but she is always fun to sail. Small dinghies need depth, beam and freeboard; the shorter waterline means that waves are not taken so easily and the smaller hull causes the water to be more abruptly forced around its curves.

Masthead buoyancy gives a feeling of security. A simple airbag slipped into the head of the sail is not too conspicuous, and should stop the dinghy inverting in the the event of a capsize.

Cruising dinghies rely on quick reefing of the main, and this can easily be done afloat as well as ashore; it should be practised in good weather. The furling jib – with the line from the drum taken beneath the dinghy's foredeck to a cleat within reach of the helmsman – is another safety factor should the weather blow up quickly. I used to think I needed cruising sails, but now I find that full sails that can be reefed are a more practical suit for a small dinghy, where stowage is at a premium.

Ken Jensen, a longtime Norwegian sailing friend and a fine Wayfarer sailor, devised a sail for heavy weather. He called it a genoa-trysail. I have made one up from an old sail, and in heavy weather it has proved to be an excellent way to continue a passage safely. A slider needs to be sewn on to the leading edge of the genoa by the top eyelet. Once the slider is fed into the mast slot, and the main halyard attached to the top of the sail, it can be hoisted in the normal manner. The foot of the sail is pulled down by a lashing (or the kicking strap) fixed to the eye on the foot of the mast, and this boomless sail is secured. It can be operated by the jib sheets which are led through a fairlead on the sidedeck near the stern. Using this sail it is possible to work to windward; it is also safer when running because there is no boom to drag in the water or scythe across the boat in an unexpected gybe. It is easy to handle. Ken mentions that if the genoa has a rope luff instead of wire, this is a simple modification to thin down the head so the sail will run up inside the mast grove.

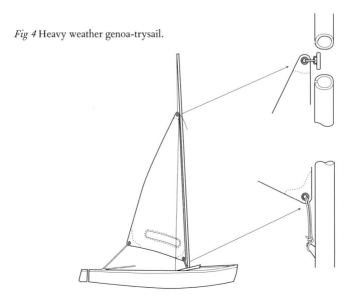

Fig 4 Heavy weather genoa-trysail.

I carry a lifeline and also a short warp attached to the thwart, with a loop permanently knotted at one end. I was out sailing in early February; my crew was a 76-year-old man. At the end of the sail, he got stiff, and fell out of the boat. In the cold water he rapidly lost heat and strength, and the only way he managed to get back onboard was with a loop in the end of the mainsheet into which he could place his foot and lever himself back on the dinghy.

A log book should always be kept up to date. It should record what is planned and what has happened. The human mind is great at forgetting what it doesn't want to remember. The log book forces the sailor to examine his mistakes in detail.

Even in small dinghies a GPS system is now considered an essential piece of equipment, and the small handheld battery-operated type is eminently practical in a cruising dinghy. However, the skills of estimating speed and distance, using transits, working out tides, laying a course to make a landfall upwind of an unknown and featureless shoreline, are basic navigational essentials that must never be forgotten. One day, the GPS batteries may go flat!

When I first considered down-sizing, I knew that whatever dinghy I opted for had to have a centreboard not a daggerboard, a foredeck, sidedecking and a bermudian rig. It also had to have sufficient space to be comfortable afloat for long periods, and a flat floor so that I could sleep afloat. Dry stowage was also an important factor, as was a double-chine hull shape. As I have previously mentioned, I found all these things in the Gull Spirit, and I am continually amazed at how much heavy weather this little eleven footer will take.

Cruising in company

Sailing in company is one dimension of sailing that increases confidence to the newcomer, and old hands usually enjoy passing on their enjoyment and skills. Competitiveness is part of man's inbuilt ego, and when I first began organising cruising rallies, it was horrifying to find how quickly the fleet got spread out, with the experienced sailing off while the inexperienced needed time to rig and get afloat. This was easily rectified by giving the least experienced sailors the job of 'leading the fleet' along the coast. People could sail anywhere within sight of the fleet, provided that they remained in a zone behind the leader dinghy.

Many sailing clubs organise rallies, picnics in company, and foreign cruises. The Wayfarer and Wanderer Cruising Sections are very active – with the Wayfarers dividing their cruising rallies up into various categories according to the seamanship skills likely to be required. Some individuals make lifelong friendships this way. Individual skippers must be responsible for checking that their dinghy and gear is reliable, with likely-needed spares carried, and that their insurances are up to date; organisers usually arrange tolls, licences and launching, pulling-out sites and club hospitalities.

Sailing in foreign waters can have an added dimension in that meeting with like-minded enthusiasts all round the world can produce real benefits and new experiences for all. For example, once we arranged to meet Wayfarer friends and to cruise around Florida. Our American Wayfarer friends had to trail over two thousand miles from Canada, while we had to ship our Wayfarer from England to the United States. 'See you at Fort Myers,' we said on the phone in a carefree way one dark night in November. Some months later we all met up at the appointed place, and learnt that our friends had endured a gruelling drive trailing their dinghy through snow drifts and ice, while we had to sail hard, dodging gales and storms, northward enduring long days afloat. Needless to say, after all the effort involved, our shared Wayfarer cruise was special.

In the 1970s when crossing Georgian Bay in Canada, the first organised Wayfarer international rally, Don Davis (the organiser) and I talked long about communication between dinghies. Watching as the six Wayfarer dinghies struggled with stormy weather we realised that if one dinghy got into trouble all the others would be able to do would be to watch visually in case of capsize, then stand by. Aural communication in such wild weather would have been impractical. That evening, over the campfire, we worked out a communication system. All dinghies would carry a brightly coloured flag on their shrouds. Should they need assistance, the flag would be pulled down, and the other dinghies would sail close in.

In this new millennium, mobile phones are both a blessing and a curse, in that communication is a 24-hour affair. Provided

Many sailing clubs and dinghy associations organise rallies, picnics and other social events. Gatherings like this are great fun and are a good way of picking up all sorts of tips and information about equipment and cruising areas. Some organisers now carry mobile phones so communication between boats is assured whilst cruising.

that this is not abused, there are obvious advantages; however, one does hear stories of people ringing in to ask the lifeboat to bring petrol out to a yacht, or of climbers asking for rescue on a mountainside when it's not really necessary. Once the callers have been located (by people who are prepared to risk their own lives to answer the distress signal), the callers are sometimes found to be badly equipped. Tidal and weather forecasting is faster and more reliable these days, and all dinghies and yachts cruising in company should keep updated with this information on a regular basis.

Once Frank set sail on the tide to singlehand his Wayfarer from Brancaster Staithe through the creeks using the flooding tide. Another dinghy skipper signalled that he and his crew needed assistance. Frank sailed over. He requested Frank to organise a tow back into harbour by the locals as their outboard had broken down and they were aground. The boat was well found, equipped with oars and anchor; they were sheltered, and it was a balmy summer's evening. All they needed to do was to anchor and wait an hour for the tide to turn and the ebb current to carry them back home without effort.

When families decide to trail, and sail in company, the companionship of both children and adults is stimulating. If several dinghies congregate, it takes more planning in dealing with rubbish disposal, or cleaning up after a beach barbecue or evening campfire. The golden rule is to leave no trace of your presence. Canadian sailors seem very caring over their environment. On my cruise with them, each boat carried a small trowel, and where appropriate biodegradable waste was buried. Plastic and tins had to be carried in black bin bags until a refuse disposal site was found. I sometimes despair when I look at beaches and campsites in my area of East Anglia. Plastic bags can take 10 to 20 years to break down, tincans over 50 years, and glass bottles over 1000 years.

The enjoyment of dinghy sailing can be the close connection with locals. An evening at the local pub gives insight into different areas, customs and traditions; connections not so easily made by bigger boats who anchor off or overnight in a marina. Listening to the locals in this wired-up modern world produces pearls of wisdom about local weather patterns, local sailing dangers (perhaps not identified on the chart), and, if we care to listen, it keeps us in touch with the countryside and coastal communities.

Forward planning of the cruise area is an enjoyable exercise. Timing is also something to think about. The period of neap tides usually produces kinder conditions in that the tides are smaller and currents are minimal.

The first spring of the new millennium has come early in East Anglia: today I stripped off *Wanderbug*'s winter sails, replacing them with her summer suit, delighting as I did so in the clumps of daffodils close to my berth and the urgency of birds' mating song all around me.

Winter sailing has been good, but now a new season is about to erupt for us all. Hopefully, most of us will sail far during it, exploring different areas, learning new cruising skills, and become exhausted, exulted and grateful for our new experiences.

Doubtless, new designs, new materials, different ways of building dinghies and innovative gear will develop in future seasons, but what will never change for me is the absolute joy in dinghy cruising: the friendships worldwide that such a shared passion generates; and the pleasure of sharing one's life with a working boat.

18
Magical moments

It seems like betraying a trust to talk about beautiful secretive places. Over-population and over-visitation can so easily destroy habitats and quiet spots. Yet to reach such a place slowly, by open boat or on foot, can enrich the body and stimulate the soul, and for me this has been one of the great joys that dinghy cruising offers. Therefore it seems selfish not to share such pleasures.

Luckily, the places most easily reached are often not touched with any special magic. It seems that part of the charm lies in the effort made to reach these out-of-the-way spots.

Scotland

One very special place we sailed to was St Kilda. It was my first big cruise in *Wanderer*. In fact I was so inexperienced I had never before sailed at night. All my life I had wanted to visit St Kilda, one of the most remote inhabited parts of the UK. Luckily Frank was equally curious about this bleak and spectacularly beautiful island group, about which so little has been written. So my wedding present was this first cruise. The Army and the National Trust both had interests in this uninhabited island, some 130 kilometres (80 miles) off the mainland of Scotland, but both were very dismissive that we should sail there in an open boat.

Late one July evening we launched from Skye and set out westwards. Wind against tide and gusty force 7 southwesterly wind set up a heavy sea in the Minches. Falling backwards out of the boat, unconscious with seasickness, my husband quickly taught me that determination and self-reliance are vital factors in the enjoyment of dinghy cruising!

About midday the following day I was preparing a sandwich while Frank was on watch. Without warning, a great wind blew across a calm sea from the west, driving the dinghy sideways for at least half a mile. Both sitting out at full stretch we were lucky not to capsize. We had read about these sudden katabatic Atlantic storms swirling around the mountainous St Kilda range, but there was no way we could have prepared for one. Five minutes later the sea was calm and blue again and we beat slowly towards the smudge on the horizon that was St Kilda.

It was a spectacular landfall. There is only one safe landing on this group of islands, which is Village Bay on Hirta, the largest island of the group, and that landing is only practical in an offshore wind. The sheer cliffs on Dun rose over 300 metres (1000 feet). Puffins, comical clown-like birds, tumbled off the cliff slopes into the blue sea, while above us the screaming gulls and aerobatics of fulmars and gannets served merely to accentuate the immense emptiness of this abandoned island.

The National Trust and Army personnel gave us kind hospitality in the form of hot showers, freshly baked bread and locally caught lobster, so it was the following day before we went for a walk over the island. This walk, 25 years on, still remains one of my deepest cruising memories. We found the deserted village; after walking along the cobbled main street, ruined houses on each side, we sat down on a large moss-covered stone just outside the village chapel. I had been given a little Austrian candle to burn on the happiest day of my life, and so it was lit and placed in the chapel while we wandered in and out of the closely clustered houses. In one, an iron bedstead still remained, in others a rickety table and chairs, pots and pans, and a fire grate with the peats still evident. Silently we recalled the facts. In 1930 the remaining 36 inhabitants of St Kilda had asked to be taken off the island. Their lifestyle, viable for 1000 years, was no longer economically or genetically practical or bearable. The close-knit, hard-working, God-fearing families who lived off a diet of seabirds and puffin eggs, spinning wool from the Soay sheep for clothing, chose to tidy their cottages, board the *Harebell*, and start life afresh on the mainland. Mary Cameron, daughter of one of the islanders' last missionaries, recalled an earlier storm that left the villagers deaf for a week, while another storm totally destroyed the village and blew most of the sheep over the cliffs to drown in the boiling surf below. It was a hard life on St Kilda.

The presence of a happy albeit ghost community was oddly and powerfully present in that deserted village, and we sailed away a day later very moved by the place. We felt very privileged to have had the chance to experience St Kilda for ourselves.

Suffolk

I wanted to celebrate my new dinghy by taking her to one of my favourite places. Launching from Slaughden, one of the friendliest sailing clubs I know, *Wanderbug* and I sailed along a grey River Alde. The long mudflats were coated in rain clouds. Quickly we got through the moored yachts, and turning a bend in the river, saw only a high sky, long lines of cornfields and belts of tall pine trees. Nothing special, just a lovely Suffolk estuary with nobody about.

Sailing on, Iken church lay beyond the withie way in a smudge of farm buildings and a clump of trees. Just as the tide was turning the last withy led me towards a narrow reed-lined channel alongside Snape quay. Barges plied this routes last century, and I tied up to one that was being restored and converted for modern living. Wet and muddy I climbed ashore and mixed with the holiday crowds enjoying Snape art galleries, tea shops and craft shops. Regretfully aware that the unacceptable face of commercialisation had now reached even this beautiful spot, once the dream project of Britten and Pears, I turned away from the imposing Maltings, now one of the finest concert halls in Europe, and walked towards the old staithe buildings where the grain barns and converted sheds now house the music school for advanced studies. To my delight, I found that master classes for violin and cello were in progress. Buying an observer ticket I lost time for several hours. This was not a concert, but an intriguing glimpse into interpretation and the technical studies that precede one.

As the great artists of the last generation, and talented youth of the next, packed away their music, I returned to *Wanderbug*. The tide had ebbed, leaving her in a great sea of mud. Sliding down the barge, I made supper aboard, then prepared to go to bed.

Everyone had gone home. Snape shops were closed, and the marshes were gloriously empty. A full moon, unblinking and golden, rose over the whispering reeds. The wind died, and the night was too warm to bother with a tent. Putting on a hat and extra socks, I crept into my sleeping bag and arranged the sails over to me to keep off the dawn dew. 'Shall I turn out the light?' said a voice from the barge. I fell asleep still laughing.

Before dawn next day I made tea, and sat snuggled up in my sleeping bag to enjoy it. The moon was still bright, then it faded as a brilliant pink dawn flooded the marshes to the east. A flash of turquoise caught my attention; a large kingfisher had landed on the bows of the barge. For a long moment I looked at the red-rust breast and jade-turquoise back feathers of this shy beautiful bird before he flashed into the water to catch his breakfast. Slipping my mooring lines I rowed away from Snape, letting the ebbing tide do all the work – my head full of Britten's music, and my eyes were enjoying the long, lonely marshes. Anyone can visit Snape Maltings Concert Hall by car, enjoy a concert and walk by the river, but to sail there, camp overnight and leave at dawn made my visit a magical, musical moment in my summer with *Wanderbug.*

Canada

I was invited to cruise with a fleet of dinghies crossing Georgian Bay. One particular day stands vividly in my memory. The day's sail had been a sunny peaceful affair over calm blue water. Anchored off a white shell beach on Snake Island, everyone busily prepared supper; Pete walked along the remote bay, billycan in hand, calling, 'Blueberry pancakes – come and get them.'

After a delicious supper I walked away from the camp to the other side of the island. The pine trees seemed to sing in the dying breeze, and as far as you can see there was blue unruffled water with just the smudge of the next island in the distance. Snakes slithered across a tree stump I was sitting on. A loon called his mate, and the liquid bursts of his music were the only sound to be heard. It was hard to break away from that magical spot and return to people and the dinghies.

East Norfolk

I rarely sail now on the once lovely Norfolk Broads, where I grew up in boats. All my youth I used to hire old gaff rigged yachts and sail over the Broads. When I visit now I am saddened to see how the peace and loneliness of these ancient peat-dug broads and their connecting rivers has been almost wiped out. A long row of grossly oversized holiday motor launches and lines of moored boats replace the once quiet freshwater habitats. Just once more I had to recall the past, so early one misty April day *Wanderbug* and I pushed out from Hickling Staithe. A windmill and a fishing heron loomed up out of the wet mist as I turned off Heigham Sound. Chuckling along with no appreciable wind, I sailed about for an hour or two, content with my own company.

Gradually the moored yachts came to life, and as the first big launch roared by I turned off the main channel into a backwater, close to a notice that read, forbiddingly, 'Shallow water', while on its other side it said, 'Refrain from entering November–March'. I brewed coffee and looked out over the broad, over clusters of cheeping coots and statuesque swans and geese. Then a cuckoo began to call – the first I had heard that spring. What an amazing English landscape was all around me: the long low skyline and big skies, so typical of Norfolk. A British-designed dinghy, built in Britain, and an early cuckoo calling as though he would burst with joy. How Elgar or Delius could have used that moment, how Constable or Turner could have painted it. I simply sat in my dinghy home, happy in a moment of magic.

That night, too, was memorable; it was my last on the Broads that year. Night-time on the Broads often has a special charm. When the wind falls light, the hire boats tie up, and the animal life goes to bed, wonderful smells float over the water. There was a frost that night, and the starry sky seemed more brilliant than ever before. As I laced up the tent flaps I saw a shower of meteorites fall over the skyline of windmill and church tower.

Egypt

The cold pre-dawn air, or the hard floor, woke me. Had I been in my own dinghy I would have got up and made tea, but four huddled figures slept on. Peering out through a gap in the canvas boat tent, I watched the River Nile steaming. A white mist bubbled off the water, like lacy curtains and over the dark Nile

Fikry, the Sudanese captain and owner of the dhow on which I was to cruise the Nile. Fikry was explaining to me how the dhow was constructed. Aswan, Egypt. *Photo: Barry Adalian*

currents. A pale mauve-pink dawn light showed palm trees, sugar cane plantations and small palm thatched huts clustered along the narrow fertile band bordering the river. As the starry sky faded into a luminous dawn our Sudanese boatman handed round cups of tea, then, pulling the felucca into the bank, helped us along a wobbly plank on to the sandy shore, indicating we should go and explore. A small group of us climbed up the rocky shoreline and along a sandy road where a great temple stood ahead. The chill dawn quickly turned into another hot blue day as the sun climbed over the eastern temple walls and chased away the cool shadows. What a fantastic way to reach the Temple of Edfu, from a traditional Nile work boat.

Edfu is half way between Luxor and Aswan. This temple took 180 years to build and is the best preserved of all Egyptian temples. The construction was begun in 237 BC during the reign of Ploterny III for the worship of Horus. Enchanted by the colossal sandstone pillars carved in low relief, the vast courtyards, the long walls of the outer chambers, I stood alone, but not lonely. Everywhere ancient Egyptian life was recorded. The pharaohs, priests, deities, rows of slave girls, dancing youths and rows of animals told stories of highly organised society. I crossed the time warp; my inner eyes saw pride in the faces of pharaohs as they engaged in the rituals of eternity of the sun, entering the afterworld nightly over the west bank of the Nile. My inner nose almost smelt the ripe melons and grapes in the great dishes held high by the rows of slave girls. My inner ears just caught the hum of humanity and the beating gongs as the shuffle of sandalled feet passed by, with scribes and officials hurrying to perform their ritual ceremonies to please the gods.

Whether I stood in the vast courtyard open to the sky an hour, a day or a year I could not tell – the experience had been vivid enough to obliterate time. Years earlier we had planned to ship *Wanderer* to Egypt to explore the Nile, but it seemed right to walk from the temple back to the limp lateen sails of the felucca and sail on in that historic craft. A modern dinghy there may have removed some of the magic of the place.

Norway

Ken, a long-term dinghy friend, telephoned on a grey overcast English summer afternoon. 'Come over and we'll sail down the Oslo fjord to our summer house,' he suggested. Two days later I flew low over fjord country to find Ken standing on the tarmac to greet me. Sparkling sun, wooden Norwegian houses smothered in roses and hydrangeas, and an under-populated country awaited me. No bustle, no thronging crowds, just lots of rocky uplands and open water.

Maitken, their Wayfarer, sailed us a mile or so along the fjord to the Oslo Boat Museum. Tying our modern glassfibre dinghy next to the open double-ender Viking long boats, moored out in the arm of the fjord next to the lovely wooden museum buildings, made a peculiarly strong impression on me. I sat on the shore, looking at both past and present in our boats, and marvelled at the Viking journeys. Little boats have brought out the best in human endeavour.

Home waters

You don't have to travel far to capture moments of magic or peace. Only last week *Wanderbug* and I had some days afloat, finding evening moorings as remote and peaceful as any I have found hundreds of miles from home. One particular morning I awoke to a brilliant sunny dawn. It was just 0500 hrs, and I reached for a thermos flask to make my morning tea. Opening the tent flaps I lay with my face in the sun. The dawn chorus was shrill, sweet and insistent, and water lilies lapped the hull. This was the first time I had erected my summer tent of beige canvas – so much lighter and more comfortable than the heavier dark green Ventile tent I used earlier in the year. Feeling the warm dry canvas walls, I thought, 'Who could wish for a better Hilton Hotel than this?'

Denmark

Cruising often brings a spiritual awareness with the magic. I recall launching *Wanderer* after she had travelled by container ship to Esbjerg. Frank gave me a course to steer while he stowed the gear and prepared supper. Night replaced a slow pink sunset, and as my watch ended Frank said, 'You're off course,' and prepared to take the tiller. Without speaking, I pointed to the moon which had risen over a calm dark oily sea. *Wanderer* and I were sailing about 25° off course to travel down her path. Frank sat motionless and I carried on helming. In companionable silence we sat together broad reaching down a silvery carpet of balmy light. The moon bathed us in ethereal moonshine. We had two weeks holiday ahead of us, and planned to sail around Denmark; I had never been happier in my life.

A week later a violent storm battered us in the shallow waters of the Kattegat. Deep reefed and shipping lots of water, we rushed into the harbour on the island of Anholt and tied up between two large cruising yachts for shelter. The wind screamed in their rigging. Out of the stinging rain hands tapped my shoulder; two cups of steaming coffee were handed down from the yacht into our little waterlogged dinghy, followed by two sweet dabs, cooked and wrapped in rye bread. What a feast!

An hour later, with our tent up and the boat snug and dried out, we realised it was Sunday. In anticipation, we walked across the grassy island, through a charming little village of brightly coloured Danish cottages, and on to the village church looking out over the sand dunes on the lee side of the island. The church was small, whitewashed, and its wooden pews were filled with villagers mostly wearing colourful traditional Danish costumes. We crept into a side pew by a window. Just in front of the altar was a large carved wooden sailing dinghy, suspended from the roof.

Outside, the storm had reached a peak; a full gale lashed the pine trees against the windows, and the moan of the wind penetrated even the thick walls of the church. Sleepily I watched the flickering candles and listened to a completely unintelligible service, looking at the weatherbeaten faces of the fishermen of Anholt in the pew next to us. In our own way and in our own language, each of us was saying 'Thank you' for protection from the storms of life.

The next storm saw us roaring across the harbour of Copenhagen, and as we passed the little mermaid statue I threw her a wild rose picked on Anholt island. It landed in her lap and I made a wish. Twenty years on, I know that the charming little mermaid heard my wish, as I am still enjoying sailing.

North Thailand

Over the years, our dinghies have often tied up alongside workboats. As we sailed away from interesting encounters with the skippers of wherry, dhow, barge or skipjack, I always wanted to know more about the life and workstyle of these unique people.

Cruising a rice barge in north Thailand was an attempt to begin to satisfy this curiosity. Flying into Bangkok, that cosmopolitan, car-congested, chaotic city of contrasts, I was visually stimulated wherever I wandered. Travelling by tin-tins (local taxis) trishaws, long-tailed boats, elephants and bambo rafts, I caught glimpses of jungle-clad, mist-wreathed mountain passes, lush tropical valleys rampant with bamboo and orchids; paddy fields, opium and coffee terraces, an hour's walk from the ancient hill tribes of the Lisu, Akha and Meo who worked them, dressed gaily in their beautiful tribal clothes. The real culture shock, however, was not in visiting night street markets, snake farms, orchid nurseries or jade factories, but in the temples – the most famous and spectacular being the magnificent Doi Suthep temple. Tucked in the mountains 1072 metres (3520 feet) above sea level, it had been built in 1383 by King Gue as a monastery. A stone staircase of 290 steps flanked the area leading to the big

205

central *chedi*. In this spired pagoda, partial relics of Lord Buddha were said to be housed. In the gardens, lush with tropical flowers and fruits, I read a small carved teak board. On it was inscribed, 'Contentment is wealth'. That seemed oddly at one with my glimpse into many temples, gold wrapped, precious stone-encrusted monuments yet pervaded with great peace and a sense of space and coolness.

However, I felt like a tourist, pampered and entertained by the beautiful, smiling, serene Thai people, my every need attended to with humour, a laugh and a bow. Then one day, standing on the banks of the Kok river, a muddy opaque fast-flowing river flanked either side by banks of lush vegetation, I felt great excitement. Our rice barge, pulled by a small red and green painted tug, swept round a bend and was coming to collect us. Rushing into a nearby park I gathered wild orchids and bamboo palms, which I presented to the rice barge deckhands. Her skipper's brown walnut face wrinkled into smiles, and he showed me round his tug where the family lived. Hanging baskets of silk roses and paper orchids decorated the walls of the cabin.

The rice barge was run by a Thai family. It was 12 metres (40 feet) long and built in teak, and previously used to pick up rice at the mills and transport the sacks to Bangkok. Other rice barges now carry cement and agricultural products, but *Prasert Somthawin* carries tourists, and was bought three years ago by Singha Travel, now travelling some 320 kilometres (200 miles) from Ayuthaya to Bankok by the Chao Praya and Noi rivers.

The first evening, sailing at 4 knots, we left Borommathat lock and headed south. The barge was steered by a curved 12 metre (39 foot) high teak carved tiller, the toilet was two planks housed in a small wood hut built over the stern of the barge, and the 12 metre hold in which we cooked, ate, slept and lived on the wooden floor was protected by a painted curved wood cabin top. Each meal was cooked in a wok, and consisted of sticky rice, sprouted beans, chilli and meat sauces. I especially enjoyed the slices of fresh pineapple and pawpaw fruits. I helped with the domestic chores of the barge, and every time I looked up I was entranced to see river people, untouched by tourism. Their little bamboo woven huts built on stilts, thatched with elephant grass and clustered into little communities, the inmates busy scrubbing have many memories to thank the rice barge for. She gave me a journey back into time before Christianity had even been founded.

Shetland Islands

Most of us do not need solitude in over-large doses, and meeting people while cruising always brings an element of pleasure. The sea brings even the most self-centred humans down to size, and all the people we have met from our dinghies have been people we have loved to share time with. I doubt one would meet such people when stepping out of a plane or car.

'You must go to see Laurie and Jeannie,' said somebody while we cruised the Shetlands one summer. So we set off to visit the 'loneliest croft in the British Isles'. Landing on the beach on the most northerly island, we walked towards a small whitewashed croft with a present from *Wanderer*. We were not *asked* to stay for tea – the kettle was already singing on the peat fire when we arrived and a snow-white cloth covered the table loaded with oatcakes, fresh cream and butter. We sat and talked, ate and laughed with Laurie and Jeannie as though we had known them for years. Later, after looking around their beautifully maintained croft, we took them out for a sail.

The Solent

The peace of a happy homestead was also vividly enjoyed as we sailed along the Solent one year. The sound of a mallet tapping on wood caused us to stop off and explore. We walked up the banks of the river estuary to the workshops of Jack Whitehead, a famous wood sculptor who had travelled the world exhibiting his craft. What a pleasure it was to watch a skilled craftsman work in this age of mechanical wizardry.

That evening Jack and his wife invited us home. We sipped elderflower champagne aboard their beautiful floating home and talked of boats and travels. A small wood carving of a praying monk now sits at home and reminds us of a brief encounter with a couple we loved sharing time with.

United Arab Emirates

Another blue-water cruise one year gave us magic in the United Arab Emirates. On Christmas Eve we sailed over a bubbling bar into a pure blue creek, very similar to our Norfolk bars – except the UK water is usually grey and cold. Al Khan creek was deep blue and warm, and the tide swept us rapidly inwards towards a shallow sandbank. Anchoring, we sat silent and absorbed. To our left, the modern city of Shajah towered above the creek, with white towerblock offices and hotels, wide tarmac roads, high bridges and a stream of smart cars. In contrast, on the other side of the flooding creek, crouched an ancient village. The crumbling, coral walls of an old fortress guarding the creek were grandly protecting the site, while shabby little Arab houses, festooned with lines of washing and overrun with grazing sheep and goats, small black boys, and fishermen mending their nets, provided a vivid contrast to eye and ear. Two thousand years spanned the two towns. Where oil-rich businessmen now build and develop the desert beside the coastal sand dunes, ancient dhows rot on the seashore. Pearl fishing has ceased to exist, yet oil drilling is enlarging its grip on the area. Somebody's car radio played European carols; across the water, the Muslim call to prayer drowned them. The smell of curry blotted out the more sophisticated smells of hotel filtered coffee. As the sudden subtropical dusk descended we put up our tent, and fell asleep to the drone of distant Dubai. A clear full moon lit up the water where one small Wayfarer and dozens of working dhows lay quietly at anchor.

North Norfolk

Camping in *Wanderbug* on the first day of my holiday the rain fell in a ceaseless patter on the tent and leaked through on to my sleeping bag. 'I have no regrets', I consoled myself. 'Think of all those horrible jabs for cholera, typhoid and polio you might have to have, think of the awful crowds at the airport, ferry cancellations, traffic jams and filthy car fumes'. So, falling asleep in a damp depression, lulled by the insistent rain, I rather wished I was not holidaying at home that summer. However, I woke at dawn to find myself in a wonderful anchorage. Stiffkey harbour was deserted except for one or two anchored workboats. The depression had passed though, and a brilliant blue sky, calm azure sea, empty marshes that were pink with sea lavender, and a warm westerly force 2 wind enveloped me. Noisy larks, oyster catchers and terns and the frothing flood tide kept me company.

My breakfast backcloth was a heavenly spot. To the east, Blakeny church highlighted the low-lying coast, East Hills smudged the dunes to the north, and the lonely, lovely seawater marshes stretched into infinity. Never had honey and stale bread tasted so good. How lucky I was to be holidaying at home! Time was endless, no housework or cooking to have to worry about. Fresh samphire and cockles lay waiting to be collected for lunch.

One can travel the world, enjoying it hugely, yet sailing in Norfolk is never an anticlimax. Sailing from home always has a special magic.

We snatched an unexpected passage one wild, winter Sunday. The tide was fair, and with shelter from the land from a strong southwesterly force 7, we roared deep reefed along the north Norfolk coast from Brancaster eastward. The tide turned against us hours later, and we pulled the dinghy ashore on Sheringham beach.

Walking into the town cold and hungry, hoping to find a cafe, hotel, pub or church where we could shelter from the biting wind, we walked through the cobbled unlit streets, passing no one. At the far end of one street the Salvation Army Hall was open. A large placard announced that a Service of the Sea was in progress. Peeling off our damp oilskins, woolly hats and salty wellingtons, we tiptoed into the back of a full hall. Fishing nets and oars decorated the walls of the hall, and the platform lectern was draped with boat lanterns and seaweed. A man in a navy blue fisherman's jersey, peaked cap beneath his arm, was reading what I thought was the lesson. I later discovered that it was the Fisherman's Twenty Third psalm. (I also discovered that the man who read it had recently been decorated at Buckingham Palace for bravery at sea; he had taken the Wells lifeboat out in a force 11 to rescue a stricken ship.)

That was a moving, magical church service, all the more special since we had arrived there by boat.

'The Lord is my Pilot
I shall not drift
He lighteth me across dark waters
He steereth me in deep channels
He guideth me by the star if Holiness
for his name's sake.

Yea, though I sail mid the thunder and tempest of life
I will dread no danger, for thou are near me.
Thy love and thy care they shelter me.
Thou preparest my harbour before me in the homeland of eternity
Thou anointest the waves with oil.
My ship rideth calmly.
Surely sunlight and starlight shall favour me on the voyage I take
And I will rest in the port of my God for ever.

Canada revisited

In this life it is not too often that one gets second chances. Ten years ago, I walked away from our beloved Wayfarer dinghy, some 900 miles into our long-awaited retirement dinghy cruise. Worn out by the severe conditions, and believing myself a useless crew, I felt I was holding my husband back from completing what he and *Wanderer* were capable of achieving (anybody who has read Frank's book, *Sailing to the Edge of Fear*, may understand my feelings of inadequacy).

We have spent the last ten years singlehanding dinghies. There has been a lot to enjoy and achieve, but something has been missing.

In 1999 Frank telephoned from Canada saying, 'You'll enjoy this, come over and join me.' A few days later I flew into Toronto with a sketchy plan of finding him somewhere near Peterborough on the Trent–Severn Waterway. Stepping into our tented Wayfarer, I was horrified to find how battered and travel-worn our dinghy had become – although the old magic was still there.

A week later, beating into cold head winds, we were approaching Healey Falls lock. By then I had read up on the history of the Trent–Severn Waterway. It linked the Bay of Quinte with Georgian Bay in central Ontario. This unique waterway was completed in 1920 at the cost of 24 million dollars. It linked natural rivers and lakes with man-made lock basins, following the ancient Indians' canoe routes. Later, the French settlers learned to use these canoe routes for exploration: they had grasped the enormous economic significance of the development of this natural waterway route.

Nowadays, this route is used by pleasure boats. The waterway comprises thirty-six conventional locks, two flight locks, two hydraulic lift locks and a marine railway. Each lock station is beautifully cared for by enthusiastic, uniformed lock keepers, and several were keen to share the history of their surroundings. A century ago the area boomed with freight of post-Confederation Ontario trade. Timber barons, farmers, merchants, steamers and grain barges all travelled along this water stairway, passing marshes rich in wildlife, lush farmland, rocky gorges, waterfalls and natural lakes. The huge distances we travelled through vast expanses of unpopulated landscape made us recall that Canada has the largest area of fresh water in the world – quite a shock to we UK sailors who sail in one of the most populated islands in the world.

Since *Wanderer* does not carry radio, we were unaware that Healey Falls lock was due to close early for the weekend, enabling it to be emptied and the valve gear inspected and repaired. Thus the waterway might be closed for several days.

'I kept the glasses on you – we couldn't close until we were sure if you were coming in,' said a friendly lock keeper as we took our position in the lock behind two enormous motor cruisers. Wondering why our boat companions maintained a frosty silence as we locked into the next level, then roared out immediately the gates opened, I learned later that they had been forced to wait for us when they were desperate to reach a big marina where they could plug in and keep their deep freezers and fridges operational.

The magic of this remote place overcame our coldness, tiredness and hunger when I realised how much more free and unhurried we were than most other boaters travelling our way. We went for a walk and found an osprey nest built on a pylon close by the lock. In that untidy raft of twigs and branches sat a fluffy white chick. We watched in awe at the aerial display of the adult bird, as her great wings dropped her out of the blue sky on to her nest. With gentleness she fed the anxious chick with tasty morsels held in her great talons. The vast silence of this spot, the endless landscape steeped in history of Indian canoe explorers, and the real freedom we had in dinghy cruising made this a moment of magic.

The next few weeks were difficult ones, in that the sweltering heat, high humidity and daily dawn and dusk raids by mosquitoes into our tent made this climate less than easy for dinghy travellers. We were looking forward to passing into the

Rideau Canal system. Anchoring at the base of the four-lock rise into the Rideau we lounged the afternoon away, because the lock keepers warned us of choppy conditions and freshening winds on the lake above. Several large motor cruisers roared into Kingston Mills lock, then a yacht motored by. They paused, and then – before tying up to enter the bottom lock – came back with a plate of biscuits to ask if we needed anything. The skipper wrote something on a piece of paper, passed it to us, then said, 'We live in Ottawa, if you need anything here is my telephone number.' One always seems to meet such kind and helpful people when cruising in Canada.

That evening seemed cooler, and the mosquitoes did not drive us into our tent. Sitting in the dinghy, enjoying the sunset, we rolled back the tent and absorbed the peace of this great granite gorge. Across the narrow rocky river an overhanging tree branch caught my attention. It was the lookout perch for a kingfisher. Frequently the bird flashed into the dark river, returning to its branch with a silver fish dangling from its beak. Clusters of pearl-like droplets of water showered off its iridescent feathers as it preened them after its meal, in preparation for its next dive.

The water all around us turned into an oily darkness; the silence was almost like a physical presence. Suddenly rings appeared to ruffle the surface of the water beyond *Wanderer*'s stern. A beaver was swimming towards us; and along the shore a chipmunk was busily foraging. Had an Indian canoed across our view, I would not have been surprised. The sense of Canada's history in that deep silent gorge was almost as potent as the present. It was an evening of complete tranquillity and isolation, and a time of pure magic.

Oman

Because dinghy cruising is so eco-friendly, one can get away from crowds and explore wonderfully lonely places.

For years I have read and re-read the travel accounts of Freya Stark in the Middle East, and of the pioneering journeys of Wilfred Thesiger through the Empty Quarter of Oman. I longed to walk in their footsteps to places of isolation.

One cold wet day I flew out of Heathrow, landing in Oman many hours later. The sunny, dry country charmed me immediately, as I blinked at the golden domes and painted minarets and walled forts in Muscat. My plan was to camp in the desert and sail on a local dhow.

A four-wheel drive vehicle took us to our first wilderness camp: Wadi al Shuwaymiyah, a dry river bed running through a wild mountain gorge. The background to our campfire was a spectacular amphitheatre of cream sandstone topped by darker brown weathered rock. Eagles soared in the thermals above. The silence was incredible. Dropping away behind were endless sand dunes, sculpted by the weather; a warm wind brought a fragrance of frankincense and herbs, wafted from gnarled trees and clumps of vegetation that we had driven past as we climbed into this silent gorge.

The others put up tents, but I slept out in the open, anxious not to miss even one moment of magic as I laid out my bivvy bag beneath a panoply of stars. Sparkling satellites orbited around the constellations. The air was pollution free and you felt you could almost taste its freshness.

Sailing along the coastal desert, with rugged mountain ranges flanking the oasis and small remote villages squatting around the verdant wadis and palm plantations, was a visual delight. A spiritual delight was to hear the call to prayer from the tall minarets dotted along the coast. Once we saw a fisherman climb out of his dinghy and prostrate himself on the damp sands of the lagoon, beside a flock of pink flamingos, as the dawn prayers floated upward towards a blue endless sky. We felt we were sailing past a veiled curtain of history.

From the turbulence of 10,000 years of history, the Oman of the 21st century is emerging as a thriving country, yet still largely untouched by mass tourism. Despite the oil-rich industries, dhow boat building (traditional trading boats since the 9th century) continues to thrive and the fishing fleet is the pride of the nation. Families build the coir-bound hulls and the poops are carved with intricate Islamic patterns.

Legendary home of Sinbad the Sailor, Oman is a seafaring nation famous for its dhows. As long ago as the ninth century, locally built dhows, their planks sewn together with palm fibres, reached China and the Malay Peninsula, carrying frankincense to all parts of that world; our desert drive was to take us to a fishing village and dhow boatbuilding yard. Oman is two-thirds desert, and for some days our vehicles transported us through it, past clusters of ramshackle huts; Bedouin communities and nomadic tribesmen herding their flocks of camels and goats. The brown sugar-like stretches of desert were flanked by huge sand dunes.

All this was a mind-blowing experience, but to arrive at Sur and see the magnificent dhows lined along the boatyard, in various stages of completion, was worth all the discomforts of the journey. The sounds of the adze rang in various parts of the yard, and these majestic dhows, some up to 21 metres (70 feet) in length, lapped the sawdust and sand floor until reaching the blue sea beyond the beach. A crew of five or six fishermen use these locally-built dhows to ply their fishing trade, and a day later I boarded one for a short trip along the fjord-like coast of Musandam. Geological forces have thrust sheer cliffs up from the waters. Dizzying layers of limestone strata in contorted patterns, some 914 metres (3000 feet) of sheer rock, drop into the dark sea. Majestic, awe-inspiring and desolate, these fjords had a strange unworldly quality.

'I must return to your beautiful country and sail further,' I smiled as I said goodbye to Galeeb, our Omani guide – regal and grave in his traditional floor-length white cotton *disfasha* robe, topped with a *kuma*, an ornately embroidered cap. 'If Allah is willing,' he replied.

This remote, culturally rich country is still so little touched by tourists – currently, only about 150,000 visas are issued annually. I feel I must return to this magic again. The desert's austerity, quiet elegance and breathtaking lunar beauty are unmatched, and the enlightened leadership of Sultan Qaboas Bin Said, who has only recently guided his oil-rich country out of a feudal world into the twenty-first century, by building roads, hospitals and schools, appears to be determined to preserve his country's great peace and its unique Islamic history and grandeur.

The mobility and flexibility of an ever-ready dinghy over a yacht snug in a marina was never more easily demonstrated than on Christmas Day 2005.

'Weather settled', I said hopefully at dawn on Christmas Day. Frank agreed, so wordlessly I tipped the chicken, cranberry sauce, mince pies and fruit into a rucksack, and made flasks of tea and coffee. We hitched up my dinghy and drove away from home with no real plan except to escape.

There is a public slipway outside the city and we launched *Wanderbug* from it into a grey still Broad. A passing shower of sleety rain reminded us that it was winter. Nobody stirred; even the ducks and geese hardly flapped a feather as we glided past them along the grey waters beyond Norwich city. Passing beneath two low bridges at Wroxham we crept out into the wide, low-lying countryside. We relaxed and soaked up the emptiness of the winter landscape. A flash of turquoise along the dew dripping banks was the first of eight sightings we had of Kingfishers that day, as the bare alder branches and low-lying scrub lined our route. Neatly ploughed fields and little country cottages newly glamourised into city dwellers' retreats with their designer gardens told us that we were passing through a village.

Later that day, as cold wind bit into our bones, we moored in a sheltered bend of the river and tucked into our Christmas feast.

Releasing our mooring lines from the bank, I noticed signs of an otter that had passed that way recently, and in the fields beyond the bank seagulls were quarelling. 'Bad weather on the way', I said, 'better get back'. I pointed to the grey sky that now had a metallic bronze sheen spreading over it. 'It'll be dark in an hour, and the roads will get icy quickly', replied Frank.

Christmas night in the house was welcomingly warm, but I only tolerated its confines because we had known freedom, space and silence on the river that day.

That a dinghy can be so many things – a home, a weekend cottage, a church, a magic carpet to foreign lands, a means of making friends worldwide, and the best way to real adventure that I have yet discovered – may seem far fetched. Yet *Wanderer* and *Wanderbug*, our Wayfarer, and my Wanderer and now my Gull Spirit *Wanderbug II*, are all those things to me. It is probably also true to say that I respect and love them more than most people I know.

Index